W9-BVI-784

Poverty, Regulation, and Social Justice

Poverty, Regulation, and Social Justice

Readings on the Criminalization of Poverty

Edited by
Diane Crocker & Val Marie Johnson

Fernwood Publishing • Halifax & Winnipeg

Copyright © 2010 Diane Crocker & Val Marie Johnson

All rights reserved. No part of this book may be reproduced or transmitted in
any form by any means without permission in writing from the publisher,
except by a reviewer, who may quote brief passages in a review.

Editing: Mary Beth Tucker
Cover design: John van der Woude
Printed and bound in Canada by Hignell Book Printing

Mixed Sources
Product group from well-managed
forests and other controlled sources
www.fsc.org Cert no. SW-COC-003438
© 1996 Forest Stewardship Council

Published in Canada by Fernwood Publishing
32 Oceanvista Lane
Black Point, Nova Scotia, B0J 1B0
and #8 - 222 Osborne Street, Winnipeg, Manitoba, R3L 1Z3
www.fernwoodpublishing.ca

Fernwood Publishing Company Limited gratefully acknowledges the financial support of the
Government of Canada through the Canada Book Fund, the Canada Council for the Arts, the
Nova Scotia Department of Tourism and Culture and the Province of Manitoba, through the
Book Publishing Tax Credit, for our publishing program.

Library and Archives Canada Cataloguing in Publication

Poverty, regulation and social justice: readings on the criminalization of
poverty / Diane Crocker and Val Marie Johnson, editors.

Includes bibliographical references.
ISBN 978-1-55266-347-9

1. Poverty—Government policy—Canada. 2. Poor—Government policy—Canada.
3. Homelessness—Government policy—Canada. 4. Low-income single mothers—
Government policy—Canada. 5. Social justice—Canada. 6. Criminal justice,
Administration of—Canada. I. Crocker, Diane II. Johnson, Val Marie, 1967-

HC120.P6P6868 2010   362.5'0971   C2010-900060-9

Contents

In memory of Amy Collins
1981–2006

Contributors

MARIO BERTI is a geography student at Simon Fraser University researching rights consciousness among panhandlers on the Vancouver streets.

AMY COLLINS was an anti-poverty activist and window washer in Halifax. She was active with the Ark Youth Outreach. Amy died in 2006 after having a serious epileptic seizure.

DIANE CROCKER teaches criminology at Saint Mary's University. Her research focuses on the effect of criminalizing social problems including violence against women and terrorism.

JEANNE FAY is a social justice activist who has taught social policy and community social work at Dalhousie School of Social Work and poverty law at Dalhousie Legal Aid Services. She focuses her work on advocacy for and organizing of grassroots groups of people directly affected by systemic injustices.

LISA M. FREEMAN is currently a PhD candidate in the Department of Geography and Planning, a Junior Fellow at the Centre of Criminology at the University of Toronto and a Trudeau Scholar. Her five years of experience in Ottawa's activist community have greatly influenced her academic work.

GRACE-EDWARD GALABUZI is an associate professor in the Politics and Public Administration Department, Ryerson University, Toronto and a research associate at the Centre for Social Justice in Toronto. He is the author of *Canada's Economic Apartheid: The Social Exclusion of Racialized Groups in the New Century* (CSPI, 2006) and co-editor of *Race and Racialization: Essential Readings* (CSPI, 2007).

AMANDA GLASBEEK is an assistant professor (criminology) in the Department of Social Science at York University. She is also affiliated with the Graduate Program in Women's Studies and the Graduate Program in Sociolegal Studies.

TODD GORDON teaches political science at York University. He is the author of *Cops, Crime and Capitalism* and the forthcoming *Imperialist Canada*.

TREVOR W. HARRISON is a professor of sociology at the University of Lethbridge. His areas of specialty include political sociology, political economy, and public policy.

VAL MARIE JOHNSON is an associate professor in the Department of Sociology and Criminology at Saint Mary's University in Halifax, Nova Scotia. Her research and teaching interests centre in histories and theories of how we produce and govern the self, others, group dynamics, and social spaces and institutions, particularly through unequal power relations.

JEFF KARABANOW is a professor in the School of Social Work at Dalhousie University. His areas of expertise include youth homelessness, international social work, and political economies.

WAYNE MACNAUGHTON spent several years cycling through homelessness and inadequate housing before becoming stably housed in 2002. Since then he has been volunteering with several groups and committees engaged in the fight against poverty and homelessness, working especially to dispel myths and break down stereotypes.

CLAIRE MCNEIL works as a lawyer and has provided legal advice and representation to individuals and community groups in Halifax, Nova Scotia for over twenty years, particularly individuals living in poverty.

JEFF SHANTZ is a longtime community activist. For the past year he has been organizing against social cleansing and criminalization in the lead up to the 2010 Winter Olympics. He has written for publications such as *Briarpatch* and *Labor Notes*.

JEFF SOMMERS has worked as a union organizer, community worker, and social researcher. He is currently employed as a health research administrator.

GRANT WANZEL teaches the history, theory, and design of housing in the School of Architecture at Dalhousie University. His academic labours support and benefit from his practical commitments as a housing activist, community organizer, architect-planner and developer of non-profit housing.

GREG X has lived in Halifax and been active with Ark Youth Outreach.

Acknowledgments

This book began with the editors' conversations about how state and non-state actors were increasingly over-regulating people with severely limited economic resources in Canada, including through the use of criminal law. There was a developing body of published work in this area, but we were particularly interested in how actors in under-documented places such as Halifax, Nova Scotia, and from non-academic perspectives, could fruitfully join in conversation with researchers and others concerned with these issues.

Toward that end the editors and the Halifax non-profit organization Community Action on Homelessness (CAH) organized a public colloquium on the criminalization of poverty, with funding from the Law Commission of Canada, the CAH and Saint Mary's University's Faculty of Arts. The editors are grateful for the assistance of Angela Bishop and Steven Bittle, Neil McCallum, Ian Mingo, Dorothy Paterson (at Ark Outreach) and for the participation in the colloquium of Costas Halavrezos, many students, concerned community members, front-line workers, policy makers, academics, and those directly impacted by poverty and over-regulation. It is out of their dialogue and work that this book ultimately comes, and it is our hope that this volume will widen and deepen the discussion on the criminalization of poverty and alternatives to it.

The published volume could not have come to conclusion without the insights and hard work of our diverse authors, a number of whom participated in that forum, and others who joined the project afterward. They not only offered their own ideas, experience (some of it quite painful), and research, but engaged as well in extensive dialogue with the editors over their contributions, and provided tenacity and patience in bringing the project to completion. The editors also offer heartfelt thanks to Amanda Nelund and Lindia Smith for steadfast editorial assistance, and to Errol and the rest of the folks at Fernwood for helping to bring the book's questions to a larger audience.

Finally the editors offer particular acknowledgment of the strength and dignity of the first-person participants in the volume, and those unpublished, who have lived with the over-regulation and criminalization that often accompanies poverty in Canada and elsewhere.

Introduction

Reading the Criminalization of Poverty

Val Marie Johnson

In November 2004, the editors, with the non-profit Community Action on Homelessness, organized a public colloquium on the criminalization of poverty in Halifax, Nova Scotia.[1] The event emerged out of the editors' concern about the growing use of criminal law to regulate the poor in Canada. We were particularly concerned about the possible emergence of a local version of legislation along the lines of the provincial "safe streets" acts passed in Ontario (1999) and British Columbia (2004). These acts criminalize the life-sustaining activities (such as panhandling and squeegeeing) of the poor in urban space, and arguably their very presence in the public realm.[2] The 2004 event was co-sponsored by the Law Commission of Canada, whose interest in the proceedings stemmed from its What Is a Crime? project, which sought to develop a framework for understanding why certain behaviour is criminalized and the consequences of criminalization.[3] The colloquium explored the problematic dimensions of criminalization as a response to poverty and attempted to redirect public debate into non-criminalizing solutions. Academics, policy makers, community advocates, and those with lived experience of poverty and the intense regulation that often accompanies it were gathered into public conversation. The response to this event suggested that a widely relevant book could be built from the proceedings.

The resulting volume investigates, in various locales and in broader terms, how state and private practices have increasingly come to over-regulate people with severely limited economic resources. It examines how this trend is part of broad socio-economic dynamics in contemporary liberal capitalist societies such as Canada, as well as rooted in their histories, and how various groups have resisted this criminalization. The editors hope that the book will contribute to solutions that minimize the use of criminal law or intense regulation to deal with poverty and that maximize potentials for a more imaginative and compassionate future.

Theory and Context: Neoliberalism and the Criminalization of Poverty

Theorists argue that one of the central recent developments in "advanced" liberal capitalist societies is the shift from a collective (or socialized) framework for risk and responsibility to ideas and practices centred in individual (or individualized) risk and responsibility (Rose 1996, 1999). The more socialized framework, often referred to as *welfare liberalism*, was enacted through mass industrial production and an economic partnership between capital and nation states associated with the ideas and strategies of economist John Maynard Keynes (Keynes 1936). State social welfare and insurance provision were also developed to buffer the harm and unpredictability produced through capitalism. What is termed *neoliberalism* (or advanced liberalism) has been increasingly produced over the past four decades by a range of state and non-state actors in the context of local and global capitalist dynamics. Through these developments various bodies — cities and states, corporations, communities, families, and individuals — have been constructed as competing in allegedly free (but actually widely state facilitated) realms including, and modelled on, capitalist markets. More limited state regulation of capitalist harm and resource distribution through the citizenry accompanies this "freedom" and competition.[4] This shift has produced a widening gap between rich and poor globally and locally in liberal capitalist societies. And for all but the wealthy it has created a situation of increased labour for decreased or relatively stagnant rewards (Harvey 2007; Comaroff and Comaroff 2001; Duggan 2003; Larner 2000; Munck 2002; Stiglitz 2002; Adam, Beck, and Van Loon 2000; Barry, Osborne, and Rose 1996). At the same time, through the neoliberal "saturation of social and political realms by capital" (in Wendy Brown's apt terms),[5] this increase in inequality and decrease in socialized responsibility for ordinary folk is perceived as the natural (or only possible) order of things.

The ideas and techniques of market capitalism are prominently featured as the ideal template for this neoliberal individualization. As Thomas Lemke summarizes, a key feature of neoliberal ideas and practices is the overlap they seek "to achieve between a responsible and moral individual and an economic-rational individual" (2002: 60). Importantly, however, one of the key characteristics of this shift from socialized to individualized responsibility is the marked extension in the state and private regulation of individuals and populations perceived as failures or sources of "risk" in this new order. Under welfare liberalism such individuals and populations tended to be regulated through techniques of social management developed in the areas of poverty, welfare, immigration, and so on. Under neoliberalism those framed as problematic have been increasingly governed through security, policing, and criminal justice ideas and practices (Adam et al. 2000; Beck and

Beck-Gernsheim 2002; Rose 1996; Ericson and Haggerty 1997; O'Malley 1998; Harcourt 2001; Kelley 2001; Simon 2007; Mosher 2008; Pratt and Valverde 2002; Wacquant 2001). Thus the criminalization of poverty is the hard edge of individualized constructions of risk and responsibility under neoliberalism.

The Book's Overall Contributions

What is perhaps most striking about this set of dynamics is that neoliberalism itself — through various state and private actors, the imagined demands of competition, the devaluing of labour, the privatization of care, and so on — increasingly produces structural insecurity, vulnerability, and deprivation, and criminalizes its most extreme victims (Bauman 2004). This book argues on multiple fronts that the criminalization of our society's most vulnerable — the poor, women, the racialized, the disabled, youth — is in fact materially and symbolically central to neoliberal politics and economics in at least four ways.

First, the criminalization of poverty fortifies market capitalism and the neoliberal policies that reflect and make it possible. This is enacted through the explicit criminalization of non-market activities and through the ways in which formal and informal criminalization are used to justify both state withdrawal from the provision and distribution of resources to ordinary people, and the state and private extension of policing and security against individuals and groups who somehow prove a problem with regard to the market.

Second, the criminalization of poverty (and linked ideas and practices) masks the structural sources of vulnerability produced by capitalism and linked forms of social inequality: institutionalized racism and colonialism, patriarchy, and so on. Vulnerability is reconfigured as individual (and at times family or community) failure, deception, and criminality.

Third, through this masking, the criminalization of poverty reframes the structural creation of vulnerable individuals and populations (and the refusal of collective risk and responsibility for the non-wealthy) into a neo-liberal vision of responsible and irresponsible (or simply bad) individuals in competitive markets. At the same time these stigmatized individuals carry, at a safe symbolic distance, the burden of social fears and anxieties inevitably produced in our structurally uncertain age.

And finally, the criminalization of poverty empowers less vulnerable and insecure (and slightly more politically influential) groups and individuals — who are nonetheless either close to living in or at least surrounded by profound insecurity — to invest in this program for reality by imagining themselves as hard-working tax payers who should police, and who are victims of, the extreme poor as public menaces.

As is demonstrated in multiple ways in this book, this investment is most obvious when individuals and groups are moved to action through what Jonathan Simon calls "governing through crime" (2007: 4–5).[6] For example, "snitch lines" are established to police welfare fraud, and neighbours report neighbours. This book also shows how investment in, and resistance to, the criminalization of poverty operates through ideas and practices with explicit sources and functions outside criminal justice, but that effectively translate into, or are linked with, governing through crime. Our authors demonstrate that struggles over the criminalization of poverty are struggles over the allocation of state and private resources, including the organization and explanation of labour markets, formal and informal political power, the definition and rights of social citizenship, the production of urban space and social relations, and so on. Thus, for example, the potential threat of that neighbour's call encourages welfare recipients to constrict their networks for the exchange of resources and communication.

In other words, criminalization serves functions beyond preventing formally criminal acts and need not target or lead to actual prosecution of precise deeds. The impact of criminalization is arguably more widely felt through its operation as a broad and vague set of social constructs. The threat of formal criminal justice action and the vague stain of criminality are as crucial as formal charges and prosecution (Mosher and Brockman 2010; Law Commission of Canada 2004). In fact it is often precisely criminalization outside the formal context of criminal law that allows for surveillance, regulation, and punitive measures without the checks and balances at least theoretically built into the criminal justice system (see, for example, Fay's chapter on the monitoring of the always potentially fraudulent welfare recipient).

The work in this volume provides insights relevant to research i) that seeks to understand how, in liberal capitalist societies, a multitude of actors at various social levels produce and employ governing methods, and the ways of thinking that make them possible over time, and ii) that rethinks political economy as a framework for understanding the practices of, and relations between, individual or social bodies and broader patterns of governing under capitalism (Foucault 1978; G. Burchell et al. 1991; Lemke 2001; Wacquant 2001). Thinking about governing practices and ways of thinking as co-produced is especially valuable because neoliberal capitalism — and here the criminalization of poverty through which it operates — is "a political project that endeavors to create a social reality that it suggests already exists" (Lemke 2002: 60) and presents that reality as inevitable. In a related way, if we are to critique neoliberal capitalism and the criminalization of poverty as inevitable, we require a sustained analysis of how economy (poverty, wealth, independence, competition, and so on) and formal and informal politics are also co-produced: as Lemke notes, "economy is always political economy" (2002: 60, 57).

Our volume contributes to this work by illustrating the wide and complex web of power relations enacted around the criminalization of poverty, and related ideas and practices. By adding to our understanding of how neoliberal governing tactics and ways of thinking work, the volume as a whole breaks open Canadian analyses of neoliberal politics and the criminalization of poverty. By way of illustration, a significant amount of the rich work on Canadian neoliberalism, and poverty and its criminalization, has concentrated on the Ontario- and Toronto-based effects of these dynamics beginning in the 1990s (Mosher et al. 2004; Hermer and Mosher 2002; Pratt and Valverde 2002; O'Grady and Gaetz 2004; Ranasinghe and Valverde 2006). This concentration in part reflects the high profile political leadership of the provincial Conservative Party government of Mike Harris (1995–2002) in the production of neoliberal ideas and practices, represented in legislation and policies such as the Ontario Safe Streets Act and that government's high profile campaign against welfare fraud. However, this concentration also reflects the dominance of Toronto and Ontario in Canadian knowledge production. Because they look elsewhere or differently in multiple ways, the chapters in this volume suggest that this concentration on neoliberalism and the criminalization of poverty dating from the mid-1990s, and prominently produced through C/conservative politics, may have influenced how we think about the politics and history of these dynamics more generally in Canada. The chapters here build on this research by continuing to expand and deepen the analysis of the longer histories and wider contexts of the political economy of neoliberalism. There is consideration of how these dynamics play out over time, space, and locale, and of political complexity across and within parties, and levels and types of governing.

Many chapters in the volume locate the criminalization of the poor in longer and broader histories of socio-economic practices and ideas under liberal capitalism. Gordon finds precedents in classical liberalism predating the welfare state for current law-and-order policing that is used to fortify the capitalist labour market. His insights are particularly important given that *neo*liberalism involves a push for mass labour conditions to increasingly resemble those of the nineteenth century (non-unionized, low wage, insecure, etc.). Fay examines the Nova Scotia social assistance policy's "man-in-the-house rule" for single mothers in the context of the development of, and shifts in, the welfare state in that province beginning in the 1930s. Gordon and Fay's strong emphasis on class and gender inequality in this longer history of liberal capitalism remind us that welfare states were developed in North America and elsewhere out of intense class conflict, economic crisis, and working-class organizing, and that although welfare liberalism responded to this by collectivizing resources and responsibilities somewhat, this was always constricted through hierarchies of class, gender, race, and colonialism, sexual norms, age, and ableism (Gordon 1994; Fraser and Gordon 1994; Katznelson 2006; Campeau 2004). It is through very similar hierarchies that the current desocialization of resources and responsibility, and the extension of policing and security functions by the state and its private partners, impacts ordinary citizens.

Accordingly, Galabuzi scrutinizes how the regulation and punishment of poverty in Canada is shaped by longstanding histories of racism and the more recent racialization of immigration and urban poverty and segregation. Berti and Sommers trace the gradual development of neoliberalism and the criminalization of the Vancouver poor in the last three decades. This began in the early 1980s in the context of both provincial level fiscal constraint and the Vancouver-based intersection of private property interests and a crime prevention framework that first emerged through residents' association activism. Berti and Sommers then document the intensification in the punitive dimensions in municipal policy and discourse around "street people" from 1993 to 2005.

The meaningfulness of these longer histories of neoliberal capitalism and the criminalization of poverty can be further illustrated by highlighting aspects of Harrison's analysis of the governing of Alberta welfare "fraud." One method of unpacking the thinking that makes specific governing forms possible is to trace it backward from the time with which it is most commonly associated. Their advocates and many commentators explain neoliberal tactics — such as cuts in state social welfare and the policing of welfare fraud — as responses to fiscal crisis and scarcity, especially in the 1980s and 1990s. Harrison expands the commonly understood timeframe for welfare state retrenchment back into the mid-1960s and early 1970s, a period of economic plenty in Alberta and one associated with a significant expansion of Canada's welfare state generally. Further, Harrison's long view demonstrates how lower levels of state social provision often continue long after recessions pass and deficits are eliminated. This is evident both in welfare policy under the Alberta government of Ralph Klein and at the federal level, where the Canadian government enjoyed huge budget surpluses repeatedly, but continued to refuse serious budget transfers to facilitate social investments that benefit the non-wealthy, such as affordable housing, higher education, and daycare.[7]

In at least three further ways our authors show the complex governing practices and ideas of neo/liberal capitalism and the criminalization of the poor: first, through the transnational and intranational migration and the local emergence of such practices and ideas in a range of places; second, through the formally political intricacies of these dynamics across multiple levels of the state and party lines; and third, through the intricate network of state and private actors and tools used.

With regard to the translocal and local production of criminalization, Karabanow extends the lens widest, arguing that we must see continuities between the brutal public cleansing of poor youth in Guatemala and the intense regulation of street-engaged youth in countries like Canada. Berti and Sommers investigate the unique combination of Vancouver's and British Columbia's specific municipal and provincial political and economic developments, with the importation of Ontario's legislation for policing the street poor in the Safe Streets Act and the largely New York City-based rhetoric and tactics of the Broken Windows model. Harrison examines the local and fragmented emergence of welfare policies in Alberta from the 1960s. Fay offers a longer history of the gradual and sporadic development of the intense regulation of poor women in Nova Scotia. This was shaped by both local dynamics provincially and in the capital of Halifax, and national-level shifts around policies such as the Canada Assistance Plan.

As these few examples indicate, the volume also brings us research on how these dynamics work outside Canada's dominant city and region, in as yet under-examined ways. Our authors do consider Toronto, but through gender- and race-critical analyses of the criminalization of poverty. Vancouver and Montreal are examined, but so are Halifax and Ottawa; Ontario, Nova Scotia, and Alberta policy and politics are all addressed.

The chapters also explore how players across state levels and parties deploy the formal politics of liberalism and neoliberalism and the criminalization of the poor. This includes consideration of the roles played in these dynamics by provincial and federal representatives of the Liberal Party, provincial and federal representatives of the Conservative Party, regional conservative variations in the British Columbia and Alberta Social Credit parties, municipal governments, and leaders from municipal parties such as the centre-right and business-oriented Non-Partisan Association, which has given Vancouver three of its last four mayors (current B.C. premier for the Liberal Party Gordon Campbell, Philip Owen, and Sam Sullivan).

This web of formal political actors, policy, and rationales is further filled out by our authors' investigation of the society-wide spectrum of state and private agents active in connection and conflict with politicians around the regulation of the poor: police, security guards, and para-military, lawyers and judges, business and residential property owners and their organizations, case workers, civil servants, financial institutions, non-profit organizations and advocates for the poor, media outlets and consumers, writers of letters to the editor, urban drivers and pedestrians, tourists, neighbours, and over-regulated but resilient poor men, women, and youth. Our contributors show this plethora of actors employing amazingly diverse tactics in their struggles. Military, para-military, and military-like policing techniques are employed against street youth in Guatemala and racialized youth in Toronto

(Karabanow, Galabuzi). Canadian provincial "safe streets," trespass, and motor vehicle legislation and municipal by-laws (regulating everything from panhandling to sign usage) have been designed, resurrected and enforced to effectively criminalize the public survival activities of the urban poor (Berti and Sommers, Glasbeek, McNeil). Social assistance recipients are surveilled and criminalized through provincial regulation (Fay, Harrison), at times with the assistance of the Canada Revenue Agency or local private actors (Fay). The poor and their advocates and sympathizers produce counter-governing forms through anti-poverty activism, subsistence economies, alternate communities and political alliances, and legal challenges (Shantz, MacNaughton, Karabanow, Glasbeek, Freeman, McNeil), and the struggles continue.

Chapter Overview

The authors and editors represent the diverse voices of academics (in sociology, criminology, history, political science, geography, architecture, public administration, social work, and legal studies), as well as front-line workers and people whose daily existence is lived out under regulatory systems enacted and analyzed by others. These diverse authors are reflected in the range of styles in the volume, from chapters written in an academic style to material centred on front-line professional experience and first-person accounts.

The chapters in the book's first section examine the criminalization of poverty as formal and informal policy and politics. The piece that begins this section, by political scientist Todd Gordon, argues that law-and-order policing in Canadian cities is not aimed at fighting crime, as its supporters insist, or criminalizing poverty, as its critics assert. Rather, he argues that urban policing through tactics such as the enforcement of anti-vagrancy statutes and zero tolerance policies enact neoliberal capitalist political economic aims by criminalizing public subsistence labour alternatives to the low-wage labour market, such as panhandling and squeegeeing. In fact, Gordon convincingly argues that law-and-order policing is the state's response to people's public socio-economic resistance to coercion at the bottom end of the neoliberal labour market.

We are reminded here of the dynamics around the long-standing pattern of the policing of the underground economy more generally in capitalist societies. Gordon's focus on the functions of policing beyond criminal justice importantly underscores the neoliberal (rather than the neoconservative) dimensions of specific "governing through crime" initiatives that are not just or even primarily about crime at all, but rather further state neoliberal economic policies prioritizing capitalist market relations and profit accumulation. This is especially resonant if Gordon's analysis of law-and-order policing as reinforcing capitalist labour markets is read together with the ways in which state and private policing works to cleanse urban publics for capitalist market operations through shopping, tourism, commercial recreation, and commuting (see Berti and Sommers, Wanzel, McNeil in this volume; Brenner and Theodore 2002).

In a related way, sociologist Trevor Harrison details how the crackdown on welfare fraud in Alberta, allegedly launched to prevent improper use of public funds, actually served a broader political purpose. As noted above, Harrison expands the commonly understood timeframe for the development of welfare state retrenchment and criminalization of "fraud" back into the 1960s and 1970s, a period of plenty in this province, and further illustrates that low levels of social provision continued under the Klein government after deficits and debts were eliminated. Given that economic scarcity has been both a key political rationale for state social provision cuts and a factor in how people date its history, Harrison complicates explanations of the welfare state, state retrenchment, and forms of liberal capitalism.

Harrison's cost-benefit analysis reveals that, when the large costs and small returns of policing are calculated, the primary "benefit" of welfare fraud campaigns is not cost savings from fraud, but rather legitimizing cuts to social service provision and upward wealth distribution through tax cuts.[8] In line with the insights of others working on welfare fraud in Canada, Harrison also further debunks the crime prevention explanation of fraud policing by demonstrating that state efforts to locate, publicize, and prosecute welfare fraud (which as he documents has always significantly involved administrative error) effectively produces this "fraud." Finally, Harrison's documentation of the Alberta government's criminalization of welfare recipients, despite its knowledge that policies were already in place to ensure that fraud was infrequent, provides evidence that governing through crime can involve very deliberate political tactics.

Anti-poverty advocate Wayne MacNaughton provides a first-hand account of how the security climate produced through longer standing neoliberal dynamics, and exaggerated through the events of September 11, 2001, has impacted the experience of being homeless in cities such as Montreal. MacNaughton describes how the security efforts of bus terminals, baggage claim agents, and security guards further criminalize those living on the streets and attempting to use public space. He describes how homeless people — who often move around a lot precisely because of the criminalization patterns described in this volume — attempt to counter these practices by circulating local "street-savvy" knowledge to newcomers in their midst. However, MacNaughton argues that more structural responses are essential, beginning at least with the development of multi-function urban drop-in centres.

Geographers Mario Berti and Jeff Sommers examine how the criminalization of poverty in Vancouver, British Columbia, allows private actors and their property interests to govern urban public policy priorities and space, in cooperation with police and local and non-local politicians. They trace this recent history back to provincial and municipal developments beginning in the 1980s, but primarily explore how private downtown business improvement associations "have deployed the Broken Windows theory of crime and neighbourhood decline as a discourse of neoliberal governance," through which they present themselves as *public* guardians. Berti and Sommers illustrate that "spatializing poverty" through Broken Windows discourse frames it "as a local problem" centred in problematic individuals rather than in "structural and institutional" factors. Solutions are thus to be found in the "management and regulation" of the street poor, "rather than political intervention" that addresses the long-term and structural conditions that have produced their situations.

However, Berti and Sommers also demonstrate that this regulatory construction of public space is profoundly political: it "aims to decrease homeless and marginalized people's use of public space for private functions, in an attempt to increase the use of public space for the private functions of business and corporate control." Further, this cleansing of public space for commerce does not eliminate poverty; it simply removes it from the public realm, discourse, and politics (Hermer and Mosher 2002; Mitchell 2003). Through extensive interviews with homeless people, Berti and Sommers also bring the consequences of this purification of urban space on behalf of the capitalist market down to the most basic level: a street-engaged person asking for help is read as "disorder" by a more privileged person moving through reluctantly shared social space (see also Glasbeek, Collins, Karabanow, Greg X, Shantz in this volume). The discomfort that relatively privileged people (including business owners and politicians and media representatives) experience with confronting poverty, and with calls to recognize their relation (or even responsibility) to that poverty, is central to how these people invest in the criminalization of poverty. Finally, the street-engaged who are interviewed by Berti and Sommers indicate that if the homeless are ever victimized through exchanges with others, the law is of little help. In this way the law is a weapon and a damaging failure for the poor: it is used against them by virtue of their being poor in public space, and they are refused justice through it when they themselves are harmed by others directly.

Architect and urban planner Grant Wanzel addresses related themes in his chapter, further arguing that the social exclusion effected through the criminalization of poverty is part of a broader "impoverishment of public spaces" through their increasing regulation with reference to narrowly defined private sector interests. He asserts that this is reflected in and enacted through city, neighbourhood, and site specific planning and design. One of the main results is an urban public catering to high-end consumers and tourists, who are sought after by state and business agents acting on the perceived demands of a corporate-dominated global economy.

While we may be familiar with this dynamic in large cities (Brenner and Theodore 2002; Ruppert 2006), Wanzel demonstrates its impact in small cities like Halifax, convincingly arguing that this not only affects those already facing high levels of social exclusion, but also undermines the democratic interests of all citizens and our ability to interact as communities. To this impoverishment of public space, priorities, and citizenship we can add questions about the long-term economic sustainability of the growing gap between rich and poor, and urban development of the sort Wanzel describes. In Halifax, for example, recent waterfront development has almost exclusively involved residential and commercial projects that operate primarily for a high-end and tourist market in the summer months (selling souvenirs, candy and snack foods, "boutique hotels," and deluxe dining). The waterfront is drastically under-used the rest of the year.[9]

The book's second section contains three chapters that enhance our understanding of how poverty is criminalized at the intersection of class, race, and gender. Politics and social justice scholar Grace-Edward Galabuzi demonstrates that the racialization of poverty is linked with criminalization and that the intense marginalization of the racialized poor in Canada's cities is itself criminalizing, as urban neighbourhoods become increasingly segregated by the disadvantages of racialization, immigration status, and class. Through analysis of socio-economic data, immigration policy, and media and political discourse, Galabuzi makes a strong argument that socio-economic discrimination and deprivation co-produce victimization, violence, and criminalization through cultural stereotypes and hyper-policing and -incarceration. He also considers how the recent racialization of immigration to Canada and the events of 9/11 add new rationales and intensity to historical dynamics of racism and criminalization.

Galabuzi gives us at least two strategies for carefully and compassionately approaching the racist co-production of poverty, victimization, violence, and criminalization. First, he urges us to see how race is central to the production of poverty and its criminalization in Canada. In particular, he illustrates how racism shapes the media, public, and political production of practices and ideas around African Canadian low-income neighbourhoods and crime. This racism means that class and other structural forms of deprivation (including racism itself) get read out of dominant constructions of harm and violence. Galabuzi shows us how racism and the criminalization and urban segregation of poverty in Toronto mean that "crime" is defined as centred in the violence of individuals. Alternately, a small minority of African Canadian young men's misbehaviour is construed as (racialized) organized crime by "gangs." This presents the structural inequalities experienced by urban

African Canadians (including their vulnerability to violence) as a problem of failed and/or criminal individuals, families, and communities, who are explicitly or implicitly racialized. His analysis is especially crucial in understanding these dynamics in Toronto, but Jennifer Nelson (2008), for example, has demonstrated related patterns in the context of Halifax.

Second, Galabuzi calls our attention to how racism is co-produced with gender and sexual norms in the interpretation of low-income urban African Canadians as both violent and victimized. He argues that, on the one hand, "competing narratives of domineering masculinity and disemboweled blackness… contribute to some young Black men's attraction to violence as a means to assert power." On the other hand, Galabuzi shows us that although this means that women in these men's lives "are likely to be prominent victims of their violence," dominant institutions stigmatize non-normative family forms in urban African Canadian communities and so define women in these communities as sources of crime (through their children) rather than as victims of violence and structured deprivation.

Social work lecturer and community activist Jeanne Fay further enriches our consideration of how gender, sexual, and class norms shape the criminalization of poverty. Fay provides two key things: extensive front-line evidence of poor women's experience of criminalization and moral regulation in an under-analyzed region of Canada, and documentation of the historical continuities and complexities in this set of dynamics. In the contemporary period, Fay essentially provides a local political economy analysis of the bodies, resources, and social relations of single mothers regulated through a welfare regime, and especially the man-in-the-house rule, which disallows women access to social assistance if they are deemed to be in an intimate relationship with a man. Drawing on historical research and long experience as an advocate, Fay historically and socially locates the legal, civil penalty, and informal regulatory landscape that has shaped the lives of women on social assistance since Nova Scotia's adoption of the Mother's Allowance Act in 1930.

Fay's history draws our attention to the fact that the intense regulation of poor women receiving public funds dates from the early development of welfare states (and really back to the new British poor laws). In this she demonstrates that although the formal and elaborate criminalization of welfare fraud dates to the second half of the twentieth century, the state's call for private actors to help them police assistance recipients (a decidedly neoliberal tactic) dates back to the Nova Scotia Mother's Allowance Commission in the 1930s. Fay also brings us insights on the contemporary era, documenting how the criminalization of welfare recipients through a combination of state and private governors — provincial welfare officials, the Canada Revenue Agency, local financial institutions and employers, landlords, school administrators, neighbours — intimidates, invades the privacy, and shrinks the life space and support networks of poor women. The fact that these techniques operate primarily outside the context of formal criminal law does not in any way lessen their impact on poor women. As Fay reminds us, welfare regulation "presumes single mothers to be ineligible (guilty) until they can prove otherwise." Under this largely administrative regime "there is no presumption of innocence."

Finally, precisely through her historical analysis, Fay highlights that the intense criminalization of welfare in the late twentieth and early twenty-first centuries has pushed the figure of the innocent poor child — earlier emphasized by women reformers lobbying for mother's allowances — out of any central place in public discourse around welfare and its recipients. A similar dynamic is at work in practices and ideas around street-engaged youth and "risky" youth generally today. We are reminded here of theorists' arguments that neoliberalism's "war" on childhood and youth — effectively the refusal of childhood through holding youth as responsible as adults without the latter's rights — is a refusal of any future except more of the neoliberal same. Given that the "child savers" were a product of nineteenth- and early twentieth-century liberalism and industrial capitalism (Platt 1996), the absence of the innocent child in various aspects of the criminalization of poverty raises disturbing but important questions around relations between children and youth, and neoliberal capitalism (Kelly 2001; Grossberg 2001; Giroux 2004).

Criminologist Amanda Glasbeek brings us an intersecting class and gender analysis of how the criminalization of poverty originates in broader political agendas. She thereby adds to our understanding of the linked class and gender dimensions of neoliberal practices and ideas, and how feminist concerns can be used in service and resistance to neoliberalism. Drawing from media coverage and political debates surrounding the enactment of the Ontario Safe Streets Act, Glasbeek shows how feminist concerns for women's safety were deployed (predominantly by male Conservative Party politicians and journalists) to legitimize a neoliberal campaign to criminalize the life-sustaining activities of the street-involved poor.

In this way, Glasbeek brings fresh insights to the consideration of how victimhood is a key tool through which neoliberalism constructs law-and-order policies, and governing and citizenship generally (Stanko 2001; Simon 2007). She shows us how forms of empowerment and protection constructed in such "crime" prevention campaigns allow an enhancement in the self-image of the participants through a projection of fear onto others and a construction of the self as benevolent and brave. As Glasbeek reveals, intersecting gender and class dynamics are at play here: public spaces in Toronto as a neoliberal city are ultimately defined through this campaign as protected by and most safe for men, and as purified for the movements of the upper classes and capitalist markets. Thus gendered fear of crime discourse is effectively employed to mask men's fears and the class interests (mostly male but also female) of politicians, business owners, and relatively privileged city dwellers. In Glasbeek's terms, "women's anxieties about violence in the public sphere," and the social deployment of them, "become a conduit" for the neoliberal criminalization of the poor.

Glasbeek's analysis reveals how the gender stereotypes required in this class work render invisible young street-involved women, the class interests and anxiety expressed by women participating in the neoliberal agenda (business owners, those wanting undisturbed access to leisure or commuting space, and so on), and an alternate feminine voice of class recognition and responsibility expressed by other women. Legislators' assertions that panhandlers or squeegeers approach women because they are "a soft touch and easily frightened" turns the possibility that women might be compassionate into women's vulnerability to crime. Glasbeek's exploration shows us how the neoliberal shift away from collective social provision and toward law-and-order solutions constructs the emotional and psychological tone and the limited political content of public life (fear, law, and order *is* the politics). Here the possibility of feeling obligated to each other is reframed as women's fear of crime and need of masculine protection (see also Hermer and Mosher 2002). As Glasbeek argues, this sort of commentary by the Ontario Conservative Party in the "safe streets" campaign fit well with their neoliberal policy drive to privatize all forms of care; she illustrates how the class dimensions of this drive meant that the definition of private and public boundaries around care and security were centrally informed by property interests.

Halifax anti-poverty activist Amy Collins' posthumous contribution to our volume is a poignant personal witnessing of the consequences of this definition of care; it seems unlikely that she would have died in 2006 at the age of twenty-five if she had not struggled with abuse, years of extreme poverty, homelessness, and substance use. However, it is precisely this sort of young woman who is erased through the construction of menacing and implicitly male squeegee kids. Collin's refusal to accept being treated on the street as an "unjust criminal for simply trying to survive" is an apt bridge into the final section of the book on regulation and resistance in urban publics.

The three chapters here by Karabanow, McNeil, and Freeman, and the two first-person accounts by Greg X and Jeff Shantz provide an appropriate end to the volume because they can be read as a conversation about what citizenship and justice mean in contemporary societies. The first chapter in this section, by social work researcher and youth advocate Jeff Karabanow, brings us rich evidence of how street youth are regulated and resist. Relying heavily on the words of youth themselves, he tackles the way in which street youth are constructed as non-citizens in Canada and Guatemala. While the criminalization affecting street youth in Canada is not as severe as the torture and death squads they face in Guatemala, his piece reveals how the processes of social exclusion can be quite similar. His comparison makes us want to know more about how the specifics of the regulation and criminalization of the poor are linked to the political system at play in different locales here and around the world. Karabanow reveals differing and overlapping versions of inclusion and exclusion, including the largely informal production of non-citizenship in these regimes. These are shaped by how the militaristic character of the state permeates Guatemalan society and a combination of government retreat from social provision and linked tactics that criminalize the poor in Canada.

Crucially, Karabanow provides further evidence that (in Canada and Guatemala) victimization and criminalization are fundamentally intertwined (see also Berti and Sommers, Galabuzi, Collins, Greg X). He describes how individual youths' histories of abuse — which often are experienced in the normative institution of the family and lead to street engagement in the first place — are so intense that many report street life *as an improvement*. On the street, however, they are then criminalized and victimized by para-military, police, and members of the public, most frequently in connection with their survival techniques and requests for assistance. This brutal catch-22 of refusing life sustenance while criminalizing their attempts to attain it is particularly expressed through homeless youth voices in Karabanow's narrative and our multiple first-person accounts in this volume. On a more positive note, Karabanow illustrates how street youth forge collective identity and community in the context of exclusionary dynamics; he argues that social solutions to the deep issues around youth homelessness must be built precisely in alliance with street youth skills and networks, and those working in cooperation with them.

The next two chapters in this section consider the complex social and legal mechanisms and strategies used to criminalize the poor, and to resist their criminalization. On the one hand, the legal and law enforcement dynamics around the criminalization of the poor reveal what Debra Parkes (2005) summarizes as the Canadian conflict between law-and-order culture, and "Charter culture" grounded in the principles of the Canadian Charter of Rights and Freedoms.[10] On the other hand, these case studies of the criminalization of the poor and legal resistance to it highlight both the uses and the limits of liberal law.

Lawyer Claire McNeil provides analysis of a legal case that emerged from Halifax police charges against "squeegee kids" from 2002–2004, deploying an obscure municipal by-law around sign use and a rarely used section of the provincial Motor Vehicle Act. In particular, McNeil examines the reported decision and public record of the provincial court trial that resulted, in which she defended twenty-year-old Mr. McCluskey. Court proceedings revealed that local police selectively enforced these obscure statutes in a way that criminalized the survival activities of young street people but not a charity campaign by local students soliciting in exactly the same intersections and time period. In the words of Greg X, author of the first-person narrative that precedes McNeil's chapter: "I don't think run-ins with the 'law' ever benefit me or my well-being" (see also Collins and Shantz in this volume).

Yet McNeil emphasizes that the Halifax police presented their mission in policing squeegeeing as centred in public roadway safety. While this explanation was already questionable in light of the double standard for students, McNeil also demonstrates that the anti-squeegee campaign does not appear to have been spurred by public complaints to the police. Evidence she presents from the local press shows that other Haligonians did not support police tactics against squeegee kids (here again we see violence and policing versus compassion as competing responses to poverty). McNeil demonstrates that this police campaign actually appears to have been motivated by two primary things: assumptions by the Halifax police force that street youth were a problem, grounded at least partly in information from other urban Canadian police forces, and local political concerns that appear to have been centred around business and especially tourism interests.

In addition to placing anti-squeegee policing in the context of a double standard and debunking the "public safety" rationale, McNeil also defended her client by claiming that the policing strategy violated squeegee kids' Charter rights to freedom of expression, the "principles of fundamental justice," and equality under the law. In 2005 the provincial court ruled that the Motor Vehicle Act (MVA) section "relied upon by the police was overly broad."[11] While Charter challenges to the criminalization of the poor have failed elsewhere, this Nova Scotia legal case forced state actors in the province and city to shift governing tactics and constrain their policing of street youth in some measure. However, the result so far is that legislators simply invented a new law to criminalize squeegeeing, through an amendment to the MVA.[12] Moreover, McNeil considers the severe limits on how individual poor people might engage with the legal system as a venue for justice. By way of illustration, precisely because the regulation of the poor is often enacted through low level policing and charging strategies (by-law and traffic offences, etc.) formal legal aid can be of limited use to the poor who are criminalized in this manner (see also Freeman). At very least McNeil's point underscores the strategic importance of funding for community and alternative legal organizations for those battling against criminalization (and, for those with opposing political goals, cutting state funding for such organizations or programs).[13]

Geography PhD candidate Lisa Freeman examines how a group of squatters confronted liberal conceptions of law outside and inside the courtroom. First, these squatters defied property law through their 2002 occupation of an abandoned building in downtown Ottawa, 246 Gilmour Street. When they were prosecuted for this two years later in *R. v. Ackerley et al.*, they directly challenged liberal criminal law and its focus on the isolated acts of individuals rather than the harms produced by social structures and organizations. In their strategic engagement with criminal charges and trial procedure, and in their acquittal, the squatters forced the court to acknowledge the social context for their criminalized actions, effectively redefining these actions as non-criminal. The squatters' tactics in squatting and in the courtroom can be read as a two-pronged strategy of civil disobedience against an unjust system of property ownership and the law as its guarantor, a strategy that fits in a long and more recent history of civil disobedience (Fudge and Glasbeek 2003).

The extraordinary bail conditions that local authorities attempted to impose on the squatters — a defendant curfew and a ban on association and political activity among them — and their refusal to consent to these conditions, reveal the explicitly political character of the squatters' actions and of the criminalization of poverty as a tactic on the part of state actors. Freeman's account of the Gilmour Street squatters' occupation, prosecution, and trial further documents poor people's socio-economic resistance to the coercions of the neoliberal market (here represented in the profound lack of affordable housing in Canadian cities) and to law-and-order strategies as part of that network of coercions. Perhaps most importantly from the perspective of building future anti-poverty activism, what was achieved in the squat and the legal case was in great part made possible by alliances among street-involved youth, other anti-poverty activists, Canadian labour unions, and local community members and politicians.

Our volume closes with a dialogue Shantz provides between theories of inequality and his personal experience. As he describes, in a political economy in which citizenship equals the capacity for consumption and mobility is linked with private property, "being homeless is an experience of bodily and spatial confinement." Shantz, and the volume as a whole, show us how the criminalization of poverty costs a great deal in terms of time, money, and energy, as well as further impoverishing the life zones, activities, and liberty of movement of those with limited socio-economic resources. Their access to space, shelter, and support, and to protection from anecdotal and systemic violence, their personal and social relations, their freedom of expression, their body integrity and peace of mind, are all impacted. While other contributions to the volume document long-standing histories of discrimination and punishment or suggest a contemporary return to nineteenth-century policing and labour tactics, Greg X and Shantz show us that in the richest countries on earth, society's poorest experience conditions of human warehousing that reveal the surreal characteristics of "advanced" liberal capitalist societies. Let us begin this volume, and our consideration of the neoliberal criminalization of poverty therein, with Shantz's words in mind:

> In hostels and shelters our bodies are crammed together in small spaces under conditions that do not even meet United Nations guidelines for refugee camps. Going to shelters can leave us beaten up, having our few belongings stolen, or contracting tuberculosis, supposedly a disease of the past that is rampant in contemporary shelters. Ironically, given our immobility, our bodies are time travellers picking up ancient illnesses that the rest of the population only reads about in history books.

The editors hope that this volume will illustrate the multiple ways in which the criminalization of poverty makes us all poor even as it relies on varying degrees of privilege, and reflects how we have lost sight of what is valuable and possible. Let us also begin here to imagine and produce something better.

Notes

1. For information on Community Action on Homelessness see <http://www. cahhalifax.org/>.
2. On June 14, 2005, Halifax Regional Municipality councillors voted 21–3 to recommend that the provincial government implement a Safe Streets Act in Nova Scotia. See Halifax Coalition Against Poverty, 2005, "Why the Safe Streets Act is a BAD idea for Nova Scotia," available at <users.eastlink.ca/~hcap/0605ssa. html>. On the Ontario Safe Streets Act see J. Hermer and J. Mosher 2002. On the B.C. version of this legislation see Berti and Sommers in this volume. See also Claire McNeil's chapter in this volume about the successful legal challenge against the policing of squeegeeing under the Motor Vehicles Act in Nova Scotia Provincial Court (*R. v. McCluskey* 2005). Bill 7 (2008), an amendment to the Nova Scotia Motor Vehicle Act, makes it illegal to "stop or approach a motor vehicle for the purpose of offering, selling or providing any commodity or service or soliciting the driver or any other person in the vehicle" (Chapter 293, Section 173A (1) at <gov.ns.ca/legislature/legc/bills/60th_2nd/1st_read/b007.htm>). For issues surrounding the bill see L. Lowe, 2008, "Squeezing squeegers: The war against Halifax's street peddlers has nothing to do with safety, and everything to do with criminalizing poverty" (*The Coast*, January 10).
3. Saint Mary's University and Community Action on Homelessness also sponsored the colloquium. The Liberal government of Pierre Trudeau established the Law Reform Commission of Canada (1971–1993), an independent body intended to undertake a systematic review of Canadian law. This body was eliminated through spending cuts by the Conservative government of Brian Mulroney in 1993. The Liberal government of Jean Chrétien established the

Law Commission of Canada in 1997. In September 2006, the Conservative government of Stephen Harper eliminated funding to the Commission.

4. For an illustrative policy template that frames resources and responsibilities in neoliberal terms that hold individuals, families, and communities responsible, while de-emphasizing public and state responsibility except in managerial terms, see the current Nova Scotia government's Social Prosperity Framework at <gov. ns.ca/coms/department/noteworthy/WeavingtheThreads.html>.

5. By this Brown means "the extension of economic rationality to all aspects of thought and activity, the placement of the state in forthright and direct service to the economy, the rendering of the state tout court as an enterprise organized by market rationality, the production of the moral subject as an entrepreneurial subject, and the construction of social policy according to these criteria" (Brown 2003: 19).

6. By governing through crime Simon means the following: the prevention and fighting of crime and behaviours "analogized to crimes" have become strategic tools that bring legitimacy to governing actions across institutional settings; governing through crime is used "to legitimate interventions that have other motivations"; and "technologies, discourses, and metaphors of crime and criminal justice" have become more prominent across social institutions, creating "new opportunities for governance."

7. Between 1997 and 2008 the Canadian federal government repeatedly underestimated its resources through what it termed "surprise surplus." The government announced a "surprise surplus" in ten out of those eleven years, with those ten surplus surprises valued at $85 billion. See Certified General Accountants Association of Canada, 2008, *The Federal Budget Surplus: Surprise or Strategy?* By 2008 that budget was substantially reduced and by 2009 Canada's deficit (brought on by the global capitalist recession) approximated the value of those surprise surpluses. In another illustration of neoliberalism in action, the more constrained federal budget situation immediately preceding the recession (and ensuring that Canada did not have a substantial cushion to meet that crisis) was produced primarily through the Conservative government of Stephen Harper's aggressive tax cuts, combined with an economic downturn spurred through the neoliberal economic policies and neoconservative foreign policy of the two U.S. administrations of George W. Bush. On the reduced surplus and neoliberal economics in Canada see the Conference Board of Canada, "The 2008 Federal Budget: The End of Surplus?" at <conferenceboard.ca/budget/> and B. Evans, 2008, "Canada's Budget 2008: Taxes and the Forward March of Neoliberalism," *Global Research* at <globalresearch.ca/index.php?context=va&aid=8235>.

8. For further analysis of welfare policy as a diverse set of tools for the enactment of neoliberalism see also Y. Hartmann, 2005. "In Bed with the Enemy: Some Ideas on the Connections between Neoliberalism and the Welfare State," *Current Sociology* 53, 1.

9. See "Planning & Development" as laid out in the website of the Waterfront Development Corporation, the provincial crown corporation that controls the Halifax waterfront <wdcl.ca/pages/PlanningDevelopment.aspx>. See also the overviews there of Bishop's Landing and South Battery Plaza, and the proposed Salter Street and Queen's Landing Developments. A coal firing power plant

and a massive oil refinery also hold prominent places in the Halifax Basin and Halifax–Dartmouth Waterfront, holdovers from an earlier liberal capitalist era. The refinery on the Dartmouth side is the first thing tourists see from the waterfront after leaving Halifax's cruise ship terminal.

10. For a copy of the Charter see <laws.justice.gc.ca/en/charter/>.

11. Canadian Charter of Rights and Freedoms, Part I Constitution Act 1982, Schedule B to Canada Act, c. 11; *R. v. McCluskey* (2005), at para. 27.

12. For the Bill 7 amendment, see Motor Vehicle Act 1989 R.S.N.S. c. 293 s. 173A, as amended S.N.S. 2007, c. 45, s. 13.

13. For example, in the same year that it eliminated the Law Reform Commission, which made the use of criminal law problematic (2006), Harper's Conservative government eliminated funding to the Court Challenges Program, a national non-profit organization established in 1994 to fund court challenges against laws thought to violate Charter rights. Undoubtedly in an attempt to appease voters in Quebec (where the Conservatives are weak politically), funding for language rights cases only was restored in 2008. See M. Sheppard, 2008, "Partial Restoration of Court Challenges Program," available at <slaw.ca/2008/06/20/partial-restoration-of-court-challenges-program/>.

Chapter 1

Understanding the Role of Law-and-Order Policies in Canadian Cities

Todd Gordon

Over the last two decades law-and-order policing has become prominent in many advanced capitalist countries, including Canada. Supporters justify this trend by pointing to allegedly increasing crime rates, fear of crime, and the need to maintain the thin blue line between order and criminal chaos, particularly in cities. Critics argue that law-and-order policing criminalizes poverty. This chapter challenges both views and demonstrates that law-and-order policing promotes neoliberal economic and political aims. At the heart of the neoliberal project is the re-imposition and expansion of market relations, including the wage relation as people's principal means of subsistence (Sears 1999; Bonefeld 1993). Policing is at the core of this project in so far as it responds to low income and poor peoples' resistance to the new neoliberal labour market.

Law and Order, Gentrification, and Fear of the Poor Other

In social activist circles, law-and-order policing is often viewed as a bulwark for gentrification or as a response to the fear of the Other: the poor represent an unsettling reminder, especially to the affluent, of the darker side of economic restructuring that needs to be removed from sight. In my own involvement in anti-law-and-order policing activism in Ontario in the late 1990s and early 2000s, I commonly came across the gentrification and fear of the Other argument. While these arguments have some merit they do not sufficiently analyze the influence of neoliberalism on the emergence of law-and-order policies, especially as they have been pursued in non-gentrified communities.

Certainly, gentrification has been a significant social force affecting the landscape of urban centres in North America and elsewhere. Wealthy residents and business associations (supported by local police and/or private security forces) have sought to remove panhandlers, and others deemed undesirable, from their neighbourhoods or business districts. Some formerly poor and working-class urban areas are being transformed into higher income neighbourhoods for living and shopping, and police have played a role in defending this development. But if gentrification is the primary reason for law-and-order policing, then how do we explain the fact that it is not limited to gentrified neighbourhoods? Clearly neoliberal states have a broader interest in policing initiatives that we are unable to fully grasp if we reduce law-and-order policing to gentrification (Committee to Stop Targeted Policing 2000; Pivot Legal Society 2002; Parenti 2000; Davis 1992).

Law-and-order policing is not so much about the targeting of a certain socio-economic condition (such as poverty) embodied in an Other, as it is about the targeting of forms of behaviour. For instance, in their efforts to establish a capitalist labour market, and thus a class of wage labourers, nineteenth-century British designers of the new poor laws and the first modern police in a capitalist society were concerned not with poverty but indigence: the condition of the able-bodied poor who refused wage labour and thus market relations. Vagrancy laws and public-order policing in early capitalist Britain criminalized indigence, not poverty (Neocleous 2000).[1] This same sentiment is being expressed today through the intersection of law-and-order policing and the restructuring of the economy and the welfare state. The poor being targeted under law-and-order policies are most often seeking an income outside the wage form (through panhandling, for example) in public or semi-public space. At a place of legitimate employment, the poor are less at risk of being targeted by police.

This intersection in law-and-order policing and economics is made clearer if we note the broader ways in which wage work is intimately bound up with a person's moral standing in capitalist society. The poor who rely on welfare, begging, or squeegee work, which grew as a practice in major Canadian cities through the 1990s, have been derided by conservative and liberal politicians, government officials, and mainstream media, as lazy, undeserving of public support, and overly dependent on handouts. Critics often present wage work, a marker of self-discipline and respectability in capitalist society, as the solution (Neocleous 2000). Signs of indigence are treated as automatic expressions of disorder that must be policed. In this respect law-and-order policing under neoliberalism cannot be reduced to attempting to remove the Other from sight.

Neoliberalism

Advanced capitalist countries, such as Canada, have undergone significant political and economic transformations over the last three decades. Neoliberalism represents a break from the policies of the Keynesian welfare state, when large sections of the working class won an increased standard of living and a measure of state-provided social security, such as unemployment insurance, welfare benefits, and healthcare (Palmer 1992). The shift toward neoliberal policy, which emerged most visibly after the economic crisis of the

1970s, is in some important respects a return to the liberalism of the nineteenth century, when the free market and capitalist profitability were largely unimpeded by such things as labour legislation or welfare provisions (Sears 1999; Gordon 2007).[2] Neoliberalism includes strategies aimed at increasing capitalist profitability by, among other things, aggressively restructuring the labour market to create a cheaper and more flexible workforce, particularly at its bottom end.

The establishment of such a workforce is a significant diminishment of peoples' expectations in terms of job and living conditions. Business and political leaders (both conservative and centrist) have mobilized the state to ensure the development of a neoliberal workforce. Social programs like employment insurance and welfare have been cut drastically in order to force people into the bottom end of the labour market. Labour protections and the right to strike for better wages and job security have been scaled back. Even as education requirements for all levels in the workforce rise, the education system is being redesigned to teach greater individual responsibility and prepare young students for an unpromising labour market. In other words, the neoliberal state and its private partners are forcing people into market relations that are most beneficial to capital by denying people alternatives for subsistence. Contrary to the commonly held perception that neoliberalism involves a retreat of the state, measures such as coercive welfare policy and anti-union legislation actually expand the coercive role of the state.

Locating the Emergence of Law-and-Order Policing

Law-and-order policing must be understood in the context of neoliberalism, rather than as simply a policy whim of conservative governments who play on fear of crime for electoral gain. The emergence of law-and-order policing in advanced capitalist states at this time suggests that it represents more than political opportunism. Law-and-order policing needs to be seen as one tactic in a gamut of policies, including cuts to social programs and the attack on workers' rights, designed to impose a specific wage experience on the working class, particularly those at the lower end of the labour market.

As noted above, the current use of law-and-order policing is reminiscent of the emergence of the modern police in nineteenth-century Britain. As Neocleous convincingly argues, the modern police were organized, in conjunction with the new poor laws, as part of the state's efforts to produce a class of wage workers by hindering alternatives for subsistence beyond wages (Neocleous 2000). The use of criminal law regulating vagrancy and public order laws regulating loitering, public disturbance, and breach of peace, and the broad discretionary power to target and detain the poor contained within them, were means toward this end (Neocleous 2000). Early police forces in Britain inspected labourers at their workplaces to forcefully end the labouring class's use of customary traditions through which they appropriated some of the product upon which they laboured; also referred to as ancient entitlements, this custom would allow, for example, a dock worker to appropriate spilt cargo or colliers some of the coal they mined. Capitalists and the state saw these traditions as a barrier to the working class's dependence on the wage and the authority of private capital. The police's attention quickly extended to street life, where they targeted begging, vending activities, sex trade work, and recreational activities, all of which were seen to undermine the discipline of wage labour by providing labourers opportunity to avoid the formal market. The aim of nineteenth-century moral reformers, police, industrialists, and politicians who crafted, supported, and executed these laws was not the criminalization of poverty; it was the able-bodied poor who avoided wage work, and their activities, that such measures criminalized (Bortich and Hagan 1987).

A more aggressive style of urban policing emerged in Britain and the United States in the late 1960s and early 1970s in response to rising industrial and political unrest (Parenti 2000; Hall et al. 1978). But the consolidation of a law-and-order policing strategy targeted at the systematic recomposition of the working classes developed with the political shift away from Keynesian labour relations and towards neoliberal state and employer efforts to create a cheaper and more flexible labour market (Sears 1999; Bonefeld 1993: 140).

By the late 1970s and early 1980s in Britain and the United States, and the mid- to late-1980s in Canada, police began consistent, targeted interventions in poorer, often racialized and immigrant, neighbourhoods that were hardest hit by recession, unemployment, and government cutbacks (Bonefeld 1993: 156; Parenti 2000; Gordon 2007). These policies came in tandem with cuts to unemployment insurance and welfare, freezing minimum wages, and curtailing union rights, among other things, and have provided many reasons for their aggressive interventions, including allegedly rampant criminality or, especially in the United States, the gang scare. Commentators have argued that these claims are more likely pretexts for the targeting of specific communities through controversial methods such as the stop and search (Davis 1992; Parenti 2000; Greaves 1986; Gordon 2007), a tactic that provides police broad discretionary power to stop people they deem suspicious on the pretence that the person may be considering illegal behaviour. It has been used overwhelmingly against young, poor, and unemployed persons, especially in communities of colour.

It was also in the 1980s and 1990s that zero-tolerance policing began to be widely adopted in all three countries (Parenti 2000; Greene 1999; Pollard 1998). This meant the systematic deployment of greater numbers of police in poor neighbourhoods, often with large immigrant communities, the aggressive targeting of low-level signs of disorder, and an increase in reported violations of civil rights by police. Wilson and Kelling, whose "Broken Windows" theory (which posits that low-level forms of public disorder are gateways that, if unchecked by police, will lead to more violent forms of crime) is considered a cornerstone of zero-tolerance policing, are quite explicit on who police targets should include. "The unchecked panhandler," they argue, "is, in effect, the first broken window" (Wilson and Kelling 1982).

In Canada, several municipalities and provinces adopted laws targeting panhandling in the 1990s. By 1999, thirteen of Canada's sixteen largest municipalities had such laws. Many of these restrictions came in the form of city by-laws that prohibit begging, which is framed as aggressive or intimidating and thus threatening to the safety of the public (Collins and Blomley 2001). The by-laws usually restrict panhandling at night or near bank machines or other urban spaces where someone is likely to have spare change handy. They also come with stiff penalties for offenders, including heavy fines and jail sentences (National Anti-Poverty Organization 1999). In 1999 the Ontario government passed the Ontario Safe Streets Act (OSSA), explicitly modelled on zero-tolerance policing strategies that emphasize the targeting of the poor and low level forms of disorder as the biggest problems facing communities (Schneiderman 2002). The OSSA was designed, in part, to forcibly remove squeegee persons, who are often in their teens or early twenties and often homeless, from the province's streets (Gordon 2007). Like other anti-panhandling by-laws, the OSSA targets supposedly aggressive solicitation that prohibits safe passage for pedestrians (implicitly defined as not visibly poor) along city streets. As Schneiderman notes, no research data documented this aggressive begging, and the act's definition of "aggressive" panhandling or squeegeeing is loose enough to provide wide discretionary scope for police (Schneiderman 2002; Moon 2002). Municipal by-laws and the OSSA make it de facto illegal, in the words of older vagrancy law, to "wander or trespass without means of support," or to seek that support outside the market (Schneiderman 2002: Esmonde 2002; O'Grady and Bright 2002).

"Get a Job!": Policing and Resistance to the New Labour Market

Law-and-order policing, with its emphasis on low level forms of disorder such as begging and hanging out in public spaces, also expresses the particular character of state power in a period of the neoliberal re-composition of wage labour. Research on squeegeeing and panhandling has shown that many people who are withdrawing from wage labour are doing so as a conscious form of resistance to the new neoliberal labour market. Thus, law-and-order policing is central to the extension of market relations further into peoples' lives and to driving down wages and expectations at the lower end of the labour market. As with the early role of British police described by Neocleous, contemporary law-and-order policing forcefully restricts activities that encourage or enable people to live outside wage relations and the order of capital. As Sears argues, "state disciplinary activities reinforce market discipline by visibly suppressing forms of deviant conduct which threaten the norms of commodity exchange" (Sears 1999).

In key respects law-and-order policing is a response to socio-economic resistance at the bottom end of the labour market, when people seek to avoid the worst paying and most dead-end, unsatisfying, and insecure forms of market work. This is expressed, for example, in the policing of vagrancy and panhandling. Greater government and police scrutiny of panhandling in recent years has particularly targeted the young and able-bodied, as with the squeegeers who were a principal target of the OSSA. Police and law-and-order advocates suggest that they are targeting criminals or criminal hotspots, as they have in Toronto under the Community Action Policing program (also known as targeted policing). However, the targets of such crusades actually represent low-level public disorder: they are predominantly the poor, panhandlers, squeegeers, youth hanging out in parks, and sex trade workers. These are poor and working class people seeking an income outside of the formal labour market or engaged in recreational pursuits rather than enduring wage discipline (Committee to Stop Targeted Policing 2000). Indeed, the remarks in legislature debates surrounding the adoption of the Safe Streets Act in Ontario, of politicians and other anti-squeegeeing and panhandling commentators in the media, and of the coordinator of Toronto's squeegee employment training program, all make clear that a major concern of policy makers with regard to this legislation is peoples' efforts to live outside of market relations (Gordon 2007).

People panhandle, squeegee, or sell sex for a number of reasons; however, people also consciously try to avoid the drudgery of wage work at the bottom end of the labour market. As Kelley (1997) argues with regard to the urban U.S. context in the 1980s and 1990s, when economic restructuring means that much of the higher paying and more secure wage work has evaporated in working-class communities, especially communities of colour, people turn to different strategies to avoid some of the more unfulfilling jobs. One response of African American youth to economic restructuring was to turn the pursuit of fun and creative expression into cash, engaging in breakdancing, rapping, and pick-up basketball on streets and in parks for money. These contemporary forms of "play" are part of a history of working-class street performance aimed at generating income outside the formal labour market. Kelley argues that African Americans' use of "play" in this manner has provided "a range of strategies within capitalism ... intended to enable working-class urban youth to avoid dead-end wage labor while devoting their energies to creative and pleasurable pursuits" (Kelley 1997: 45).

In their study of policing in 1970s Britain, Hall et al. (1978) noted a similar response to economic restructuring by working-class youth, especially in Black communities. They argue that the preference for street-based income-generating activities — such as panhandling, drug dealing, and running numbers — over waged work steadily increased as formal market prospects for decent paying work decreased through the 1970s. Likewise, O'Grady, Bright, and Cohen (1998) found in their ethnographic study of Toronto squeegeers in the mid- to late-1990s that squeegeers quite explicitly considered their street work "to be preferable to most 'legitimate,' low wage employment." For many poor youth, earning an income off the streets, although not without its difficulties and dangers, is often a more appealing option than very poorly paid wage work, the conditions of which they have no control over. As O'Grady, Bright, and Cohen note, "working the streets… [is] a form [of] resistance to low wage employment" (O'Grady, Bright, and Cohen 1998: 322).

Legislators, policy makers, and police systematically target these activities that refuse the market. As Kelley notes, Black youth have been arrested for "disturbing the peace" when they use art, such as break-dancing, in public spaces to earn cash (Kelley 1997). As suggested above, despite policing claims to the contrary, little evidence has been provided to prove that panhandling, squeegeeing, public breakdancing, or simply hanging with friends in public space represent a significant threat to urban public safety. Yet they have all been recent policing priorities. The real danger to public order being suggested here, then, lies not in the acts in and of themselves — the break-dancing, the cleaning of a car windshield, or the request for spare change — but in the possibility of participants earning an income from them. The order being defended is very specific: it is the order of capital, which demands the complete subordination of labour to wage relations in a market structured for capitalist profit. Earning an income outside of this market is an affront to that order and as such is intolerable.

The contemporary targeting of the able-bodied and unemployed poor by policy makers, legislators, and police is also informed by corporations' introduction of lean production methods. Lean production is guided, Sears notes, by the ethos of the "lean person," which requires workers to produce more, work longer hours, multi-task, and, if necessary, carry more than one job to make ends meet (Sears 1999). Personal sacrifice and self-discipline, bound up with the willingness to work a lot harder for less pay, is the norm that the state and employers expect today (Sears 2003: Moody 1997).[3] The inability or refusal to live by this ethos speaks, in the eyes of the state and employers, to a person's weak moral and potentially criminal character.

The emphasis on this ethos can translate into real anger towards poor people who are on the streets panhandling, labouring for spare change, or simply hanging out, particularly from police officers responsible for enforcing laws against these acts. Thus, "Get off the streets and get a job you pieces of shit" is a form of verbal abuse that some police officers direct at squeegee persons (O'Grady and Bright 2002). Such comments express how law-and-order policing is fortified by the way in which wage work is strongly imbued with moral connotations. Peoples' choice to seek alternatives to the market, and not simply the condition of being poor, is an affront to respectability and the moral order.

Thus a great deal of police energy in recent years has been directed at the typically young and able-bodied panhandler, squeegeer, or poor hanging out in public space (Gordon 2007).[4] By way of illustration, the removal of large numbers of beggars from public spaces was an important result of Toronto's zero-tolerance-inspired targeted policing campaign in 1999 (Gordon 2007). Since the mid-1990s, the Winnipeg police have also strategically reoriented their foot patrols to areas police vaguely describe as high in person-to-person crime, but they have also reported that a key focus of their activity is removing panhandlers from public spaces (Winnipeg Police Service 1998). Parenti (2000) noted a similar pattern in U.S. cities in the 1990s. More police were assigned to walk the beat and were then strategically placed in areas where squeegeers, panhandlers, and the poor were known to hang out. While it has the veneer of a friendlier approach, community policing is another significant policing trend that serves purposes similar to those of zero-tolerance policy. Community input is kept to a minimum if it is used at all, as police use the allegedly consultative angle of these programs to justify deeper penetration of usually poorer communities. Community policing research on Britain in the 1980s and Toronto in the 1990s suggests that it emphasizes foot patrols aimed at removing panhandlers, squeegeers, sex trade workers, and loiterers from public spaces (Fischer 2000; Gordon 1987). These policing practices, as part of officially adopted police department philosophies, actively criminalize the failure to adopt the ethos of the "lean person" by targeting those scraping together an income outside of the market or using public space while avoiding work.

The anger towards the able-bodied who fail or refuse to achieve the ethos of the lean person is expressed beyond formal policing philosophies. An unofficial police campaign against squeegeers and poor youth in Toronto in the late 1990s provides a good example of this pattern. Jackie Esmonde's ethnographic study on squeegeeing in Toronto shows that the police aimed to physically intimidate and remove squeegeers and other poor youth from streets and public parks. As one police sergeant comments to her, "My direction to my officers is that we don't drive by or go by a problem.... Our position is zero tolerance to this problem" (Esmonde 1999: 129). Different police departments across Toronto employed similar tactics, suggesting that an intentional and coordinated citywide policy was being pursued. Police liberally handed out tickets to squeegeers and panhandlers for various municipal and provincial offences. Offences included soliciting business on a road, impeding traffic, blocking a sidewalk, jaywalking, operating a bicycle without a bell, littering (for leaving a squeegee on the ground), and even possession of a prohibited weapon (again, a squeegee) (Esmonde 1999; Davidson 2000). Many of these charges have little to do with the act of begging itself or any danger that a squeegeers supposedly represent to the public. After its enactment in 1999, the police used the Ontario Safe Streets Act to remove squeegeers from the streets, and some squeegeers even reported spending time in jail as a result (Davidson 2000).

This mass ticketing campaign was accompanied by Toronto police engaging in the often violent harassment of street persons, the stealing of their property (squeegees, bags, and identification), and illegally detaining them — all measures clearly designed to frighten individuals. Reportedly, police regularly stopped squeegeers and other poor youth panhandling, who had not broken any law, to take their photos, physically assaulted such individuals standing on the street or sleeping in parks, and burned a squat to the ground (Davidson 2000; Esmonde 1999). By the end of 2000, the presence of squeegeers or poor youth hanging out or sleeping in parks appeared to have dramatically declined in Toronto.[5] Reports on policing in Vancouver's downtown eastside also detail aggressive campaigns that feature many of the methods used in Toronto (Pivot Legal Society 2002; Justice for Girls 2003).

Conclusion

This chapter argues that to properly understand the implications of law-and-order policing we need to situate its emergence within the context of neoliberal state and corporate restructuring and related efforts to recompose the working class. Law-and-order policing is an integral feature of neoliberal state power, rather than simply the coincidental product of conservative and centrist governments and opportunistic politicians in various countries. Law-and-order policing expresses both the state's commitment to the creation of a cheaper and flexible labour market and the aspirations of many people to avoid this wage experience. Further, this chapter challenges commonplace assumptions about the retreat of the state under neoliberalism. State restructuring clearly does not entail the eclipse of state power. To the contrary, it necessitates the mobilization of state power. Policing, often in an increasingly aggressive form, is on the front lines of that process, targeting those people who dare to resist the new neoliberal labour market.

Notes

1. While "indigence" has also been used to refer to the aged and infirm, who cannot physically obtain their own means of subsistence, it was also used by

police theorists and designers of the new poor laws, along with "pauperism," to demarcate the able-bodied employed poor from the able-bodied poor avoiding work. Neocleous (2000) cites the use of the term as an important expression of the move beyond undifferentiated notions of poverty in the early nineteenth century as the British state actively tried to establish a capitalist labour market. In some of these writings, Neocleous argues, "'Indigence' is merely coda for any attempt to avoid wage labour, to refuse exploitation" (Neocleous 2000: 55). It is in this respect that the term is employed in this article.

2.   Although nineteenth-century liberalism and neoliberalism share attributes, especially their end goals — imposing market relations deeper into peoples' lives and aggressively pursuing the interests of capital vis-à-vis workers — they are not entirely the same thing. For example, we still have remnants of the post-World War II labour relations regime and the welfare state today, which provide some, albeit increasingly meagre, relief from the vagaries of the market. At the same time, these very social welfare programs are also now part of the state's efforts to restructure the labour market. Recipients of Employment Insurance in Canada, for instance, get quite limited financial support and must also participate in jobs training programs that emphasize personal responsibility and acceptance of the new labour market.

3.   For a general overview of lean production and the ethos of the lean worker, see Sears 2003: 56.

4.   One indication of this energy is the rate of public order charges by police compared to criminal charges, as the former far outstrips the latter. While this chapter has focused on police attention towards squeegeers and panhandlers, they've also stepped up their targeting of sex trade workers and young persons of colour dealing and using soft drugs such as marijuana or, in Toronto's Somalian community, khat.

5.   This assertion is based on my own experience walking and driving through downtown Toronto.

Chapter 2

Social Assistance and the Politics of Welfare Fraud Investigations

The Case of Alberta

Trevor W. Harrison

"Seek and Ye shall find." Matthew 7:7

The 1990s saw the retrenchment of welfare state programs in several countries including Canada. This chapter[1] examines the politics underlying these efforts, looking specifically at government decisions to locate, prosecute, and publicize welfare fraud. I argue that government actions in collecting welfare statistics present a picture of welfare clients that undermines public support for the poor and provides ammunition for conservative governments bent on slashing social assistance funding. I further argue that welfare retrenchment predates the rise of neoliberalism in the 1980s and 1990s. The fiscal crisis of the 1990s, identified by various governments, can be viewed as less a cause than an excuse for welfare state retrenchment. The specific case examined here is that of Alberta during the period of the Conservative government of Ralph Klein (1992–2006). The arguments presented, however, pertain to Canadian governments at large.

Setting the Stage

Alberta suffered two significant economic downturns in the 1980s. The first — and worst — occurred in 1982, with a severe drop in oil royalties. The second came hard on the heels of the first, occurring in 1986. These events were followed in the early 1990s by a more generalized Canadian recession, which added to Alberta's fiscal woes. In this context, the Conservative government of premier Donald Getty began reining in government spending (Taft 1997). Efforts at belt tightening accelerated when Ralph Klein became leader of the provincial Conservative Party and premier in December 1992.

Throughout 1992, the Conservatives — in office provincially since 1971 — trailed badly in the polls. Klein's government skillfully employed a mix of traditional populism and neoconservative rhetoric about crime and "special interests" (Harrison, Johnston, and Krahn 2005) to turn the Tory ship around. They rode to electoral victory on a platform of fiscal austerity, having convinced the vast majority of Albertans that government spending required even more belt tightening.

The early 1990s were a tough time in many Canadian jurisdictions. The recession left much of the Canadian economy reeling. While other Canadian jurisdictions chose a mix of spending cuts and tax increases to deal with their fiscal imbalances, Alberta was singular in resorting to a massive downsizing of government and government services (Canada West Foundation 1998). Downsizing impacted all departments and services, but welfare — and welfare recipients — took a particularly large hit (Flanagan 2005).[2]

Social Assistance in Alberta

Even before the Klein government came into office, Alberta (beginning with the 1986 recession) had implemented some of the most drastic cuts to benefit levels in all of Canada, especially for single people (Roy 2004). In 1990, in response to increasing welfare caseloads, the government curtailed benefits and began a process of categorizing recipients based on their relationship to the labour market (Gorlick and Brethour 1998).

Alberta's welfare caseload stood at 98,642 in December 1992 (Gorlick and Brethour 1998). Continuing a long history of meagre assistance (Reichwein 2003), the province's social assistance rate was the second lowest in the country (Roy 2004). In April 1993, the Alberta government announced a new welfare reform initiative, based on reduced benefits and stricter eligibility rules, designed to "reinforce the principle that welfare was now a program of last resort and not a choice of lifestyle"(Gorlick and Brethour 1998: 194). Table 2.1 shows the consequences of this initiative.

Between 1993 and 2004, the percentage of people on social assistance in Alberta dropped by nearly 69.4 percent compared to a national drop of 42.7 percent. Similarly, the ratio of Albertans per 100,000 on social assistance dropped during this period from 7.4 to 1.9, compared to a national drop from 10.4 to 5.3. In short, while Alberta's social assistance cuts were not entirely unique — the number of welfare recipients throughout Canada dropped steadily between 1993 and 2004 — nowhere was the drop as great as in Alberta (National Council on Welfare 1998, 2000; Murphy 1995; Lafrance 2005: 269–84; Elton et al. 1997).

There are a number of possible explanations for the decreasing number of social assistance recipients in Alberta since the early 1990s. Certainly, the past decade has seen Alberta's economy surge, fuelled by rising world oil and gas prices. Alberta became officially "debt free" in 2004 (Flanagan 2005), and its unemployment rate is low despite the recent recession. It is also likely, however, that Alberta's welfare policies have played a role in keeping the

Table 2.1 Social Assistance Recipients, Percentage Change, and Social Assistance Rate, Alberta and Canada, 1993–2004

| Year | Alberta | | | Canada* | | |
	SA recipients	+/- (%)	SA Rate	SA recipients	+/- (%)	SA rate
1993	196,000	--	7.4	2,975,000	--	10.4
1994	138,500	-29.3	5.2	3,100,200	4.2	10.8
1995	113,200	-18.3	4.2	3,070,900	-.1	10.5
1996	105,600	-6.7	3.8	2,937,100	-4.4	10.0
1997	89,800	-15.0	3.2	2,774,900	-5.5	9.3
1998	77,000	-14.2	2.7	2,577,500	-7.1	8.6
1999	71,900	-6.6	2.5	2,279,100	-11.6	7.5
2000	64,800	-9.9	2.2	2,085,100	-8.5	6.8
2001	58,000	-10.5	1.9	1,910,000	-8.4	6.2
2002	53,800	-7.2	1.7	1,842,600	-3.5	5.9
2003	57,800	+9.3	1.8	1,745,600	-5.3	5.5
2004	60,200	+4.2	1.9	1,705,065	-2.3	5.3
1993–04	-135,800	-69.4	--	-1,269,935	-42.7	--

*Includes Alberta. Sources: Roy 2004: 3.2, Tables 1 and 2; National Council of Welfare 2005: 92–93, Appendix A.

number of social assistance recipients low. In particular, low levels of social assistance support and a notoriously low minimum wage (increased in 2005 from $5.90 to $7.00 per hour; by 2009 the wage was $8.80) may have driven the unemployed and the working poor to other jurisdictions.

Those who remained in Alberta and wished to obtain social assistance after 1993 found their situation far more difficult. Government cuts and a series of other government initiatives implemented after April 1993 were designed to make welfare "much less financially generous, more difficult to access, and easier to exit unwillingly"(Murphy 1997: 116). One of these other initiatives, for example, was to rescind a 1986 departmental directive to assistance workers requiring that they fully inform clients of their rights and entitlements. From then on, clients were responsible for knowing what they should receive beyond basic subsistence.

As evidenced by changes to eligibility rules that made benefits contingent on continued efforts to find employment (Murphy 1995), the government intended to use welfare reform as a stick for forcing recipients into the labour market. Hence, many of those cut from welfare were placed in a variety of Alberta government programs designed to provide them with job skills and employment. While a few former welfare recipients may have benefited from these programs, evidence suggests that most were able to find only low-paying jobs (Boessenkool 1997).[3]

Fuelling the Myth of Welfare Fraud

Alberta's social assistance cuts aroused little public uproar. This lack of empathy was fed by already existing popular beliefs that many, if not all, welfare recipients could work if they wanted to; that, indeed, many were working on the side, while — in the vernacular — "ripping off" the system (Murphy 1995, 1997; Lafrance 2005; Black and Stanford 2005). A national poll conducted in July 1996 showed the public estimated that about 30 percent of those "receiving some form of social assistance from the government, such as welfare or unemployment insurance" were cheating the system (Canadians Assess Extent of Social Assistance Cheating," *Gallup*, August 15, 1996). This estimate regarding the amount of cheating ranged from 27 percent of those surveyed in British Columbia to 34 percent of those surveyed in the Atlantic provinces. The same poll, and an earlier one conducted in December 1992, showed a high degree of support on the part of Canadians for electronic fingerprint scanning to reduce fraud (60 percent) and the right of governments to verify information provided by welfare clients (71 percent). According to the 1992 poll, 44 percent of Canadians also believed that government spending on welfare was too high ("Majority Believe Government Can Check Upon Welfare Recipients," *Gallup*, January 18, 1993).[4] In short, right-wing politicians in Alberta and elsewhere built upon existing negative stereotypes while also fuelling public suspicions of welfare recipients.[5]

This was informed by the fact that Alberta has a long history of hostility to welfare recipients (Murphy 1995, 1997) and of contradictory treatment towards the poor in general (Reichwein 2003). In part, the reasons are cultural, tied to the province's well-honed myth of prairie individualism. The belief that the poor should pick themselves up by the bootstraps is often voiced by politicians and is encoded in Alberta's welfare practices, along with a deep suspicion of the motives and trustworthiness of welfare recipients (Murphy 1995).

Ralph Klein's Tory government drew upon these existing perceptions in fomenting the rhetoric of welfare abuse and fraud. Some Conservative politicians and government officials went particularly out of their way to verbally denigrate welfare recipients. Bob Scott, the Public Affairs Bureau spokesperson then attached to Alberta's Department of Social Services, noted with regard to the expansion of the Job Corps program that, "this move will result in a huge lifestyle change for some people. They'll have to shave, shower, and go to work like everyone else" (Murphy 1997: 119). Scott's comments may have been particularly unguarded; they were not, however, singular (Murphy 1995).

The media — much of it fawningly uncritical of the Klein government during its first mandate (Laxer and Harrison 1995) — played a major role in highlighting welfare stories. An Internet search of newspaper headlines from January 1, 1993, to January 1, 1997, turned up 2,000 headlines with the key words "Alberta" and "welfare" (Gazso and Krahn 2008). In Edmonton, where welfare cuts were greatest, a plethora of stories appeared between 1993–97. In the early days of the Klein revolution the generally liberal-minded *Edmonton Journal* alone carried a host of stories dealing with welfare fraud in and outside of Alberta.[6] Media reporting of fraud cases during these years was assisted by the government's sustained efforts at uncovering fraud through a bulking up of resources dedicated to this purpose.

The Reality of Welfare Fraud

Welfare retrenchment is often associated with neoliberalism, beginning in the 1980s and 1990s. An examination of the history of welfare in Alberta suggests, however, that retrenchment began two decades earlier. Furthermore, the history of Alberta welfare policies contradicts the idea that fiscal crisis is the causal factor underlying welfare state retrenchment.

Under the Social Credit Party in 1966, Alberta formed its first Maintenance and Recovery Branch within its Social Services department to serve primarily an auditing function. A few years later, the branch suddenly found itself very busy. The oil boom of the early 1970s brought an influx of people into the province looking for work. Not finding regular employment, many sought out welfare assistance.[7] The suspicion that some of these new clients were being less than honest led Alberta Social Services and Community Health (ASSCH) in 1977 (with the government now under the helm of the Progressive Conservatives) to implement a pilot project to determine the amount of fraud and administrative or client error in the welfare system (Alberta Social Services and Community Health 1979). Based on a sample of 1,368 cases, the investigation team estimated a total of 17 percent of public assistance cases in Alberta involved either fraud or error, broken down as 9.1 involving fraud, 6.7 percent involving administrative error, and 1.2 percent involving client error. Those found to commit fraud were mainly single parents and employable people. While the study's final report noted, "many frauds and errors involve small or no financial losses," it did estimate total losses from error and fraud combined at 5.3 percent of Alberta's provincial public assistance budget at the time, or about $7.4 million (Alberta Social Services and Community Health 1979: 6).

Before the study's final report came out, it had already resulted in some permanent changes that, the writers of the report believed, would further reduce the amount of error and fraud in the system. Among changes noted were "a stricter requirement for personal identification and documentation of circumstances, more home visits and implementation of a standardized medical form" and the creation of a "permanent Eligibility Unit in the department" (Alberta Social Services and Community Health 1979: 15).

In short, the Alberta government in the late 1970s embarked on a series of organizational changes designed to deal with an undifferentiated combination of welfare abuse and administrative error. These changes were not the last, however. Efforts to locate and squeeze out the last vestiges of welfare fraud were renewed in the 1980s as Alberta underwent a series of wrenching economic downturns.

From 1985–86, Alberta experienced its second serious recession in four years. In this context, and following a 1987 Auditor General's report that suggested a serious level of welfare overpayments (perhaps $35 million) due to a variety of causes (administrative and client error and fraud), the Alberta government conducted another study of welfare fraud. In September 1987, the re-named department of Alberta Family and Social Services launched the Eligibility and Benefit Verification Project (EBVP) (Alberta Family and Social Services 1988). The pilot project involved a random sample of 1,484 client files drawn from district offices throughout Alberta's six administrative regions. Based on these initial findings, project administrators extrapolated potential savings, if the project were extended to the entire province, of between $5.6 and $12.3 million for the year 1988–89. Subsequently, the EBVP was extended province-wide, and forty more verification officers were hired, bringing the number to fifty. (It should be noted, however, the extrapolated savings did not include the cost of these additional hires.)

Of 7,495 client files examined under the EBVP's expanded verification program for the fiscal year 1988–89, 20 percent had minor errors not related to eligibility or benefit levels; 22 percent had overpayments, but 17 percent also had underpayments. Only 4 percent were referred for fraud investigation (Alberta Family and Social Services 1989). The expanded EBVP resulted in further government changes dealing with welfare fraud. Chief among these was the establishment in 1991 of the Fraud and Error Control Unit (FECU) with its own manager, located within the Department of Family and Social Services, and the hiring of an additional thirty-two staff.[8]

Estimates made by the Alberta government suggest that these efforts at preventing welfare fraud were hugely successful. As previously noted, a departmental study in 1979 estimated the welfare fraud at about 9 percent (Alberta Social Services and Community Health 1979); in 1989 at about 4 percent (Alberta Social Services and Community Health 1989). Just after Ralph Klein won Alberta's leadership race to become premier, a high official in Alberta Family and Social Services publicly estimated the amount of deliberate abuse at 2 percent (Helm 1993: A7). These lower estimates conformed to figures accepted elsewhere for welfare fraud (Feagin 1975).[9]

In short, departmental estimates regarding the degree of both error and fraud in Alberta's welfare system showed a steady decline throughout the 1970s and 1980s. While some might demand that all cases be weeded out, most analysts agree that some amount of error and fraud are inevitable in any large bureaucratic system, public or private (Moscovitch 1997). In 1993, Mike Cardinal, Minister of Alberta Family and Social Services and not a man known to be soft on welfare recipients, admitted as much, while also wanting to defend his department's credibility. He noted that while welfare overpayments might amount to about $2 million, they were also probably a minimum unavoidable expense: "We have a big [case] load, a $1.7-billion budget and close to 6,000 staff. Even with staff working well and hard there are bound to be some mistakes" (Helm 1993: A7). Cardinal further noted that Social Services had made great strides from five years earlier when the Auditor General had pegged overpayments at $35 million.

Welfare Fraud After 1993: The Search Continues

Despite its own evidence the Alberta government continued to foster public beliefs of rampant welfare abuse after 1992 (Murphy 1995, 1997). Indeed, it increased the amount of resources — people and money — dedicated to fraud detection. The Fraud and Error Control Unit (FECU) took on added importance, and by the fall of 1994, Alberta's FECU operated three programs: fraud investigation; eligibility review; and error detection, correction, and improvement, the last instituted to "correct policies and practices which result in client abuse of welfare" (Alberta Family and Social Services 1995). A 1999 Social Services document, identifying the FECU's mandate and procedures, adopts a somewhat less harsh tone:

> Fraud and Error Control investigates and prosecutes fraud and identifies potential recoveries through file closures, court-ordered restitution and compensation and recovery agreements. The Eligibility Review Officer (RO) and Error Detection, Correction and Improvement (EDCI) staff review client files and verify client circumstances through home visits, contact with employers, landlords, banks, etc. These reviews produce cost savings through identification of overpayments due to administrative and client error. (Alberta Family and Social Services 1999: 24)

That same year, as previously mentioned, Alberta's government departments experienced a massive reorganization of functions that saw a new ministry created, Alberta Human Resources and Employment (AHRE). The new ministry became responsible for many functions formerly performed by social services, among them the provision of social assistance and the

FECU. The latter was renamed the Fraud Investigation Unit, while the detection of administrative errors was left to Error Detection and Correction Investigations (EDCI), now a separate unit within AHRE. Unfortunately, there is no way to know whether the detection of fraud is being prioritized over the detection of error.

Table 2.2 shows a large and steady decline in the number of welfare fraud complaints, investigations, and charges between 1993 and 2005. It is also useful to note that not all charges resulted in convictions. In 1992, for example, Alberta laid 457 charges, but there were only 209 convictions for fraud (Helm 1993: A7). The following year, the province laid 346 charges, resulting once more in slightly more than 200 convictions.[10]

How much has welfare fraud in Alberta cost the government? For the fiscal year 1994–95, Alberta's Welfare Fraud and Error Control Unit claimed

Table 2.2 Fraud Investigations in Alberta, 1993–2005

Year	Complaints*	Investigations**	Charges Laid***
1993–94	11,263	3,575	367
1994–95	9,007	2,560	446
1995–96	8,644	2,040	452
1996–97	7,684	2,100	323
1997–98	8,009	2,070	227
1998–99	8,975	3,294	179
1999–00	7,574	2,822	161
2000–01	6,210	2,584	184
2001–02	5,146	1,619	167
2002–03	4,819	1,311	155
2003–04	4,600	1,736	171
2004–05	4,402	1,714	177

* Complaints include complaints or contacts received at fraud investigation offices from sources within or outside the ministry. The complaint count may include contact or information that does not relate directly to suspected abuse or fraud.
** Investigations means the number of files assigned to an investigator, who then determines if abuse has occurred.
*** Charges Laid means the total number of charges laid. There may be more than one charge per case file.
Source: The figures for the years 1993–94 and 1995–96 come from Alberta Family and Social Services 1995: 7; 1996: 8. The figures for the years afterwards come from Human Resources and Employment 2005: attachment 1. The statistics gathered from AFSS (1993–94 and 1995–96) appear to include both error and fraud investigations. The statistics afterwards deal only with fraud cases.

to have identified through fraud investigations $6.6 million in "potentially recoverable funds" (Alberta Family and Social Services 1995: 8). For 1995–96, the Unit identified $6.8 million paid to clients due both to error and fraud (Alberta Family and Social Services 1996). The amount of actual money recovered in either year is unclear, however.

The question of whether efforts to locate welfare fraud are cost effective is difficult to answer definitively. According to government sources, the answer is yes. One estimate pegged the return to investment at four-to-one (Helm 1993: A7) but the accuracy of this claim is hard to test. As we have seen, Cardinal suggested in 1993 that the amount of money lost to overpayments (i.e., not only fraud) might be $2 million. Yet the maintenance and recovery budget from 1993–97 consistently ranged around $3 million, and in 2003–04 was nearly $4 million.[11] Not surprisingly, much of the budget went to staff increases. The number of staff at the FECU went from thirty-two in 1991 to sixty-seven (full-time equivalents [FTEs]) in 1993–94, then to seventy-six (FTEs) during the period 1996–2001, before declining to fifty-seven FTEs (Alberta Human Resources and Employment 2005). In short, the 1990s saw the Alberta government cut back severely on social assistance expenditures, while increasing the amount of money spent and the amount of staff hired to identify administrative errors and fraud within the social service program. The fact that the government's own estimates of the amount of either error or fraud occurring in the system showed a steady decline from the late 1970s on, and that government statements suggest few savings compared to the costs of investigation, raises questions.

Given the apparent decline in welfare fraud cases even before 1993, what appears to be a low return on investment in fraud investigations, and the plethora of criminal actions of all sorts open to prosecution by the state, how do we explain the Alberta government's single-minded efforts at seeking out welfare fraud?

Discussion

Justified by perceptions of economic uncertainty and the prescriptions of neoliberal ideology, governments in the 1990s embarked on a series of fiscal cuts, many of them directed at the welfare state. Abroad, Tony Blair's "New Labour" government in Britain became a devotee of workfare, further entrenching policies begun two decades before under the Thatcher administration. In the United States, President Bill Clinton's democrats similarly undid America's minimalist welfare state, reducing welfare benefits and toughening eligibility criteria (Dye 1998: 128–130). Within Canada, the Conservative governments of Ralph Klein in Alberta (1993–2006) and Mike Harris in Ontario (1995–2002) became the chief poster boys for similar experiments (Klassen and Buchanan 1997; Moscovitch 1997; Ontario Ministry of Community and Social Services 1997, 2000)

Yet, as the case of Alberta suggests, caution must be exercised in assuming that welfare retrenchment began with the recent neoliberal era. While retrenchment certainly intensified during this period, similar trends were already emerging two decades earlier. In this context, the fiscal crisis of the 1990s, identified by various governments, can be viewed as less a cause than an excuse for welfare state retrenchment, including renewed attacks upon the poor and vulnerable.

Finding, publicizing, and prosecuting welfare fraud is an important adjunct to social assistance cuts, reinforcing the erroneous belief held by many that public assistance caseloads are subject to rampant abuse.[12] In turn, these perceptions undermine public support for the poor, providing ammunition for efforts by conservative governments to slash social assistance funding and promote workfare, while otherwise pursuing an upwards redistribution of societal wealth through tax breaks to corporations and the well-off. Consider that the costs of conducting fraud investigations in Alberta now outweigh the benefits of the program, but that social assistance benefits (in real dollars) have eroded severely since the early 1990s (Lafrance 2005; Black and Stanford 2005).

At the broadest political level, welfare fraud investigations, and the image of the welfare cheat such investigations reinforce, also function to distract people from asking questions about (for example) the distributive logic underlying capitalist social relations or the nature of corporate crime. In the specific case of Alberta, a focus on welfare fraud in the 1990s distracted people from more fundamental questions about the causes of the province's debt crisis, notably a series of bad investments and loans made to government cronies (Taft 1997).

The political success of the Klein government in demonizing those on welfare can be measured by what has occurred in Alberta during the years of plenty since 1996. Alberta is one of the richest jurisdictions in Canada, indeed in all of North America. It has no long-term debt (though it will run a deficit in 2010), and its economy is strong; yet welfare incomes in Alberta as a percentage of median provincial incomes in 2004 were the lowest in all of Canada in nearly every category — single employable, person with disability, single parent, one child, and couple, two children — as measured by the National Council of Welfare.[13]

There is only a small and politically weak constituency supportive of the poor in Alberta (Lafrance 2005; Black and Stanford 2005). I would argue that one reason for this lack of public support for the poor is the success of Premier Klein's government in labelling welfare recipients as unworthy of support, or even empathy.[14] Investigations of welfare fraud and the publicity surrounding them have played a role in this process.

Finally, it is important to recognize that public perceptions of crime are in part the result of government statistics regarding the incidence of such events. In turn, the gathering of statistics is a by-product of government budget decisions. Shifting more resources into policing services results in the discovery and prosecution of more crime, including — in the case discussed here — the detection of specific types of crime, such as welfare fraud. Such an argument seems obvious, yet it is often overlooked. Consider how public perceptions might be altered if there was a massive shift in public expenditures directed at locating corporate crime (Glasbeek 2002). Our perceptions of the extent and seriousness of various social problems — and whether we should do something about them — are largely determined by official statistics about their existence. But to find evidence, one must want to find it and have the resources to go about doing so. Governments want to find welfare fraud and, as a result, set about finding it.

Conclusion

No one denies that some amount of welfare error and fraud occurs. Few would also argue that, where actual fraud occurs, it should not be prosecuted, keeping in mind the dictum that punishments should fit the crime. Neither should anyone read this chapter as an attack on the credentials or impartiality of those whose work it is to locate and prosecute welfare fraud.

It is worth considering, however, that negative images of welfare clients are a kind of social construction, easily manufactured by politicians, both through rhetoric and administrative policies, while also utilizing existing stereotypes. In the context of the debt crisis that elevated Ralph Klein to premier in December 1992 and underscored his election in the spring of 1993, welfare recipients became a convenient scapegoat for a host of society's ills and the problems of capitalist development in a resource-based economy. Framed as a pariah class, welfare recipients were suitable for both verbal abuse and economic and political coercion (Lafrance 2005; Black and Stanford 2005; Murphy 1995, 1997).

The Alberta government went even further, however, in ensuring that public sympathy could not attach itself to those on welfare or, indeed, to the poor and vulnerable in general. The government, aided by the media, used its considerable power to systematically reinforce existing public perceptions that large numbers of welfare recipients were abusing the system and to imply that this was a major cause of public deficits. The government knew these assertions to be false. By the 1990s, welfare policies were already in place to ensure that welfare fraud was a minor and infrequent occurrence; yet the government's investigation branch was enlarged and the search for miscreants intensified. This endless ferreting out of welfare fraud must be understood not as crime control *per se*, but rather in the broader political context of policing the poor.

Notes

1. I want to thank Terri Saunders for her valuable work in obtaining some of the data used here. I also want to thank Ken Collier for his comments on an earlier draft of this paper, and Val Marie Johnson and Diane Crocker for their comments on this much later draft. An early version of this was presented at the first Parkland Institute conference in Edmonton, Alberta, in November 1997. A revised version of this paper was presented at the National Social Work Conference in Halifax, Nova Scotia, in June 2006.

2. While health care expenditures in the province declined from 1992/93 to 1994/95, and education lost 6.6 percent, welfare expenditures declined by 22.1 percent (Canada West Foundation 1998: 12). Even today — long after prosperity has returned to the province — social service expenditures in Alberta continue to lag behind other areas of provincial spending.

3. Boessenkool (1997), writing for the very conservative C.D. Howe Institute, argued that most of those forced off welfare found employment. Two studies conducted by the Canada West Foundation (CWF), examining a small sample of people who left Alberta's welfare system between 1993 and 1996, arrived at different conclusions, however. The studies found that about half those surveyed had located full-time work, but most of these didn't make enough money to cover their food and shelter needs (Azmier and Roach 1997). A fourth study, conducted by Richard Shillington at the University of Alberta, found results similar to the CWF studies, with most former welfare recipients in poor paying jobs with few benefits (Shillington 1998).

4. The 1992 poll surveyed 1011 respondents. The 1996 poll surveyed 1002 respondents. Both had a margin of error of 3.1 percentage points nineteen times out of twenty. Surprisingly, the 1996 poll showed women and respondents with lower educational levels tended to have the most negative and/or punitive attitudes towards welfare recipients. For example, the average estimate regarding the prevalence of cheating was 33 percent for women and 27 percent for men. The average estimate of prevalence of cheating among those with public or high school education was 36 percent as opposed to 29 percent for those with community college or university education.

5. During the 1995 Ontario election, the Mike Harris's Tories declared that "estimates of welfare fraud have ranged from a few million to hundreds of millions of dollars" (D. Camp, 1997, "Renegade Revolutionaries," *Maclean's*, November 10). Comments by Harris and others regarding welfare were particularly strident at this time, but should be understood also as fed by a long-standing differentiation within Anglo-democracies (in particular) between the "deserving" and "undeserving" poor, the latter a rather elastic group capable of being discursively expanded at any time.

6. See Richard Helm, "Welfare Abused to Tune of $2M, Minister Says," *Edmonton Journal*, February 10, 1993; "U of A Researcher Jailed For Welfare Fraud," *Edmonton Journal*, February 20, 1993; "Panhandler Faces Welfare Fraud Charge," *Edmonton Journal*, May 6, 1993; "Welfare Ends if Job Training Refused in B.C.," *Edmonton Journal*, September 23, 1993; "Fraud Charges in Welfare Probe," *Edmonton Journal*, October 5, 1993; "Cross-border Welfare Fraud Under Attack,"

Edmonton Journal, November 4, 1993; "Welfare Spies Trim Fraud," *Edmonton Journal*, November 10, 1993; "B.C. Tightens Welfare Rules, Cracks Down on Cheaters." *Edmonton Journal*, January 21, 1994; "LaserCard Promoted as a Fraud-preventer," *Edmonton Journal*, February 10, 1994; "Data Sharing Urged to Curb Welfare Fraud," *Edmonton Journal*, July 6, 1994; "Life After Welfare," *Edmonton Journal*, July 23, 1994; "Suspended Sentence for Welfare Fraud," *Edmonton Journal*, September 3, 1994; Joan Crockatt, "Provinces Attack Welfare Fraud," *Edmonton Journal*, September 7, 1994; "Ontario Announces Tough New Program to Cut Welfare Costs," *Edmonton Journal*, August 24, 1995; Chris Montgomery, "Cheats May Feel Heat," *Edmonton Journal*, January 26, 1995; "Welfare Mom Admits Hiding Extra Income," *Edmonton Journal*, August 10, 1996; Greg Crone, "Search Warrants for Social Workers Part of Agenda Against Welfare Fraud," *Edmonton Journal*, August 20, 1997; Helen Plishke, "Few Inmates Collect Welfare Illegally," *Edmonton Journal*, March 21, 1997; Kerry Powell, "Pair Accused of $225,000 Welfare Fraud, Income Hidden, Says Crown," *Edmonton Journal*, May 6, 1997; "Ontario Nails 1,000 Welfare Cheats," *Edmonton Journal*, November 14, 1998.

7. Up until 1975, there were separate municipal and provincial assistance caseloads in Alberta. The Alberta government took complete control in that year.

8. It should not be assumed that these thirty-two positions were added to the fifty positions hired under the EBVP. The latter was a special project. It would seem likely that the thirty-two new hires were drawn from the project staff (Richard Helm, "Welfare Abused to Tune of $2M, Minister Says." *Edmonton Journal*, February 10, 1993).

9. Random samples of welfare recipients conducted in the United States in the 1970s, for example, showed that ineligibility rates were 6 percent at the state level and 5 percent at the federal level. But the ineligibility proportion due to agency error was higher than that due to client error. Moreover, little of the latter proportion was found to be due to intentional fraud. In these instances, the prosecution rate for fraud was about 1 percent of all welfare cases.

10. The discrepancy between *Western Report*'s figures and those in Table 2.2 appears to be explained by the fact that the former is using the calendar year of 1993 while the latter uses the 1993–94 fiscal year (Peter Verburg, "No Fraud Too Serious to Forgive: A Sweep Nets 300 Welfare Cheaters, But It's Illegal to Deny Them Benefits," *Western Report*, Sept 19, 1994).

11. Alberta Auditor General, 1993–99, *Public Accounts 1993/94–1998/99*, Edmonton: Government of Alberta; Alberta Human Resources and Employment, 2003, *Annual Reports, 1999/00–2002/03*, Edmonton: Alberta Human Resources and Employment; Alberta Human Resources and Employment, 2004, *Supplementary Estimates, Program Funding*, Edmonton: Alberta Human Resources and Employment. As a comparison, total social assistance expenditures in Alberta dropped in nominal dollars from $765 million in 1993–04 to $283 million in 2003–04, or 63 percent. During the same period, total expenditures on maintenance and recovery rose in nominal dollars from $3.3 million to $3.9 million, or 18 percent. Calculated from the Government of Canada, Social Development Canada, n.d., *Social Security Statistics Canada and Provinces 1978–79 to 2002–03*, Ottawa: Social Development Canada; Alberta Auditor General, 1993–99, *Public Accounts 1993/94–1998–/99*. Edmonton: Government of Alberta; Alberta

Human Resources and Employment, 2004, *Supplementary Estimates, Program Funding*, Edmonton: Alberta Human Resources and Employment.

12. It is also likely that another function of welfare fraud prosecutions is that they send out a message of general deterrence to actual or potential welfare clients, further controlling and pacifying them in their relations with the State. Unfortunately, verifying this conclusion is beyond the scope of this study.

13. To take a particularly striking example, consider the comparison of Alberta with Newfoundland and Labrador, intil recently one of Canada's poorest provinces (Table 2.3):

Table 2.3 Welfare Incomes by Family Type, Alberta vs. Newfoundland and Labrador, 2004

	Alberta	Newfoundland and Labrador
Single Employable	$5,044	$7,401
Person with Disability	$7,846	$8,930
Single Person, One Child	$12,151	$15,228
Couple, Two Children	$19,166	$18,468

Source: National Council of Welfare, *Welfare Incomes 2004*, 106–7.

14. During the November 2004 provincial election, Premier Klein got into some trouble for remarks he made to some Conservative supporters about two women on AISH (Assured Income for the Severely Handicapped). "They didn't look severely handicapped to me; I'll tell you that for sure. Both had cigarettes dangling from their mouths and cowboy hats." Many scolded the premier, though a surprising number of Albertans did toss off the comments as "just Ralph being Ralph." Had the two women not been visibly handicapped, only poor, it is unlikely the premier's remarks would have drawn any significant rebuke. Indeed, a similar incident a couple of years earlier, when the premier late at night stumbled, drunk, into a homeless shelter and verbally abused its patrons, raised scant comment from most Albertans.

Chapter 3

Homelessness after 9/11

Reflections on How Our Society Treats Homeless Individuals

Wayne MacNaughton

When I say homelessness after 9/11, I am not talking about someone who was living in a crawl space at the World Trade Center and had to search for a new place to squat. I am referring to the manner in which our society, and in particular police, security forces, and some business operators, exploit the public fear that follows events such as the horrific terrorist attacks on 9/11 in order to justify cracking down on the homeless. This was in fact driven home to me personally when, in the fall of 2002, I returned to Montreal after spending a couple of years in Halifax.

I arrived by train early in the morning and later in the day went to the central bus station to place my heavily laden knapsack in one of the public lockers there. This bus terminal has been trying to limit access by homeless people to their lockers, as well as their public washrooms and waiting areas, for years. When I found an available locker, I looked around for the automated token dispensers that used to be nearby. The token dispensers were nowhere to be found so I went up to the baggage claim counter and asked the agent, "How do I get a token for the locker?" He said that he sold them, and so I asked him for two tokens and moved to give him my money. He asked me for my bus ticket. I explained that I didn't have one; I just wished to use the lockers for the day. He informed me that I must present a bus ticket or a current ticket stub (if I had just arrived on the bus, for example) because the lockers are for customer use only. When I enquired of friends of mine in Montreal they told me that the terminal had changed their policy in the aftermath of 9/11 in order to prevent someone from placing a bomb in a locker.

For many months prior to 9/11, eighteen men lived in the U.S., paying rent and expenses, paying thousands of dollars for flying lessons, and then on September 11, 2001, bought last-minute first-class tickets (in order to be close to the cockpit) on transcontinental flights (in order to have full fuel tanks). Somehow I doubt that individuals with those kinds of resources and that kind of determination would be slowed down by having to buy a bus ticket from Montreal to Ottawa. The simple fact is that the terminal operators had finally found an acceptable excuse to prevent homeless people from using their lockers.

You might say, "What's the big deal?" Well, simply put, when you are homeless, access to storage lockers, public washrooms, and a place to sit for a bit out of the cold and wet take on incredible importance. I know of two gentlemen who used to sit quietly at a table in the Complexe Desjardins Shopping Mall in downtown Montreal and would be harassed continually by the security guards. In their case they were being singled out for their clothes and, sadly, for their race. That is one case and I know of many others. Mall managers have also played on the public fear of terrorism to justify increasing their security staff, and then used that staff to harass peaceful and law abiding individuals.

I was entering into the Place Bonaventure one day during this 2002 stay in Montreal when a security guard asked me out of the blue where I was going. When I said I was going through the mall to VIA's central station he said, "Keep going. Don't stop in the mall." This guard didn't know me and judged me entirely on my appearance. (I was overdressed for the weather as quite often homeless people are, given that we must spend so much time outdoors.)

I mention these things that happened to me in Montreal in 2002, and unfortunately similar things are happening every day right here in Halifax. To try to cope with this reality, someone at the local Metro Turning Point men's shelter who knows the city will take a newcomer under their wing to help them find their way around. A street-savvy individual, for example, will quickly pass on the unwritten rules of behaviour for the various downtown shopping malls.

It is particularly frustrating to me that there is another answer, a positive and humane way to reduce loitering and panhandling: provide drop-in centres for people living in poverty, especially downtown in cities. In Montreal, old church buildings downtown have been converted into drop-ins. These are places where people can go to get out of the elements, have a coffee and a doughnut, use toilets, and in one case showers. In the case of another drop-in, people can leave a bag or knapsack overnight. Obviously the drop-in doesn't assume responsibility for people's possessions but at least people have an option available when they can't get access to lockers. Such a drop-in could exist in downtown Halifax and central Dartmouth, supported by faith organizations and local businesses. It is not uncommon in Montreal for someone to drop off leftovers at one of the drop-ins or emergency shelters downtown after a business luncheon or office party. Some local businesses in Halifax would like to do this but it is often out of their way to go to Hope Cottage or Metro Turning Point, for example, because they are not right downtown.

As a "come from away" in Halifax, I've noticed the strong local pride here and an attitude of "we want our own local solutions." But we can take solutions from elsewhere and adapt these to our own needs. A classic example of this for me is Halifax's very own Shining Lights Choir. Inspired by Montreal's homeless choir, we have created a unique group here, one guided by local culture and traditions and unmistakably Haligonian. The choir makes homeless issues visible to the public and provides support to those living in marginal circumstances.

We need to stop criminalizing the homeless. Individuals who commit criminal acts need to be dealt with, but this a very small minority of homeless individuals. Closing doors will only increase marginalization and make the job of outreach workers more difficult. Business and government need to be more constructive and creative in finding ways to help people get back on their feet and rebuild their lives. This starts by helping those who are homeless to get through their day, not putting more barriers in the way of them meeting their basic human needs. By all means, let's work on long-term solutions to poverty; let's work to eliminate racism and the criminalization of the poor. But let's not forget that the homeless need help right now, not tomorrow, or next month, or next year. Let's use our creativity and work together to build community.

Drop-ins can provide a venue for people to connect to health and social services, housing, and employment. Such centres exist already but on a small scale and are chronically under-funded. A drop-in could be started in one of the churches in downtown Halifax and move to the current Spring Garden Road library once the library's new central branch is built. This would be an ideal long-term home. The ground floor could serve as the drop-in, with various health, training, housing, and employment services using the other floors. Partners in this could include the local businesses on Spring Garden and local organizations such as the YM/YWCA, Teamworks, and Youth Live. I know that it is still in the future, but the location would be near perfect.

While all this may seem idealistic, consider the costs of doing nothing. We can do a great deal to reduce poverty and eliminate homelessness if we work together on positive solutions. Let's get at it!

Chapter 4

"The Streets Belong to People That Pay For Them"

The Spatial Regulation of Street Poverty in Vancouver, British Columbia

Mario Berti and Jeff Sommers

The street person has emerged as an increasingly troubling — and troubled — figure on the landscape of Canadian cities over the past two decades. Evoking at once feelings of pity and fear, sometimes even revulsion, the term functions as a label that designates profound social difference across a range of axes, but especially in relation to moral and aesthetic norms. As the number of people thus labelled has proliferated in urban areas, so too have official and unofficial efforts to regulate street people, usually under the banner of restoring public order, which is portrayed as threatened by their presence. In this chapter, we look at the role that private sector groups, particularly downtown business improvement associations (BIAs), have played in promoting fear of "street people" and advocating the criminalization of the most marginalized citizens in the city.[1] With a particular focus on Vancouver, we examine how BIAs have deployed the Broken Windows theory of crime and neighbourhood decline as a discourse of neoliberal governance (Kelling and Coles 1996; Wilson and Kelling 1982), enabling them to constitute themselves as custodians of public space, conduct widespread surveillance, act in concert with the police and other state agencies, and campaign for policies designed to penalize street people and enhance the authority of BIAs beyond the bounds of the private property of their members.

We then examine a selection of the ways in which this change in custodianship of public space has resulted in an increasing impetus towards sanitizing the downtown core, an effort that increasingly dictates the allegedly proper uses of public space through legal remedy, reifying the privatizing vision of the BIAs specifically and neoliberal principles in general. We illustrate the results of this effort from the viewpoint of those on the street, utilizing data gathered during a 2004 project in Vancouver, and discuss the effects of these changes both for marginalized people and with a view to the larger implications for spaces of community and citizenship.

Disorder and the Fear of "Street People" as a Political Issue in Vancouver

The figure of the street person entered Vancouver's official discourse in the early 1990s through the final report of the municipally sponsored Safer City Task Force. Among the report's many concerns, which included gangs and domestic violence, was the "growing phenomen[on]... of street people," who "provoke feelings of frustration, helplessness, and anger in many citizens" (Safer City Task Force 1993: 90). The members of the Task Force reported that while citizens may fear and feel threatened by street people, it is actually the latter who are most at risk because, "by circumstance or behaviour, [they] are left to survive on the street" (Safer City Task Force 1993: 90–91). While recognizing that fear of "aggressive, professional panhandlers" and "street people affects the use of public spaces and increases the general anxiety of people," the Task Force noted that "street people [are] not responsible for the majority of crime in Vancouver" and argued that in order to address the issue, authorities must confront "the underlying problems of poverty, addictions, mental illness, and unemployment" (Safer City Task Force 1993: 91).

By early 2005, the B.C. government (under the Liberal Party) adopted the Safe Streets Act almost verbatim from Ontario's 1999 legislation, following a prolonged campaign by business groups centred in downtown Vancouver and Victoria. The B.C. law was designed to purge squeegee kids from the streets and tightly regulate the activities of panhandlers. It also provided security guards with additional powers of detainment on private property.[2] Less than two years later some of these same business organizations submitted an open letter to the municipal, provincial, and federal governments arguing for even more rigorous regulation of public space to cope with a "crisis... an urban malignancy manifested by an open drug market, rising property crime, aggressive panhandling and a visible growing population of the homeless."[3] Within a month of this submission, the mayor of Vancouver announced Project Civil City, a package of measures that formulated the demands of these business groups into a series of policies focused primarily on street people. According to the mayor's report, the project was "produced in partnership with Councillor Kim Capri, a trained criminologist with 20 years of experience and former Executive Director of the B.C. Crime Prevention Association, whom... [the mayor] asked to take a lead role in Council on this major public policy issue" (Office of the Mayor 2006: 3). The mayor's report stated that Project Civil City was produced through a crime prevention perspective and framed explicitly as an effort to "improve order on the streets," with a particular eye toward the city's hosting of the 2010 Olympic Games. By May 2007, former Attorney General Geoffe Plant became Vancouver's Civil City Commissioner.

The distance between 1993's Safer City Task Force, with its concern about the health and welfare of street people, and the current decade's Safe Streets Act and Project Civil City, which advocate punitive action and control, is marked by a fundamental shift in discourse around public space in Vancouver. The first document is imbued with what theorists of neoliberalism term a welfarist perspective that constitutes the presence of street people as a consequence of poverty and sickness. The latter two documents, in contrast, draw directly on neoliberalism and Broken Windows theories of crime to constitute street people as the problem. The rise and acceptance of neoliberalism and punitive models of social regulation provided a means by which local elites could articulate both their unease with the human evidence of growing inequality and their proposed solutions.

Broken Windows

Broken Windows emerged as the central discursive frame for understanding the social geography of crime in North American cities over the 1990s, not least due to its deployment as the guiding concept of New York City's vaunted crackdown on street crime and disorder. Its key theoretical innovation, a proposed link between petty crime and nuisance behaviour, on the one hand, and, on the other, urban disorder, served to reconfigure "our notion of what constitutes 'crime' and... how we determine the relative seriousness of particular types of crime" (Kelling and Coles 1996: 27). Broken Windows proponents contend that activities once approached as nuisances should actually be treated as criminal acts because they are the cause of even more terrible deeds. By this logic, signs of public disorder such as rowdiness, public urination, begging, and public drinking, as well as graffiti, uncollected garbage and litter, and deteriorating buildings, reach a critical mass that invites an escalation of criminal acts if left unchecked. As indications of disorder mount, they provide evidence to the criminally disposed that nobody cares about the area in which they are taking place. Such individuals are thus encouraged to engage in progressively more serious acts (Kelling and Coles 1996).

According to this theory, the more disorder there is, the more criminal acts take place and the more disorder is tolerated, and so forth. Once residents begin to fear for their safety in public places, a spiral of decay sets in as public space is taken over by the disorderly and the criminal. Businesses close or move as their customers stay home behind locked doors. Disorderly behaviours and situations are not simply nuisances but criminal acts that, in sufficient numbers, lead inexorably to neighbourhood or even city-wide decline (Harcourt 2001; Skogan 1990). However, Broken Windows' proponents hold out the hope that the decline that results from disorder can be halted, and even reversed, through police and community intervention.

Brown and Herbert point to a core spatial logic that underpins Broken Windows, which is based on the premise of an essential territorial imperative, especially the notion that both built and human "landscapes… communicate signals of neighbourhood vulnerability to the criminally minded" (Brown and Herbert 2006: 758). Places must therefore be defended from potential wrongdoers, and their residents and/or users must seek to actively exclude "the criminally minded." Broken Windows thus constructs public space in terms of a division between good residents or passive users of space and the dangerous strangers who seek to harm the former. This social division is constituted spatially, as the two sets of actors are embodied and present in particular places (Herbert and Brown 2006). Indeed, as we will see, it is the embodied presence of the stranger that makes them such a problematic figure.

Broken Windows theory does not simply diagnose problem situations. It also prescribes two main types of action. First, building on the notion of situational crime prevention, Broken Windows advocates careful attention to the design and maintenance of the built environment, arguing that such activities will effectively discourage criminal acts not only by decreasing opportunities but also by sending the message that the place is cared for. Second, and more contentiously, Broken Windows promotes the active exclusion of people from local spaces via aggressive policing. Critics argue that such exclusionary action primarily targets the poor, especially the homeless, who are obliged to live in public space (Gibson 1004; Mitchell 2003). However, proponents of Broken Windows claim that the measures they advocate target not social groups but individuals and their unacceptable conduct, particularly "disreputable or obstreperous or unpredictable people: panhandlers, drunks, addicts, rowdy teenagers, prostitutes, loiterers, the mentally disturbed" (Wilson and Kelling 1982: 30).

In seeking to defend Broken Windows from the charge that it primarily afflicts the poor and homeless, Kelling and Coles maintain that the homelessness-disorder nexus can only be properly understood through social classification that distinguishes "the truly homeless" — a category in which they include "the genuinely poor" and people who are "seriously mentally ill and addicted" — from "those for whom living on the streets and hustling, including criminality, has become a lifestyle." The directions for exclusion in each case are different. While the latter are to be aggressively policed, the former require assistance that amounts to sequestration in shelters and other institutions and forms of management that remove them from public space (Kelling and Coles 1996). Ellickson (2001) advocates another kind of spatial fix, suggesting a return to well defined containment zones like the old skid rows in which the police exercise wide discretion in dealing with nuisance activities and misbehaviour.

It is little wonder that, despite a clear lack of systematic empirical validation of these theories, a range of authorities, from police to business groups to civic leaders, have mobilized Broken Windows and its preoccupation with public order. By spatializing poverty, the discourse constitutes it as a local problem centred on individual conduct. Broken Windows gives its proponents a way of talking about poverty without dealing with the structural and institutional conditions through which poverty is generated. Poverty is rendered as a problem of public order, which can be treated through questions of management and regulation rather than political intervention.

The Rise of Neoliberalism

The type of public order management that currently prevails in Vancouver began to emerge in the early 1980s in the west end, a high rise neighbourhood adjacent to the downtown shopping and business district, when a group of local residents initiated what was essentially the city's first resident vigilante organization. The Concerned Residents of the West End (CROWE) started what they called a "shame the johns" campaign, targeting sex workers who worked on local corners, as well as their customers. In 1984, the intensity of this campaign prompted B.C.'s then attorney general, Brian Smith, to apply for a Supreme Court injunction against thirteen women and "persons unknown," prohibiting them from loitering in the west end (Lowman 1986).

The injunction effectively banned street prostitution from the west end and the western edges of the business district, pushing it eastward across the city, and initiating an almost twenty-year process in which the growing street sex and drug trades were pushed from neighbourhood to neighbourhood, dislodged by successive resident campaigns pressuring participants in the street scene as well as the police and civic authorities. Such campaigns marked a historical shift in the role of neighbourhood residents' groups in Vancouver. Until the early 1980s, they had been concerned primarily with issues around community services, property development, and zoning controls.

It is worth noting the wider context in which this emerging preoccupation with street people took place. While it may only be coincidental, CROWE's campaign began just as British Columbia's Social Credit government was implementing its infamous "restraint" program, an early Canadian exercise in neoliberal budget cutting and program restructuring precipitated by ideological predilection and the collapse of the province's primary-industry economic base (forestry, mining, and fishing) in the wake of the Reagan-era recession. In the aftermath of the 1986 World Exposition in Vancouver, an escalating flow of capital began to pour into property development, particularly the downtown peninsula and surrounding districts. This transformed the urban landscape and propelled a wave of gentrification throughout the inner city that continues unabated. It is in many of these gentrifying sites that conflicts over public space and the presence of street people have been most acute (Reid 1998; Sommers 2001).

As noted above, the figure of the street person was also flagged as a public issue at the municipal level by the early 1990s. Panhandling appeared as a constant irritant to some residents, consumers, and businesses over the course of the decade. However, most of the concern over public order focused on the city's downtown eastside, a neighbourhood where, in 1997, the Vancouver Richmond Health Board declared a health emergency due to spiraling rates of HIV/AIDS among injection drug users. Suddenly, the attention of the news media across the country was drawn to the area's open and dense drug market. A panic erupted across the city as the downtown eastside was cast as the source of the many social problems faced by the region. The neighbourhood became synonymous with the equation of public disorder and urban decay (Sommers 2001; Sommers and Blomley 2003). Open drug dealing and use, panhandling, binning (recovering recyclable goods from garbage cans), vending (selling goods on the street obtained by binning or other means), and homelessness were interpreted as spillover from the downtown eastside resulting from gentrification or police pressure.[4] In this context, the figure of the drug addict was seen as the primary carrier of disorder (Colebourn 1997: A8; Vancouver Board of Trade et al. 2006).

The association between urban decay, drug addiction, and the various activities associated with disorder served to emphasize the difference between the street person and other citizens. A key element of this difference was aesthetic. Commenting on the proliferation of security guards hired by business improvement associations to patrol public space, a police officer argued in the local media that: "These [street] people look quite scary. Law abiding citizens and business owners get quite frightened about seeing these people on the street" (Bailey 1997: B4). It was also reported that, according to some U.S. tourists, the "once beautiful city has now turned into a city of despair, with panhandlers and runaway teenagers at every corner... [and] scenes of filth and hopelessness." These tourists asked, "Where are the police to patrol these areas?" (Myers and Myers 2000: A11). Beyond the aesthetics, the situation was cast as an infection in which the presence of street people "spread its tentacles like a cancer through the body politic." The *Vancouver Courier* told its readers that citizens were all at risk from the "runaway kids and... panhandlers [who] crash after a night's partying [in] parks, doorways and squats" (McCarthy 1998: B3).

The pervasive fear that was generated via the media, with support from the police, and especially the BIA, resulted in the city's 1998 anti-panhandling by-law. Citing a "survey of members of the Downtown Vancouver BIA [which] indicated that 73% of members polled felt that the panhandling problem in the downtown area had worsened" (City of Vancouver 1998), City Council enacted a by-law[5] modelled on one in Winnipeg. Shortly thereafter, separate challenges were launched as to the constitutionality of both the Winnipeg by-law and its Vancouver relative. In 2001, under an almost certain threat that the Winnipeg by-law would be struck down due to its unconstitutionality, Vancouver City Council repealed their version of the by-law, citing concerns that such "regulation must balance the competing rights of all people who use the streets including pedestrians, panhandlers, and those who derive their business from street traffic such as merchants and shop owners" (City of Vancouver 2001). The city simultaneously enacted an equally punitive (but harder to challenge) street and traffic by-law against "obstructive solicitation."[6]

To step back for a moment, we can consider the changing provincial political context of British Columbia in 2001. A decidedly (neo)Liberal government campaigned on a platform of "economic revitalization" and was elected under the leadership of former realtor, businessman, and Vancouver mayor Gordon Campbell. Initiating an unprecedented restructuring, the provincial Liberals made deep cuts to social and health programs. This included the introduction of a "training wage" of six dollars an hour, an almost 50 percent increase in Medical Service Plan fees, a weakened Pharmacare program, the reduction in amounts and time spans for welfare eligibility, mandatory reassessments for most people on disability benefits, and the dismantling of a large number of treatment facilities for people with mental illness, without the creation of viable alternatives (Johnson 2004; Kerstetter 2002). This dismantling of the social safety net and reorganization of health services was accompanied by changes in legislation to ensure that the penal system was ready to deal with the products of restructuring. Thus we see, in Loïc Wacquant's apt phraseology, "the invisible hand of the market and the iron fist of the state combine and complement each other" (Wacquant 2001: 404) to offer up the problems and their solution.

It is within this rendering of neoliberalism in full swing that the Safe Streets Act, and related amendments to the provincial Trespass Act, were introduced in British Columbia.[7] B.C.'s version of the Safe Streets Act, like similar legislation in Ontario, effectively regulates the time, place, and manner in which people can panhandle.[8] When introduced in the Provincial Legislative Assembly, the bill was said to:

> recognize that those who wish or feel they are obliged by circumstance to panhandle or beg are free to do so. They have the right to be on the streets, just as all of us do. But they do not have the right to use their right to be on the streets to intimidate and to belligerently verbally abuse people, to block their right of passage, to take advantage of their presence in situations where citizens are waiting to make a phone call or using a cash machine.[9]

Thus, it is all right to panhandle (if one *wishes* to be poor), as long as it is done in places where citizens can easily ignore it. Using the typical neoliberal catchall of "responsibility," those arguing in favour of the Act in the Legislature claimed that the legislation would balance the interests of all citizens, insuring that all people involved worked together for a more just society. As Jeff Bray, the MLA for Victoria–Beacon Hill, put it, "We have expectations of each of us in a society. Those shouldn't stop because somebody is perhaps less fortunate. Their responsibility doesn't automatically end. We must work together, including people who find themselves on the streets, to make our community healthy and strong"[10]

As "safe streets" acts like those in B.C. and Ontario illustrate, Broken Windows theory's preoccupation with public disorder means that the prescription offered for visible poverty is centrally concerned with intensifying spatial regulation and, in particular, with the stigmatization and exclusion of those categories of people who are labelled disorderly. The sponsoring member of the B.C. Safe Streets Act, Vancouver–Burrard MLA Lorne Mayencourt articulated the message implicit in the legislation: "what we're telling them is that the streets belong to people that pay for them" (*The Province*, "MLA Pushes 2 Aggressive-Panhandler Bills in House," May 7, 2004).

To put aside the more general dangers entailed in a dichotomization that constructs the urban poor ("them") as distinct from us (or "we"), this way of thinking about space has important implications for who has the right to access and use public spaces in the city. As Collins and Blomley have noted, such legislation signifies "a growing mistrust in the ideal of a truly inclusive public space and [strengthens] the hegemony of those private interests that assert that if cities are to compete in a global economy, they must 'purify' the urban landscape" (Collins and Blomley 2001: 42). Wardaugh and Jones further clarify that, in the neoliberal vision of poverty, "it is not marginality per se that is dangerous: rather, it is the *visible* presence of marginal people within prime space that represents a threat to a sense of public order and orderliness" (Wardaugh and Jones 1999: 112, emphasis added).

However, as scholars such as Don Mitchell have urged, the spaces of representation found in city streets are vital for political functioning. For "if the right to the city is a cry and a demand, then it is only a cry that is heard and a demand that has force to the degree that there is a space from and within which this cry and demand is visible" (Mitchell 2003: 129). If legislation and political ordering are allowed to render the poor and marginalized out of public sight, then being out of mind may quickly follow. As Mitchell argues, "insofar as homeless people or other marginalized groups remain invisible to society, they fail to be counted as legitimate members of the polity" (Mitchell 2003: 129).

Regulation of Public Space and the Criminalization of Homelessness

Immediately prior to the passage of the Safe Streets Act and the amendments to the Trespass Act we conducted a large scale study of if and how the regulation of public space was acting to criminalize homelessness in two Vancouver neighbourhoods (Sommers, LaPrairie, Bertiand, and Laviolette 2005).[11] We interviewed a large assortment of people from many perspectives, including the police, security guards, business improvement associations, the municipal government, and social service agencies. However, a large part of the study involved extended interviews with 196 homeless people. We briefly examine these interviews here to offer insight into the experience of those who are simultaneously most affected by legal-spatial regulations and least consulted with regard to their formation and enforcement.

What (or Who) Is Really Being Regulated?

There are plentiful provisions in the Canadian Criminal Code to bring intimidating and dangerous behaviour under legal regulation. Canada has long had laws against offences such as causing a disturbance, harassment, common nuisance, uttering threats, assault, robbery, extortion, intimidation, and mischief (Vonn 2004[12]).In other words, the existing Criminal Code already effectively regulates harmful behaviour on the street. "Safe streets" legislation brings nothing new to this, except for an easy framework through which to target impoverished people whose basic crime is, in the words of today's legislators, to make some members of the public "feel very uncomfortable while they're asking them for money."[13] This kind of legislation harkens back to earlier vagrancy laws that overtly targeted the itinerant poor, effectively criminalizing the *status* of its intended objects rather than an individual's specific actions (Gordon 2004).[14] We must ask what laws such as the Safe Streets Act intend to accomplish, shrouded in this diaphanous veil of public discomfort.

Within the discourse around "safe streets," those *not* living on the street consistently define perceptions of "disorder" as the main issue. Looked at through this lens, the presence and behaviour of the urban abject is an imposition that is incongruent with the enjoyment and use of space; the street person is an inconvenience and a pest, that, left unregulated, will impact the bottom line of businesses' pursuit of profit and citizens' commute or enjoyment of their Sunday stroll. If we reorient ourselves to see such regulations from a street-entrenched point of view, the picture is different.

Often it is the pursuit of sustenance that brings the homeless and poor into contact with the larger public. While the homeless person is, necessarily, always in public space, he or she does not always need to be in public *view*; hence, were it not for the street encounter where a plea for money is made, the average person might have little direct encounter with the poor and homeless. Thus, perceptions of public disorder inexorably link into poor peoples' means of income, in the form of requests for financial help that are perceived as threatening by those who receive them. It is the efforts of marginalized people to eke out their day-to-day existence that require them to become visible to more privileged others.[15] As framed by neoliberal discourse, this presentation of visible poverty is, always already, discussion of public dis/order.

It is troubling when discourse and social relations involving a gentrified public equate "public disorder" with "means of survival" as experienced by a marginalized populace. For within these legalistic and politicized definitions of disorder rests the very essence of the urban poor's attempts to eke out an (increasingly quasi-)legal and non-violent form of survival. It seems puzzling then, that this very attempt is targeted for increased regulation and stigmatized without meaningful and sustained alternatives being suggested.

This is especially evident when one looks at the survival strategies employed by homeless people in Vancouver. When asked about means of sustaining themselves, the three most common strategies were binning, welfare, and panhandling. Specifically, when asked about their income-generating strategies over the previous two years, 66 percent of respondents in our sample cited binning as a strategy, 57 percent reported using social assistance, closely followed by 56 percent of respondents who identified panhandling as a primary means of income. Many people combined these survival tactics in various ways. The Safe Streets Act and the amendments to the Trespass Act are precisely targeted at binning and panhandling, while, as noted above, welfare restrictions are continually tightening. The enactment and enforcement of these acts in Vancouver illustrate Mitchell's argument that the legal regulation of behaviour and space effectively means "that homeless people simply cannot do what they must do in order to survive without breaking laws. Survival itself is criminalized" (Mitchell 2001: 9). The neoliberal policy landscape, combined with legislation explicitly criminalizing the poor's informal means of income, create a situation whereby the apparent aim is to eliminate the primary survival strategies of the homeless — perhaps in the misguided hope that by eliminating the visible activities of the poor, we eliminate poverty.

The picture becomes more troubling with a closer look at these numbers — 57 percent of homeless people collecting welfare at some time also means that 43 percent are not. Anecdotally, many told us that a lack of identification and address, combined with the bureaucratic procedures necessary to gain access, discouraged them from seeking these resources and made it difficult to stay in the system. If we take into account the 14 percent of respondents who said they only had access to welfare sometimes in the previous two years, those who used welfare never or only sometimes over the past two years are actually the majority of respondents, at 57 percent. Thus, a majority of respondents did not make steady use of income assistance resources. This becomes even more striking when we consider that, unsurprisingly given the related difficulties involved in living on the street, 84 percent of respondents had no formal employment in the previous two years.

In other words, not only did large numbers of respondents report involvement with the informal income-generating activities more tightly regulated by the Safe Streets Act and Trespass Act, many reported *total* reliance on them. More than one third (36 percent) of respondents had neither income assistance nor steady employment over the past two years. If we include those who used income assistance only sometimes, the proportion of those with no formal means of income rises to more than half (53 percent) of the sample. Disturbing numbers of the homeless in our sample are outside any formal economy, living not just on, but even outside, the margins of society.

Safety for Whom?

Regulations aimed at sanitizing the urban core of disorder generally take as a starting point the feelings of vulnerability experienced by the public when confronted with behaviour by the marginalized. As we have seen, the nuisance presented by being asked for alms, the unsightliness of the street person, and the perceived danger posed by these things to the market economy, are seen as paramount concerns for the gentrified public. If this is allowed to go unchecked, it is argued, both tourists and local people will venture to other sanitized urban environments or stay home from the shopping districts and businesses, and the public sphere (defined here in very specific ways) will suffer as a result. Consumers, commuters, and business people must not have their passage impeded by being forced to walk around and/or ignore the poor in public space. There must be no feelings of discomfort in the daily journey to, through, and from the market.

In fact, the governmental discourse arguing in favour of "safe streets" legislation in British Columbia asserted that "feeling unsafe on our streets is not an option that any of us should tolerate."[16] Yet how does safety on the streets work for the non-gentrified public? An examination of this reveals yet another of the contradictions behind such legislation: the insistence that the streets must be made into safe spaces for the public ignores or even precludes the possibility that members of the street community are members of the public as well.

To contextualize the housed and economically more comfortable public's perceptions of discomfort, we explored how vulnerability played out among homeless people. While 33 percent of homeless respondents in our survey felt vulnerable to physical danger and victimization during daylight hours, this number rose to 55 percent at night. In contrast to the fears cited by the gentrified public, the most prevalent perceived threats among the homeless were attributed to the actions of the gentrified public, including fear of drunken suburban youth beating them up for fun, judgmental community members, and police behaviour. In addition, the homeless have no private space to retreat to, no option of staying home in order to avoid these concerns.

While much of the fear of victimization among the gentrified public is based upon fear of *perceived* vulnerability, with actual victimization through criminal acts occurring rarely, vulnerability as experienced by the homeless is vastly more common (see Roberts 2001). Of the 196 respondents we talked to, *88 percent had been victimized* in the previous two years. Most victimization that occurred was categorized as personal (assaults, etc.). However, 24 percent of respondents had suffered all of the forms of victimization we asked them about. To make the picture even bleaker, 71 percent of those who had been victimized did not report the incident(s) to anyone, including the police, a community policing station, or an outreach agency.

In stark contrast with the government, police, and business recognition of, and responses to, the perceived vulnerability of the gentrified public, the primary reason that the homeless cited for not reporting their victimization was the perception that it would do no good and would not be taken seriously. Although the law views itself and is presented as a neutral force for justice, treating all equally, the reality is not so simple. Indeed, when asked about whether they felt they had access to the justice system, 54 percent of homeless people felt they had none whatsoever. More than half of these felt that they had no access because members of the police and justice system would think that they deserved whatever happened to them. In a grim irony illustrating how the criminalization of poverty works, many of our respondents commented that the only way that they had access to the justice system was to get arrested.

Hence, homeless people are victimized at an alarming rate and are unlikely to believe that they enjoy any benefits from the law or to utilize the law as a resource. Indeed, the homeless people in our study overwhelmingly held the view that they are excluded from the justice system in cases where the system could do any good for them. They are essentially doubly victimized by a political ideology that uses the law as a weapon against them (Berti 2007). From the point of view of a homeless person, the law is to protect other people from them, not to protect them from other people.

When explicitly stated, this defines the homeless person as a second-class (or non) citizen in ways that many would find disturbing. However, this is the logical product of the concentrated effort to sanitize urban space for the workings of the market. This is a graphic illustration of how misguided legislation is that seeks to make the streets "safe" for those who are made uncomfortable by the visibly poor, rather than (or in addition to) creating safety for those whose life on the streets renders them in greatest danger, with no escape or legal recourse.

Conclusion

We have argued that private sector interests acting in the name of local residents and businesses, in cooperation with state agents, have used the Broken Windows model of crime to situate street poverty and its associated economic and social activities as indices of social disorder, and thus as objects requiring punitive sanction. Rather than calling for measures to alleviate or eliminate poverty, these actors have sought to criminalize it via the surveillance and control of public space. By spatializing poverty and rendering it into a question of maintaining order in public space, legislation such as the Safe Streets Act in British Columbia has enabled its proponents to evade dealing with the consequences of rising socio-economic inequality. This has involved minimal (if any) reference to the fiscal and welfare retrenchment and labour market restructuring through which this inequality is produced, and which these Vancouver actors have largely supported.

It seems that the ultimate intent behind legislation such as the Safe Streets Act is to purify urban space so that it is even more friendly toward investment, business, and consumers — a special concern in the lead up to the 2010 Olympics in Vancouver, when the city was to be showcased in all its glory. This involves the giving over of public spaces for use by the private few who benefit from a gentrified space inviting to consumers or at least a public who has the potential to support private business. This is tantamount to an increase in the privatization of public space for corporate and commercial interests: such regulation aims to decrease homeless and marginalized people's use of public space for private functions, in an attempt to *increase* the use of public space for the private functions of business and corporate control (Collins and Blomley 2001).

The insidious nature of such legislation becomes evident with examination of its substantive effects. Such regulation targets the very forms of survival that the homeless utilize. This appears to involve an attempt to render the homeless and marginalized invisible, disabling their political voices, and making their efforts to survive illegal. Lastly, if "safe streets" and a reasonable standard of community decency is the goal, then a focus on making the streets safe for those who experience the greatest risks on them is an appropriate start; here the focus is on eliminating poverty, rather than on eradicating the poor.

Notes

1. Safety and security issues are the top priority of the Downtown Vancouver BIA, utilizing 54 percent of the annual association budget. According to the DVBIA, "aggressive begging and squeegee nuisances top the list of member and public aggravation in the professional surveys conducted by the DVBIA." Thus, the DVBIA works in partnership with a range of municipal and social organizations "to advance a growing agenda in matters related to crime, safety, cleanliness and street behavioural matters, including aggressive begging, loitering and littering. All of these issues are intrinsically linked in the relentless pursuit of good order and discipline." See Downtown Vancouver Business Improvement Association, 2007, "Committees: Maintenance and Security," available at <downtownvancouver.net/work/maintenance_security.html>.

2. 2004 Legislative Session: 5th Session, 37th Parliament, Bill 71: Safe Streets Act <leg.bc.ca/37th5th/3rd_read/gov71-3.htm>; 2004 Legislative Session: 5th Session, 37th Parliament, Bill 74-Trespass Amendment Act <leg.bc.ca/37th5th/3rd_read/gov72-3.htm>. The Ontario legislation was Safe Streets Act, 1999, S.O. 1999, c. 8; Amended by 2002, c. 17, Sched. F, Table; 2005, c. 32, s. 1.

3. Vancouver Board of Trade, Tourism Vancouver, Downtown Vancouver Business Improvement Association, Vancouver Hotel Association, Vancouver Taxi Association, Retail B.C., Downtown Vancouver Association, Vancouver Hotel General Managers' Association, Building Owners and Managers Association of B.C., Council of Tourism Associations of B.C., B.C. Restaurant and Food Services Association of B.C., and B.C. and Yukon Hotel Association, 2006, "Letter to Prime Minister Stephen Harper, Premier Gordon Campbell, and Mayor Sam Sullivan," available at <boardoftrade.com/policy/StreetDisorderletter30oct06.pdf >.

4. Anonymous 2004, Poster Taped to Telephone Pole in Grandview Woodlands Neighbourhood of Vancouver Urging Residents to Attend a Public Meeting to Oppose a Needle Exchange in the Area; A. Davies, 1996, "Vancouver's Downtown Eastside Is a BC Problem," *Vancouver Sun*, November 20; I. Mulgrew, 1999. "Residents of the Drive Scared of Area's Newcomers," *Vancouver Sun*, August 28; B. Weikle, 1998, "Dealers, Hookers Return to Mount Pleasant: Downtown Eastside Cleanup Sends Problems Back up Main St," *Vancouver Courier*, October 11.

5. Panhandling By-law No. 7885 (Vancouver, B.C., 1998).

6. Street and Traffic By-law No. 2849: A By-law to Regulate Traffic and the Use of Streets in the City of Vancouver; Section 70a: Obstructive Solicitation (consolidated June 8, 2004).

7. B.C. Legislative Session: Fifth Session, "Bill 71: Safe Streets Act." At the same time that the Safe Streets Act was passed, amendments were made to the Trespass Act to make it easier for property owners to evict unwanted people from their land. B.C. Legislative Session: Fifth Session, "Bill 74-Trespass Amendment Act."

8. The B.C. Safe Streets Act has two distinct parts. The first prohibits "aggressive" solicitation, which is defined as soliciting "in a manner that would cause a reason-

able person to be concerned for the solicited person's safety or security." This includes, but is presumably not limited to, "obstructing the path of the solicited person; using abusive language; proceeding behind or alongside or ahead of the solicited person; physically approaching, as a member of a group of 2 or more persons, the solicited person; and continuing to solicit the person." The second part of the Act prohibits solicitation in certain spaces where there is a "captive audience." These include spaces such as near bus stops, pay phones, and automated teller machines, as well as parking lots, roadways, and those about to either enter or exit an automobile. In essence, as some have noted, this spatial restriction effectively makes most areas in the downtown urban core off-limits to panhandlers (see Nicholas Blomley, "Panhandling and Public Space," Expert Opinion to the BC Supreme Court Case, *Federated Anti-Poverty Groups of BC v. Vancouver [City]* 2002, B.C.S.C. 105," [2000]).

9. *Official Report of Debates of the Legislative Assembly (Hansard)*, 2004, B.C. Parliament, Tuesday, May 11, Volume 26, Number 17, Hon. Geoff Plant, at 11721.

10. *Official Report of Debates of the Legislative Assembly (Hansard)*, 2004 B.C. Parliament, Monday, May 10, Volume 25, Number 6 , J. Bray, at 10950.

11. The study was conducted in the spring and summer of 2004 in Vancouver's west end and Grandview Woodlands neighbourhoods using a snowball sampling method. The questionnaire focused on respondents' experiences in the neighbourhoods where they were interviewed, including their encounters with police and other residents.

12. The article also appeared in the October 20, 2004, edition of the *Vancouver Sun*.

13. *Official Report of Debates of the Legislative Assembly (Hansard).* Monday sitting. Mayencourt, 1105.

14. See also McNeil's contribution to this volume.

15. What we really mean here is, of course, a *legal* means of income. There are certainly other sources of income available (such as theft) that depend upon invisibility; thus, a rather obvious question that could be posed is, if you make forms of income that are a minor nuisance because of their visibility illegal, where will the income-generating focus turn?

16. *Official Report of Debates of the Legislative Assembly (Hansard)*, 1110 (Monday Sitting).

Chapter 5

The Intersecting Experience of Racialized Poverty and the Criminalization of the Poor

Grace-Edward Galabuzi

This chapter addresses the mutually reinforcing processes of the racialization of poverty and the criminalization of race and poverty in Canada's cities, with a particular focus on Toronto. The complex experience of racialized poverty disproportionately relegates racialized groups to low income neighbourhoods. Efforts to protect the rest of society from the threat that they are perceived to represent intensifies poor, racialized populations' exposure to criminalization and contact with the criminal justice system. Criminalization in the form of surveillance, targeted policing, and racial profiling adversely impact the life chances of racialized poor populations, and produce and reinforce experiences of social exclusion.

These processes of criminalization indicate the extent to which the experience of poverty is highly differentiated by the social hierarchies of race, gender, religion, immigrant status, and other distinctions that intersect with class to compound the experience of poverty. In periods such as the late twentieth and early twenty-first centuries, when race, nationality, and religion become more pronounced as markers of difference, the burdens born by groups defined by "othering" characteristics are accentuated by intensified regulation and economic marginality. In Canada today, issues of community safety and national security particularly intersect with racial, national religious, and class hierarchies to define relations between marginalized and dominant groups. Here, I consider the linked experience of racialized poverty and the criminalization of the poor. I look at the experience of Toronto's African Canadian community, whose members' relations with dominant groups and institutions are often mediated through stereotypical notions of their proclivity to criminality and disproportionate contact with the criminal justice system. I explain how institutions such as the mainstream media produce stories and images that reinforce historically constructed stigmas and pathologies, especially about Black youth, thus helping to generate moral panics that demand securitized responses and criminalization. These developments reproduce unequal access to employment, neighbourhood selection, life chances, and full citizenship for the stigmatized groups.

Poverty, understood here as material and social deprivation, inflicts pain and exclusion on individuals, families, and communities. Indicators of the denial of well-being such as low literacy rates, high health risks, uneven access to housing, disproportionate contact with the justice system, and low levels of community safety are sustained in an experience of poverty that matures ultimately into a denial of full citizenship for marginalized populations. Groups such as women, Aboriginal peoples, new immigrants, and racialized men and women are the disproportionate victims of poverty. This has far-reaching implications for social cohesion in a liberal democratic society that promises equality and claims multiculturalism as a core value. Today, racialized group members are two to three times more likely to live in poverty than other Canadians; this is compounded by historical disadvantages that are interpreted through popular cultural explanations for racialized poverty that blame the disadvantaged. This chapter explores the processes of exclusion manifest in racialized groups' particular experience of poverty, understood here as persistent and disproportionate exposure to low income and criminalization that together represent harm to the dignity and citizenship of racialized groups' members.[1]

Using comparative secondary data on exposure to low income, income attainment, and evidence of residential segregation, the chapter demonstrates that poverty in Canada is increasingly feminized and racialized, and that this has implications for our understanding of the criminalization of poverty. This approach departs from notions of poverty that ignore the particular characteristics that structure the experience of those living in it. In challenging the premise of anti-poverty approaches informed by liberal individualism (including the myth of colour-blindness), the chapter draws attention to the poor's varied levels of vulnerability to criminalization, which are produced through racial stigmatization and cultural explanations of criminality. Race is significant in two ways when it comes to criminalizing the poor: it structures exposure to poverty so that racialized people are more likely to be poor and vulnerable to criminalization, but it also provides cultural explanations for criminality. These dimensions intersect in racialized low-income communities in Canada's cities, where racialized groups' experiences of poverty lead to high levels of contact with the criminal justice system.

The Structural Problem of Poverty

Almost twenty years after the Parliament of Canada pledged to end child poverty by the year 2000, Canada has one of the highest rates of poverty among individuals and families in the industrialized world (UNICEF 2005). An important part of the explanation for this sad reality is that although the root causes of poverty in Canada are structural, they are not always treated as such. Too often the connection between what is happening in the economy and society generally has not sufficiently informed our understanding of poverty; we prefer instead to see poverty as a problem for which affected individuals should take moral responsibility. The impact of this misdiagnosis on anti-poverty policy at various levels of government and community has been devastating. Another critical dimension that policy makers and anti-poverty activists have often ignored is that poverty arises out of the various social distinctions that shape access to resources. It is not a generic experience. For instance, women and children experience higher levels of poverty than adult men. Average poverty among seniors has declined, though not for all seniors. Poverty is disproportionately experienced among Aboriginal people, racialized groups, and persons with disabilities. In other words, dimensions such as racial and gendered hierarchies compound the poverty-generating processes in a capitalist economy that systematically create winners and losers and distinctive experiences of inequality.

Poverty is a multidimensional phenomenon, encompassing inability to satisfy basic needs, inadequate control over access to resources, lack of education and skills, lack of shelter, poor health, nutrition, and access to water and sanitation, vulnerability to violence and crime, and lack of political freedom or social voice. We need to consider both quantitative and qualitative indicators of poverty. Qualitative indicators of the constraints on poor people include experiences of racialization and feminization, which structure access to resources, benefits, and burdens. We also need to pay close attention to quantitative indicators such as income security, health status, infant mortality, and so on. It is essential to understand the everyday vulnerabilities the poor face arising from socio-political and cultural relationships that generate powerlessness, voicelessness, and marginality. It is also crucial to be informed by how those living in poverty perceive their own lives and circumstances, as well as their own priorities for addressing them. Poverty is a human rights issue that denies too many Canadians of their right to adequate food, shelter, and a quality of life that a wealthy nation can afford for all its citizens; it denies Canadians the right to be treated with dignity. In the context of hierarchies of oppression, poverty is compounded by experiences of social exclusion that make its elimination more intractable and its violations of rights more profound.

The tenor of the public discussion on poverty is at variance with the reality of a persistent and structural set of problems. Before the latest economic downturn, the mainstream media and the political and business leadership of Canada emphasized the unparalleled economic growth of recent years. In the midst of that plenty, the reality was that many have been adversely affected by the growing polarization in income and wealth, and the loss of socio-economic opportunities. A reality gap emerged between the experiences of many groups and the dominant narrative of the times. This corresponds to the gap in well-being that developed in recent decades, but that is not well articulated in the mainstream media or the political arena, largely because the victims of economic polarization have lost their political voices, and their claims on the state are silenced and delegitimized. In the lead-up to the recession, with selective reporting on stock market performance and narratives about Canada as a prosperous, globally competitive country, we were implicitly counselled to accept government inaction on social problems and subject ourselves to market discipline; the message was that we must live with job insecurity and lower wages through allegedly free trade regimes run by undemocratic and unaccountable corporations. It has been implied that the globalized race to the bottom for workers and communities is inevitable.

Both before and since the economic downturn, poverty has been rarely discussed substantively as a core issue at any level of government because to do so would mean acknowledging it as a by-product of a presumably infallible market. Discussion of unemployment and reduced consumer spending has increased recently, somehow without meaningful examination of poverty as a central concern. One hears talk of homelessness, concern about child care, and the proliferation of food banks, but this is often limited to musings about moral failure or framed in neoliberal terms. People living in poverty are stereotyped based on popular narratives about single teenage mothers, able-bodied men and women collecting welfare and spending their days drinking instead of looking for work, and immigrants and refugees cheating their way into Canada so they can drain government programs.[2] These stereotypes inform the public debate, in part because they converge with the construction of the Other in Canadian society — Aboriginals, Blacks, immigrants, and so on — through racialized pathologies. There is a disturbing silence when it comes to talking about the structural nature of poverty and its root causes, even in the midst of an economic recession. There is also a deep denial about the racialized and gendered characteristics of the deepening problem of poverty in Canada.

Growing Income and Wealth Polarization in Canada

In March 2007, the Canadian Centre for Policy Alternatives (CCPA) published a report titled *The Rich and the Rest of Us: The changing face of Canada's Growing Gap* (Yalnizyan 2007). The report noted that Canada's economy had doubled in size since 1981; by 2005 we were the ninth-richest nation in the world. The report also concluded that the income gap between rich and poor is at a thirty-year high. According to Statistics Canada, between 1999 and 2005, the median net worth of families in the top fifth percentile increased by 19 percent, while the net worth of their counterparts in the bottom fifth was virtually unchanged. The share of total household wealth held by the top 20 percent of families continued to grow to 75 percent in 2005 (Morissette 2006). According to the CCPA report, "The poorest 10% of families earned less than $9,400. The poorest 10% of families raising children—more than 376,000 households in Canada—lived on less than $23,300, after taxes, in 2004. Half of these families lived on less than $17,500 a year" (Yalnizyan 2007: 3–4). The report notes that the real value of Canadians' earnings has been falling. Even when the economy was strong and marked by increased productivity, most Canadians were not receiving their share of this prosperity. Social inequality in Canada — specifically the income gap — is growing.

Studies show that most Canadian families are working longer than families in the late 1970s, but their incomes are lower today than they were a generation ago; today having a job is not enough (Jackson 2005). The data show a significant improvement when one compares employment and investment earnings to after-tax incomes (which include government income supports and income taxes), suggesting that governments can have a positive impact on income distribution and mitigate income disparities. But while Canada's system of taxes and transfers have helped families in the last ten years, the system of social supports has been weakened by tax and social service cuts, the former benefiting the wealthy and the latter disadvantaging all others. The after-tax income gap is also growing through these government measures (Yalnyzian 2007).

Wealth and power have become increasingly concentrated in the hands of a small group of citizens (and non-citizen investors), undermining the Canadian vision of an equitable society. The dominance of neoliberal ideas — the call to get government out of the way and to let markets run their course under threat of global competition — has meant that workers lose their power to bargain with capital. The resultant deterioration in wages, job security, and work conditions impacts vulnerable groups most adversely. The brunt of the growing precariousness in work produced by economic restructuring has been disproportionately born by working-class people, immigrants, youth, women, Aboriginal and racialized peoples, and the disabled, consolidating poverty among these groups in many Canadian cities (Galabuzi 2006; United Way of Greater Toronto and the Canadian Council on Social Development 2004; Ornstein 2000; Kazemipur and Halli 2000; Fleury 2007; Picot and Hou 2003; Picot, Hou, and Coulombe 2007; Vosko 2006). Increasingly, these experiences are intergenerational because they influence determinants of social mobility such as educational attainment, health status, access to secure employment, neigbourhoods and housing, and undue contact with the criminal justice system. The concept of the racialization of poverty describes how this process is unfolding for racialized Canadians.

The Racialization of Poverty

The root causes of poverty are not individuals without work, unwilling or unable to work, or with low-paying jobs. These circumstances are the *outcomes* of social and economic structures in capitalist societies that unequally distribute resources, and the common sense understandings that legitimize them. As Heller remarks, "the term *structure* indicates an arrangement of elements… inequality is not random but follows a pattern, displays relative constancy and stability, and is backed by ideas that legitimize and justify it" (Heller 1987: 5).

While the current deepening polarization in income and wealth can be traced to the economic restructuring and state deregulation of the last quarter century, the persistence of poverty also has longer-term roots in the structured hierarchies of class, race, gender, and ableism built into the foundation of Canadian society. From its early days, Canadian institutions operated in such a way as to marginalize people based on class, gender, and race. Canada was founded as a private-property-based settler colony that required the subordination of Aboriginal people and their way of life so that their resources could be harnessed for the benefit of British and French interests, first in Europe and then domestically. These historical inequities, arising out of internal and external colonial relations, have contemporary manifestations that shape individual and community access to resources.

Two key processes have made poverty among racialized groups an increasing source of concern more recently. One is the changing economy, through which neoliberal restructuring has imposed new vulnerabilities on working populations (Stanford and Vosko 2004). The other is the increased numerical significance of racialized groups, as the major sources of immigrants to Canada have shifted away from Europe toward countries in Asia and the global South.[3] These two processes combined build on historical processes of inequality that make factors such as race and gender significant in the distribution of opportunities in the labour market. Historical processes of stratification have intensified in the last two decades under neoliberalism, largely because restructuring has made precarious employment the fastest growing form of work (Cranford and Vosko 2006). These developments have placed all workers in a vulnerable position, but vulnerabilities are unevenly distributed because of pre-existing hierarchies that adversely impact women, persons with disabilities, Aboriginal peoples, racialized workers, and new immigrants (Vosko 2006; Zeytinoglu and Muteshi 2000). This leads to disproportionate exposure to lower incomes and occupational status and the racialization of poverty (Galabuzi 2004).

The racialization of poverty refers to the disproportionate and persistent incidence of poverty among racialized groups in Canada. It emerges out of the socio-economic features described above, including processes that structure differential access to economic opportunity and outcomes for racialized group members. The outcomes are that racialized groups disproportionately live in low-income, often concentrated immigrant communities, and thus also suffer from the impact of immigration status. Current trends indicate that the economic inequality between racialized immigrants and the Canadian-born is becoming greater and more permanent. That was not always the case; historically, immigrants tended to outperform Canadian-born counterparts because of their high educational levels and age advantage. Increasingly, however, racialized immigrants live on the margins of society, excluded from the job market and other means of upward mobility, in neighbourhoods of deep poverty with high unemployment rates, significant welfare dependency, and high school dropout rates, all conditions that perpetuate poverty (Picot et al. 2007; Picot and Hou 2003).

The changing Canadian demographic profile has made the issue of the socio-economic status of racialized groups newly significant as a public policy issue. Some argue that racialized groups, as growing populations in major Canadian cities, represent a source of concern because their vulnerability to low income can mature into threats to social cohesion such as we saw with the racialized riots in the Paris suburbs in 2005 and 2007. National and metropolitan area census data show that racialized people in major urban centres are two or three times more likely to be poor than other Canadians (Hou and Picot 2003; Lee 2000; Ornstein 2000; Kazemipur and Halli 2000; Fleury 2007; Picot and Hou 2003; Picot et al. 2007). The rates are even higher among recent immigrants and some select groups such as youth, women, and seniors of Arab, Latin American, Somali, Haitian, Iranian, Tamil, East Indian, and Vietnamese origin. The Canadian low-income rate was 14.7 percent in 2001, but low-income rates for racialized groups ranged from 16–43 percent (Linday n.d.).[4]

In cities like Toronto, Vancouver, Montreal, and Calgary, where racialized populations are statistically significant, the impact of the normalization of racially segmented labour markets and a racialized income and employment gap, combines the racialization of poverty with the racial segregation of low-income neighbourhoods, sustained school drop-out rates, and the criminalization of racialized youth. According to a 2001 United Way of Greater Toronto and Canadian Council for Social Development report, the overall Toronto poverty rate at 19 percent was higher than the Canadian rate of 14.7 percent, and racialized group members and immigrants in the city were almost three times more likely to live in poverty. About 29.5 percent of them lived below the poverty line, compared to the overall average of 11.6 percent among non-racialized groups. Between 1980 and 2000, poverty among racialized families rose by 361 percent. These conditions have created a deepening social marginalization. In a number of low-income Toronto neighbourhoods where racialized group members are disproportionately represented as tenants of poorly maintained public and private housing, the disempowerment has degenerated into a level of violence that has claimed many young lives (United Way of Greater Toronto and the Canadian Council on Social Development 2004).

Racialized Poverty and Residential Segregation in Urban Canada

Social exclusion is increasingly manifest in urban centres where racialized groups are concentrated in segregated low-income neighbourhoods. These urban neighbourhoods have been impacted by economic restructuring as well as immigration patterns over the last quarter century that have established racialized countries as key sources for immigration. Cities such as Toronto, Vancouver, and Montreal are magnets for immigrants, taking in almost 78 percent of new immigrants to Canada. The racialization of poverty has had a major impact on access to adequate housing for new immigrants and racialized groups. Immigrants in Toronto and Montreal are more likely than non-immigrants to live in neighbourhoods with high rates of poverty and increasingly are concentrated in what have come to be called racialized enclaves (see Table 5.1).

As urban housing markets become more segregated, racialized groups are relegated to substandard, marginal, and often over-priced housing (Philp 2000: A15). From 1980 to 2001, there was a sizeable growth in these neighbourhoods in Canada's three largest cities, which are home to over 73 percent of Canada's racialized population (Kazemipur and Halli 1997; see also Kazemipur and Halli 2000; Balakrishnan and Selvanthan 1990; Fong 1997; Fong and Gulia 1999, 1996; Fong and Shibuya 2000). The number of racialized enclaves increased in Toronto, Montreal, and Vancouver, from six in 1981 to 254 in 2001 (Hou and Picot 2004).[5]

These racialized enclaves have high levels of unemployment, low income, single parent households, and low levels of higher education, all characteristics of inter-generational poverty (Clark 1989).

Table 5.1 Toronto Area Racialized Enclaves and Characteristics Linked with Poverty Rates

	University degree	Unemployed	Low income	Single parent
Chinese	21%	11%	28%	12%
South Asian	12%	13%	28%	18%
Black	9%	18%	49%	34%

Source: Statistics Canada, 2003 Catalogue No. 11F0019M1E – no. 204 as cited in Hou and Picot 2004.

Studies suggest that these areas show characteristics of ghettoization or the spatial concentration of poverty: racialized concentration, high density and tightly clustered housing, and limited exposure to majority communities (Kazemipur and Halli 1997). Toronto and Vancouver had more racialized enclaves than Montreal, at 135, 111, and 8 respectively, most of which reflect the three largest racialized communities in Canada: Chinese, South Asian, and Black. These neighbourhoods, segregated by poverty, race, and immigration status, have become increasingly defined by the stresses that come with concentrated low incomes and poor allocation of government resources (Hou and Picot 2004).

The diminishing state commitment towards income redistribution and supports, services, and health and education funding are compounded with racial inequality in shaping the shift towards precarious work, limited access to employment income, and the increase in South-North immigration. The result is isolated, racially defined low-income neighbourhoods. Racialized group members live in neighbourhoods that are "hypersegregated" from the rest of society, characterized by disintegrating institutions and inadequate access to services and resources. Young immigrants living in these areas struggle with alienation from their parents and community of origin, and from the broader society (Kazemipur and Halli 2000). Homelessness, as an extreme form of exclusion, is also increasing among racialized group members because of low income incidence and the housing crises in urban areas (Lee 2000). Recent immigrants and racialized people are more likely to be homeless in Canada's urban centres than they were ten years ago. Homelessness in turn is associated with health factors such as extreme difficulty accessing health services, substance abuse, mental illness, infectious disease, and early mortality (Toronto Mayor's Homelessness Action Task Force Report 1999).

The Racialization of Poverty, Segregation, and Violence

> Poverty is like punishment for a crime you did not commit.
> —Eli Khamarov (quoted in Raphael 2007: 7)

Urban low-income neighbourhoods play a complex role in nurturing community for their immigrant and racialized residents by providing a space in which belonging is created. However, one way to understand the increase in gun violence among youth in low-income neighbourhoods in Toronto is by focusing on the high levels of poverty, marginalization, hopelessness, and powerlessness in these neighbourhoods subjected to the impacts of the neoliberal global economy, racial and class segregation, social service deficits, and a denial of government resources. These are the conditions under which violence can thrive.

Some studies have connected socio-economic crisis and deprivation on the one hand, and violence on the other (Boyd 1988). Other research suggests that generalized violence in communities represents a form of nihilism and a distorted evaluation of human life that emerges from alienation, despair, and powerlessness in environments characterized by severe exclusion. Young people are more likely to be victims of violence, and this is particularly true of racialized youth in low-income areas. These youth are also more likely to be criminalized through targeted policing, over-policing, and racial profiling, leading to high levels of criminal justice system contact for these groups. The prison population from major Canadian cities is disproportionately Aboriginal and racialized (Leonard, Rosario, Scott, and Bressan 2005; Welsh and Farrington 2005).

Critical legal theorists have provided insights into how legal regimes deploy dominant ideologies to define who or what is criminalized (Aylward 1999; Comack and Balfour 2004; Razack 2002). The assumptions of colour-blind legal regimes mask how the differential application of law criminalizes racialized and poor people. Zero-tolerance policies in education, racial profiling, the enforcement of anti-terrorism policy, and targeted policing in low-income neighbourhoods in the name of community safety, all deploy racialization to define criminality. As low-income neighbourhoods become increasingly racialized enclaves, processes of racialization offer important explanations for the over-representation of racialized groups in the criminal justice system. In the early twenty-first century, the proliferation of national security and community safety rubrics is an added dimension in how the racialization and criminalization of poverty intersect to produce racialized subjects as criminal. In turn, racialized communities thus become subject to practices and stigmas that have adverse socio-economic impacts on their members' life chances. The cultural prisms through which the racialized Other has historically been understood in Canada accentuates criminalization, as the contemporary intersection between racial stigmatization and exposure to poverty increasingly marks entire communities as criminalized, through their disproportionate experience of surveillance, over-policing, and incarceration. Here I examine how cultural explanations are used to criminalize Blacks, provide a gender analysis of criminality discourses, and follow with an illustrative case study of the African Canadian Toronto community.

Criminalization and Racialized Cultural Pathologies

The early twenty-first century has seen a re-assertion of the White settler colonial project that conceived Canada. Despite the official commitment to multiculturalism, discourses that essentialize racialized peoples are commonly used to provide cultural explanations and official justification for the othering of racialized peoples and the violation of their human rights, in continuity with historical practices such as the Chinese Exclusion Act, the head tax, and the internment of Japanese Canadians (Stein et al. 2007). Today in Canada, dominant discourses reproduce racist ideologies that deny the pervasiveness of racism while characterizing racialized people as culturally distinct Others. This is especially marked in moments of perceived national or community security crisis when discourses — such as those around the "jihad generation," criminal immigrants, and violent urban youth — depict the racialized Other as someone whose culture, immigrant status, and youth are to be feared and loathed. These discourses impact public practice, as is evidenced in the disproportionate profiling of racialized Canadians of Muslim, Arab, and Asian origin. Such discourses and practices also pathologize entire communities and intensify their extant alienation. The popular discussion that emerged with the arrest and media trial of seventeen young Muslims in Toronto on terrorism charges in 2006 portrayed them as Jihadist monsters linked with Islamic extremism of far off lands, although most were Canadian-born. The continuing preoccupation with national security and community safety, conditioned by post-9/11 moral panics, has intensified the pathologizing of racialized peoples as the dangerous Other (Galabuzi 2007).

In Toronto, this moment plays out through the pathologizing of Black, Brown, and Muslim identities using various discourses — of home-grown terrorists, guns and violence, Asian, Tamil, or Latino gangs, Black on Black crime, and so on — to produce public concern about racialized criminality. The normalization of these discourses justifies draconian policing and anti-terror measures. Racial and religious profiling become common means of maintaining law and order in Canada's cities and in the border-crossing experiences of members of racialized groups (Suljit 2001; Weber 2005; Wortley 2005).

These racializing and criminalizing discourses and practices inform strained interactions between racialized groups and Canadian state representatives, leading to withdrawal of community cooperation. This is compounded by the fact that these communities are subjected to police harassment and brutality, excessive use of techniques such as strip searches, and harsh criminal justice penalties. Racialized youth have their access to space challenged by police and private security guards. Public and semi-public space becomes a site for turf wars, which are often resolved through further police harassment and force. In other words, poor racialized communities experience policing and criminal justice through intensive criminalization.

Criminality Discourses as Gendered Masculine Discourses

These racializing and criminalizing discourses also suggest the need for a gendered analysis. Major newspapers have editorialized not just about the alleged moral deficiency of the Black community, but how it manifests in high levels of single parenting — i.e., loose women with multiple partners unable to control their fatherless children. In the wake of fifteen-year-old Jason Manners' Toronto shooting death in May 2007, *Globe and Mail* columnist Margaret Wente opined that violent youth are produced in an urban immigrant "underclass" characterized by "disorganized, single-mother families where discipline is scarce" (Wente 2007: A21). These racialized "culture of poverty" discourses that blame women for community decay and violence are reminiscent of U.S. Senator Patrick Moynihan's accusations in *The Negro Family: The Case for National Action* (1965) and Ronald Reagan's vilification of "welfare queens."[6] Using mothers as scapegoats fits with cultural explanations for crime in a period of panic; racializing and classing criminality reinforces the ideological position that this is not a Canadian problem but one of a racialized and/or immigrant underclass that exists outside the bounds of normal Canadian behaviour.

At the same time, these discourses rely on patriarchal conceptions of masculinity, which define men as powerful, competitive, controlling, unemotional, rational, and task-oriented, yet risk-taking. This conception of masculinity promotes a sense of entitlement and privilege among men in a context of assumptions around individualism and hierarchy. While such a conception lays down rules for how men are to interact among themselves and with women, the experience of masculinity is not the same for all men. Masculinity is experienced and worked out in groups of men subject to social forces in relation to race, ethnicity, class, sexuality, age, ability, religion, worldview, marital status, education, and occupation. Men's experiences of these multiple dimensions are constitutive of their masculine identity. As both an oppressed minority and a privileged gender, many young Black men are subject to contradictory discourses of masculinity. Their identity in Canadian society is formed through competing narratives of domineering masculinity and disemboweled blackness. I would argue that this experience contributes to some young Black men's attraction to violence as a means to assert power and patriarchal position; it also means that the women in their lives are likely to be prominent victims of their violence (Messerschmidt 1993; Brunson and Miller 2006).

The moral panic around the Black criminal in Toronto is rooted in a broader construction of the Black community as prone to criminality and representing a threat to community safety. These assumptions are perpetuated by an inordinate media focus on criminal behaviour by a small number of Blacks, especially poor urban youth, and by uncritical reporting of disproportionate Black incarceration rates. Coverage in major newspapers sensationalizes criminal activities involving Black suspects, using repeated images to generalize them as representative of the Black community's moral position as a group. This provides a cultural explanation for the moral panic about violent crime in Toronto, which racializes criminality as it criminalizes poverty, and reinforces the ideological position that racialized immigrant communities exist outside the bounds of a normal Canada. *Globe and Mail* columnist Michael Valpy once remarked that "The barbarians are within the gates," while *Toronto Sun* columnist Raynier Maharaj suggested that "Canadians are fed up with people they see as outsiders coming into their country and beating and killing them" (as quoted in Henry and Tator 2002).

The media regularly refer to "Black on Black" crime to discuss violence in low-income communities (Porter and Campbell 2001). Popular discourses around violence often make reference to gangs using racial designations (Chinese, Tamil, Black, Hispanic, Asian). Anti-Black and more general racializing media discourse around crime intensifies the alienation of community youth, making violence by individuals more, not less likely. Some Black youth have concluded that nobody cares and maintain their silence about acts of violence as an act of defiance or fear. Moreover, stigmas surrounding racialized criminalization and the criminalization of poverty among racialized youth represent vulnerabilities arising out of generations of stereotypes.

Frances Henry has identified three modes of historical discourse that have characterized racialized groups in Canada that help to explain the persistent mischaracterization of African Canadians and the resulting impacts on their experience. She identifies a discourse of otherness that draws boundaries between "us"" and "them" and is commonly framed in the context of the relative values and norms of majority versus minority cultures. The universalizing "we" comprises members of the dominant White culture (viewed as law-abiding, tolerant, and fair-minded) or the culture of mainstream organizations (media, police, school, workplace). "They" refers to the "Other," who possesses "different" or "deviant," but fixed, values, beliefs, and behaviours. Complementing the discourse of otherness are discourses of denial about racism in Canada and colour-blindness, both of which invalidate the experience of racialization and its outcomes (Henry and Tator 2002).

Case Study: The African Canadian Community

The African Canadian community is made up of a diversity of cultures representing the African diaspora; it draws from descendants of some of the earliest settlers in Canada and multiple generations of immigrants from the Caribbean, Africa, Latin America, the U.S., and Europe. Ethnically mixed, with dual- and single-parent families, the community (which is really multiple communities) has more women than men. Three out of five are foreign-born or recent immigrants. More than 50 percent reside in the Toronto area and over 90 percent live in urban Canada. They experience a range of socio-economic status from high-income professionals to low-income manual labourers and those on social assistance. However, in 2001, they lagged behind other income earners, with as much as three times higher rates of poverty and two times higher rates of unemployment. Canadian-born Blacks are more vulnerable to unemployment than their immigrant counterparts although they are just as likely to have a university education as other Canadians. The African Canadian community has three times the standard rate of single parenthood, and over half the children in the community live below the poverty line. African Canadians are younger on average than the Canadian population and the Black population is growing faster than the general population (Milan and Tan 2004).

The African Canadian community has doubled in the last twenty-four years due to increased immigration in the 1970s and 1980s. That growth stalled in the 1990s due to stringent immigrant selection measures and administrative action aimed at lowering Canada's refugee acceptance rates. The immigration structure, long affected by the domestic worker program, means that there are more African Canadian women than men (52 to 48 percent), far more in the 24–45 age group. Many families remain separated for extended periods of time, leaving youth with an integration challenge and limited private or public social supports (Milan and Tan 2004).

While the resulting patterns of exclusion are similar to those experienced by other racialized groups, African Canadians consistently lag behind others in relevant indicators. This is true in spite of the fact that they often have comparable levels of education and the fact that two out of every five are Canadian-born compared to one in three for most other racialized groups. Harvey, Siu, and Reil's study of ethno-cultural groups over various immigration periods shows that African Canadians and other racialized groups suffer higher unemployment rates, lower employment incomes, and higher poverty incidence than European immigrants over the same periods. Hum and Simpson found that African Canadians experience a wage disadvantage similar to that of immigrants, and Gosine notes that "Black Canadians incur the most severe penalty in the labour market as a result of their racialized status" (da Silva 1992; Hou and Balakrishnan 1996; Harvey, Siu, and Reil 1999; Hum and Simpson 1998).

Social Exclusion and Criminalization among Toronto's African Canadian Population

In Toronto, Canada's largest city, with close to half of Canada's African Canadian population, Blacks living in racialized enclaves experience high rates of poverty, especially among female-led families: this group's poverty rate of 48 percent is even higher among female-led families, who represent 33 percent of Black families in these enclaves. Unemployment rates are high in these communities, which are also characterized by a breakdown in social institutions, service delivery deficits, increased health risks, and a profound sense of powerlessness, marginalization, and insecurity (Picot and Hou 2003). These experiences set communities up for stigmatization through popular pathologies, which in turn can be internalized, especially by youth. The more the community is pathologized through generations of negative stereotypes, the more the intersection of poverty and racialization marks communities as the target of surveillance, policing, criminalization, and other forms of regulation.

Stephen Lewis (1992), appointed by the Premier of Ontario to investigate the causes of the Yonge Street disturbances in Toronto, suggested that anti-Black sentiment was at the heart of the racism problem in Ontario. Research indicates that African Canadians in Ontario experience unequal treatment from police and across the criminal justice system, beginning with police stopping, arresting, and charging, through to bail hearings, sentencing, and incarceration. The disparities are most glaring when you look at discretion points in the system (police stopping cars, justices deciding bail, judges sentencing, and so on). African Canadians are also profiled as dangerous foreigners and subject to police brutality as a perceived means of protecting the citizenry (Gittens and Cole 1995; Gittens and Cole 1994; Aylward 1999; Wortley and Tanner 2003). Low-income, marginalized communities tend to bear the brunt of the neoliberal law-and-order agenda through targeted policing. Because African Canadians are over-represented in these communities, over-policing and racial profiling involves criminalization at the intersection of poverty and racialization (Ornstein 2000).

In these urban contexts, young Black men in particular are depicted as aggressive, violent, and dangerous. Even when they are just chilling, they are lay-abouts, up to no good (James 1997). The police act on these stereotypes and enforce order in ways that criminalize these young men: young African Canadians describe their encounters with police as often characterized by contempt, harassment, mistaken identity, and harshness (James 1999). Police and security guards in malls consistently challenge these young people's access to public and semi-public space. As noted above, these spaces become a site for turf wars, which are often resolved through police harassment and brutality, and these encounters in turn often result in the imposition of harsh penalties.

A *Toronto Star* investigation published in 2002 described racial profiling by police as prevalent in Toronto, with disproportionate police stops of cars driven by Black citizens, especially Black youth (Rankin et al. 2002: A1, A2, A13, A14; Wortley and Tanner 2003). In a study analyzing 1994 stops data, Wortley found that 28.7 percent of African Canadians surveyed reported being stopped by police compared to 18 percent of Whites and 14.6 percent of Chinese. Compared to 22.1 percent of their non-Black counterparts, 42.7 percent of African Canadian men reported being stopped in the previous two years, 28.7 percent of Blacks reported being stopped twice in that same period compared to 9.9 percent of non-Blacks. Blacks were also three times as likely to be detained before trial on a drug charge (Wortley 1997). In data that suggests racial profiling also crosses class, age, and gender lines, among young African Canadian women with university education, 22 percent were stopped in comparison with 9 percent of their non-Black counterparts. Older African Canadian females with university education had a 16 percent chance of being stopped compared to 6 percent of their White counterparts.

Toronto's African Canadian Youth and Violence
In the summer of 2001, Toronto's African Canadian community was engulfed in an undeclared crisis of internecine violence. Sixteen Black youth lost their lives in gun violence over a period of four months.[7] According to Toronto's Black Action Defence Committee (2001), this loss of young life to violence added to 100 such deaths in a five-year period and 200 in the preceding ten years.[8] While Canada and Toronto's overall murder rates were stable for much of the 1990s, the rates among Toronto Blacks, particularly youths, skyrocketed. According to Gartner and Thompson (2004), the rate for Toronto Blacks was four times that of the general population at 10.1 per 100,000.[9] While the Black community represents just under 10 percent of the city's population, it accounted for approximately 30 percent of murder victims annually between 1996 and 2004. Since 1998, the percentage of homicide victims under age twenty-five has grown to 40 percent from 25 percent in the 1970s, and a majority of these have been Black youth (Gartner and Thompson 2004b).

Anti-Black discourses dominate the popular portrayal of, and official engagement around, violence in the African Canadian Toronto community. The official response to the Toronto gun killings has centred on a law-and-order containment agenda; political leaders have indulged every police resource demand. Toronto Police Services have set up a Toronto Anti-Violence Intervention Strategy (TAVIS) that operates on principles similar to those that characterize military war-zone operations, with high-visibility police vans and scout cars patrolling continuously in targeted communities, and quick deployment and intelligence gathering methods (cultivating community informers).[10] This scorched earth approach to policing, reminiscent of U.S. operations in Iraq (and policing in racialized enclaves in U.S. cities), dehumanizes communities as it sets them up for police brutality and civil and human rights abuses. In a number of incidents in Toronto's poor neighbourhoods police sweeps have broken into homes, destroyed property, and arrested scores of alleged suspects under the guise of breaking up gangs. The subsequent release of many without charges does little to save their dignity from the humiliation of arrest and media parading, ease the trauma felt in these communities, or address the loss of their already meagre property. The

Toronto Star reports that by January 2008 "TAVIS has made more than 10,000 arrests." While the *Star* notes that Ontario Attorney General Chris Bentley claims that TAVIS has "built positive relationships by making over 120,000 business and citizen contacts," the paper also reports that critics "say TAVIS officers are going beyond the proper scope of their authority and leaving young black males feeling harassed" (Powell 2008: A6).[11]

The mainstream media and state officials implicitly present this conflict as Black-on Black violence in communities over-run by criminal gangs.[12] While these characterizations invoke moral challenges to the Black community for collective responsibility, they also pathologize the entire community. Limited attention is given to the fact that there is little to suggest that the anti-social actions of some young Blacks fits the concept of gangs in the academic or official use of the word. The limited research that exists does not suggest that Black Toronto has organized criminal gangs with clear hierarchical control structures, organized economic activity and modes of operation, or numbers that suggest the organization and consistent recruitment patterns characteristic of gang culture. Rather, the evidence suggests relatively anecdotal anti-social activities among youth (Wortley and Tanner 2004). Based on self-reporting interviews of students and street youths, Wortley and Tanner conclude that there is a higher level of "criminal gang activity" among White youth than racialized youth. Even with student and street youth who claim "criminal gang membership," these researchers point to definitional problems since most of those claiming gang membership cite social activity (including hanging out) as the basis for their membership. Beyond that, what passes for gang activity involves under-organized and fragmented criminal and sub-cultural activity such as participating in fights, breaking and entering, use of and trafficking of small amounts of illegal drugs, and use of alcohol by minors (Wortley and Tanner 2004). Nonetheless, (Black) criminal gangs provide an easy descriptor that fits well with historical and contemporary anxieties about the Other behind dark faces.

The near absence of skepticism by the mainstream media around criminalizing portraits of the racialized urban poor in Toronto is explained by the fact that Canadians are conditioned by the long history of racist discourses that construct Blacks, and especially young Black men, as violent and dangerous. This can become a self-fulfilling prophesy as young men are subject to patriarchal gender codes, and the alienation and misbehaviour that racism, poverty, and social exclusion engender lead Black youth to be subjected to surveillance in malls and stores, recreation centres, public housing, schools, and ultimately prisons. Surveillance intensifies the alienation of Toronto's poor African Canadian youth and impugns their humanity, leading them to take positions of resistance, which can include showing attitude, avoiding contact with the police (including when members of their own community are victimized), and exhibiting anti-social behaviour.

Black youth in low-income urban communities know that public and semi-public spaces are areas of contest between police — seeking to impose order and often assert their own masculinity — and residents, who feel hemmed in and denied their rights. As low-income communities have become more racialized, these communities, especially young men, are disproportionately targeted, and the frequency of stops and arrests in turn comes to justify the racial and class profiling.

Conclusion

In Canada today issues of crime prevention, community safety, and national security increasingly define the relationships between marginalized and dominant groups. In this chapter, we consider the intersecting experience of racialized poverty and the criminalization of the poor. Race is central to the process of criminalizing the poor in two ways. It is significant in structuring exposure to poverty so that racialized people are more likely to be poor and vulnerable to criminalization. But it also provides cultural explanations for criminality in moments of concern about national security and community safety. These dynamics intersect in racialized low-income communities in Canada's cities, where experiences of poverty by racialized groups lead to high levels of contact with the criminal justice system.

We have looked specifically at the experience of the African Canadian community in Toronto, whose relations with dominant groups are often mediated through commonly held stereotypes about Blacks' disproportionate proclivity to criminality (today frequently read as "gang" involvement) and actual experiences of disproportionate contact with surveillance and the criminal justice system. We have explained how key institutions such as the mainstream media and the state produce stories and images that reinforce historical stigmas and imagined pathologies, especially about Black youth, generating moral panics that demand securitized responses and the criminalization of Blacks. These developments in turn reproduce unequal access to employment, neighbourhood selection, life chances, and ultimately the quality of citizenship for African Canadians and racialized Canadians generally.

Notes

1. Racialized group members are persons, other than Aboriginal peoples, who are non-Caucasian in race or non-White in colour as defined by the federal Employment Equity Act, 1995; a fuller definition of racialized poverty is provided elsewhere in this chapter and other work by the author.
2. Only 3 percent of single parents on welfare are under twenty years old and nearly half of single parents on welfare have only one child. See J. McCormack, 2007,

"Why myths about poor endure: Scape-goating needy justifies society's failure to find political solutions," *Toronto Star,* March 20; D. Chunn and S. Gavigan, 2006, "From Welfare Fraud to Welfare as Fraud: The Criminalization of Poverty" in E. Comack and G. Balfour (eds.), *Criminalizing Women,* Halifax: Fernwood Publishing; Pratt and Valverde 2002.

3.   Recent immigrants from Asia (including the Middle East) were 58.3 percent of immigrants to Canada in 2006 and 59.4 percent in 2001. In 1971, only 12.1 percent of recent immigrants were from this region. Immigrants from Europe made up 16.1 percent of recent immigrants in 2006. In 1971, they were 61.6 percent of immigrants to Canada. In 2006 10.8 percent of recent immigrants were from Central and South America and the Caribbean, and 10.6 percent were born in Africa, up from 8.3 percent in 2001 (Statistics Canada, *Immigration in Canada: A Portrait of the Foreign-born Population, 2006 Census: Highlights* <http://www12.statcan.ca/english/census06/analysis/immcit/highlights.cfm>).

4.   Data is drawn from the 2001 Census and the 2002 Ethnic Diversity Survey.

5.   These enclaves represent census track areas with at least 30 percent of the population belonging to the designated group. In 2001, each census track included about 5000 people.

6.   For the origins of "culture of poverty" explanations and the phrase itself see O. Lewis, 1966, "The Culture of Poverty," in G. Gmelch and W. Zenner (eds.), *Urban Life* Waveland Press.

7.   Gun violence remains a major concern in Toronto, claiming over forty people in 2005, most of them Black youth. This was by far the highest rate of gun homicide in a major city in Canada. See K. Roach, n.d., "Racism and Gun Violence in Toronto's Black Community," *New Socialist* <new socialist.org/newsite/index.php?id=851>.

8.   The BADC was founded by Dudley Laws, Charles Roach, Sherona Hall, and Lennox Farrell in response to the 1988 police shooting of Lester Donaldson and several other Black Toronto men. See L. Farrell, 2005, "A Return 'Into the heart of Africa,'" *Toronto Star,* February 16; K. Donvan, 1988, "Police Probe Mental History of Man Police Killed," *Toronto Star,* August 18; K.K. Campbell, 1992, "Laws Charges Metro Police Bias Against Blacks 'Worse than LA,'" *EYE Weekly,* October 1.

9.   The rates have fluctuated between 1.8 to 3.0 per 100, for Canada and 1.8 to 2.8 per 100,000 for the City of Toronto over the past thirty years (1974–2003).

10.   For the official presentation of the Toronto Anti-Violence Intervention Strategy (TAVIS) see *11 Division Community Bulletin* 2006, available at <torontopolice.on.ca/tavis/> and <toronto.ca/scfy/assets/appendix2/appendix%202%20-%20C2.pdf>.

11.   See also the statement by criminal lawyer Edward Sapiano in T. Appleby and U. Gandhi, 2006, "Toronto proves adept at curbing gun violence," *Globe and Mail,* April 11; K. Roach, n.d., "Racism and gun violence in Toronto's Black community," *New Socialist* <newsocialist.org/newsite/index.php?id=851>, and the criticisms of TAVIS' anti-drug trade practices by the Canadian HIV/AIDS Legal Network at <aidslaw.ca/publications/publicationsdocEN.php?ref=607>.

12.   See, for example, Ontario Ministry of the Attorney General and Ministry of Community Safety and Correctional Services, 2008, "McGuinty Government's

Comprehensive Gun Violence Strategy." For media portrayals see, for example, n.a., 2006, "Gang leaders 'surgically removed' in 60 police raids," *CBC News*, May 18 <cbc.ca/canada/toronto/story/2006/05/18/tor-massive-raid060518. html> and n.a., 2007, "Suspects in Toronto shooting have criminal past," *CTV News*, July 24 <ctv.ca/servlet/ArticleNews/story/CTVNews/20070724/ gun_crime_070724?s_name=&no_ads=>.

Chapter 6

The Criminalization of Poverty... and the Impoverishment of Everything Else

J. Grant Wanzel

In this chapter I argue that with respect to the public realm, urban design and planning that privileges private over public interests impoverishes everything for everybody even as it reinforces other ways in which the poor are criminalized. In the medieval era one was all but excommunicated from one's community when one was required to live "beyond the pale" — the pale being a wooden stake that marked the town's outer limit. Many contemporary parallels come quickly to mind: gated communities, shopping malls, summer sidewalk cafés, and the for-profit rock concerts that temporarily claim public parks as their own. There are many more such impoverishments of the public realm, each one just as mean-spirited, intolerant, paranoid, and controlling as the very first "pale" would have been. This chapter explores some of them, as they play out in Halifax, Nova Scotia.

Criminalizing Poverty

A few years ago, I was watching a rerun of a popular Canadian crime drama when one of the characters said to his partner:

> When did we get so afraid of homeless people, when did that happen? When I was a kid there used to be guys would come around, offer to mow your lawn, or clean out your garage, paint your house numbers on the curb, lot of 'em were just back from the war, couldn't get a job, nobody thought they were homeless 'cause they were home, you know, the whole country was their home.

I was somewhat surprised when his mate responded, somewhat offhandedly, "Yeah. We made poverty a crime."[1]

If we have made poverty a crime we have also created gated communities to secure privilege and keep poverty out. Gated communities are private enclaves that promise secure enjoyment of one's private wealth free from the unfamiliar, the unpredictable, and above all, public scrutiny. We employ architectural means such as fences, screens, electrified borders, steel and concrete, walls, and empty space to distinguish one sort of place or territory from another. By such means we can, and do, make increasingly fine distinctions on the basis of race, function, socio-economic class, and so on. As a consequence we have criminalized poverty and impoverished everything else.

Back Sides/Front Sides

Those who inhabit a territory distinguish themselves from outsiders by rules of behaviour and insider codes. For example, the European Union has done away with national passports. Every citizen of a member country enjoys a *passe partout* and, with a common E.U. passport, may now cross any border within the Union. But if you are a guest worker and not a citizen you have none of the privileges or protections of membership; we set the rules and know the signs — you do not. We belong here — you do not. If you have business here, it had better be legitimate. If you do not, you had better behave; otherwise, out you go. In this way, by conflating territory and locally acceptable behavioural expectations we embrace some and ostracize others. Those so marginalized we deem to have criminal intent.

When it comes to the residential neighbourhoods of our towns and cities we bring similar associations and discriminations to who and what belongs where. As was previously mentioned, what we build, how we build

Figure 1 West End Halifax, N.S., aerial view to the east

it, and what it looks like say a lot about who we are and how we think about things and one another. In architecture, devices such as relative size, shape, position, and directionality are employed to manipulate physical space and built form to express purpose, that is, to speak to us about ourselves. I will illustrate by reference to my own early twentieth-century neighbourhood in Halifax, Nova Scotia (Figure 1).

Our family has lived in a single-family, wood-frame dwelling on Lawrence Street (Figure 2) for more than twenty-five years. The house sits on its own long, narrow lot. Its front side or public face is rather ornate and formal while its back side is plain — not trying to impress anybody. Across the fence, its backyard neighbour has a similar

Figure 2 Lawrence Street, south side, Halifax

design. In fact, the individual buildings that form the block are all much the same: each on its own lot, close together, and each putting its best face forward.

This is now a street of neighbouring houses and the beginnings of a small community. Every house is different but roughly the same size and shape as its neighbours. None stands out as remarkably different. Together the houses make a street — critically, a neighbourhood street — a place for encounter, a place of sharing and caring. As children on such a street we encounter the unfamiliar and learn about citizenship and tolerance. As adults we can continue these encounters. John Sewell, a former mayor of Toronto, has suggested that you can tell much about a person's values by how they travel to work. In an observation about the public realm that closely parallels my own, he referred to the bus passenger and pedestrian as members of "communities in transit," who, being exposed twice daily to the diversity of the city, would share a more inclusive view of the world.[2]

Although the rules about space and its use are unspoken in my neighbourhood, they are very clear and easily read. If you are a neighbour, we would expect to meet you in the street or over the back fence, but not in our

Figure 3 Typical bungalow, Lower Sackville, NS

yard. If you are just passing through, you would enjoy right-of-way and be welcome as long as you observed the customs of the neighbourhood and were respectful of its various actual and virtual boundaries.

But, what if we triple the space between neighbouring houses? And what if we more than double the amount of space between houses facing one another across the street? Oceans of green lawns and rivers of asphalt now separate houses. Distance alone decreases contact and opportunities for neighbours to get to know one another. Further, given the distances between things, everyone who lives here has to drive. There are no sidewalks, but then no one here walks. Here anybody in the street is suspicious. Where did they come from and where are they going? We ask these questions because in this part of the city local streets neither come from nor lead to anywhere in particular. I offer in evidence the following images of Lower Sackville, a planned community on the outskirts of the Halifax Regional Municipality (Figures 3 and 4).

Alternatively, what if we single out a section of Lawrence Street for special attention? What would happen if we take twenty or thirty individual houses and place them shoulder-to-shoulder, faces in, backsides out, in the form of an enclosed square or court at the top of a street, with four of the houses forming a gate? And what if then we were to give them a distinctive two-tone paint job? Beautiful. Very exclusive.

Exclusive is the operative word. What we really have is an inward-looking group of houses, their expressionless posteriors turned to the world outside.

Figure 4 Typical residential street, Lower Sackville

Freestanding houses have been transformed into an identifiable corporate entity, quite distinctive in size, colour, form, and detail. We've emphasized the differences between them and the other houses of the neighbourhood and singled out the newly arrived residents, stigmatizing them. Recall too that in the rest of the neighbourhood, the streets continue on into other parts of the city. Here the street dead-ends at the newly built courtyard community.

Figure 5 Aerial view to the west, Mulgrave Park, Halifax

Figure 6 Where's the neighbourhood? The western edge of Mulgrave Park, Halifax

Its residents are trapped inside and clearly separated from the rest of the neighbourhood. They are on its fringes, marginalized and suspect — exactly where we can keep an eye on them.

Now if this is not familiar, it damn well should be. I have just described any one of dozens of public housing projects built in the 1950s and 1960s. Even allowing for its far greater size and isolated and steeply sloping site, this could have been a conceptual sketch for the Mulgrave Park public housing project in the north end of Halifax (Figures 5 and 6). Its design, like a lot of public housing, stigmatizes the residents and promotes a sense of them as outsiders or even criminals in the minds of those who are predisposed to such prejudices. In turning longstanding rules of order inside-out, it undermines the neighbourhood's unspoken understanding about what is public and what private, the distinctive roles of front sides and back sides, and the all-important lines between the formal and the informal, and public decorum and old-fashioned neighbourliness.

The Impoverishment of Everything Else

Classifying people, things, and activities and separating them is what planners call zoning. The principal purpose of zoning is to control the use and value of real estate. Property owners, mortgage companies, and property investors abhor uncertainty. Once enacted, zoning and land-use by-laws give predictable uses and values to the properties they protect. Their principal effect is to thus simplify every facet of the human habitat. Through the determined pursuit of numbing sameness and predictability, single-purpose zoning assigns everything and everyone a place and then fights like hell to keep them there. This way, we can also avoid urbanity and intercept cosmopolitanism. We do this out of fear of the unknown, out of a deep desire to bring the present we know into the future we can't know. In his splendid little book, *The*

Figure 7 Fox Harbour, a gated community somewhere in rural Nova Scotia

Uses of Disorder, Richard Sennett (1970) called this drive to secure the future in what is already known "purified consciousness." The GAP is everywhere and offers the same merchandise everywhere. Every major city in the world boasts a MacDonalds, and as we know, MacDonalds primarily aspires to dispense a single, standard product. This corporate sameness leaves little room for a mom-and-pop shop, unless it is a branch of a Mom and Pop franchise operation.

We have many names for this spatialization of social and cultural relations. In economic terms, we call it globalization and commercialization. In geo-political terms, we call it imperialism. In socio-economic terms, it is corporatism. Whatever it is called, what we can actually see and experience is the steady progress of a dominating, invasive culture ensuring its comfort level by extending its own comfort zone. The resulting shifts send a clear message: "This is our culture now. You are welcome to it, of course. But on our terms." Black or White. With us or against us. No in-betweens. No ambiguity. The pervasive result is the criminalization of any and every difference, including poverty, and the banal, sterile, predictable, comfortable, and above all else, privatized, impoverishment of everything else. The following examples will by now be familiar to most of us.

Figure 7 shows the main gate of a gated community at Fox Harbour, Nova Scotia. It is walled in, gated, and secured by surveillance cameras and guard dogs. Such places are promoted as islands of privilege, complacent and pleased with their panic rooms. Arguably, they are beleaguered outposts, islands adrift in a mounting sea of poverty.

Figure 8 West side of Gottingen Street, Halifax

Gottingen Street (Figure 8) was a major shopping street in Halifax and home to many fine shops, banks, department stores, cinemas, and restaurants. It is now a shadow of its former self. Its once animated sidewalks are uncomfortably narrowed in favour of wider lanes to accommodate traffic that is just passing through.

Argyle Street (Figure 9) in downtown Halifax is peppered with self-important and pushy little bars and restos poking into the public right-of-way, converting public sidewalks into private terraces, choking the roadway, and elbowing pedestrians onto temporary boardwalks. Right-of-way? An ironic

Figure 9 Pushy restos: The view south on Argyle Street, Halifax

Figure 10 Citadel Hill secured for a rock concert, Halifax

concept in this context, I'd say.

Citadel Hill dominates the skyline of Halifax. It is the city's major landmark and a National Heritage Site. Routinely now, rock concerts and festivals rent, fence off, and temporarily privatize huge portions of this piece of our patrimony (Figure 10).

Spring Garden Place and Park Lane (Figure 11) are privately owned shopping malls that front onto fashionable Spring Garden Road in downtown Halifax. Because they are aligned at right angles to the street, the commercial activity they accommodate is focused inward. By this simple means they are able to suck the life out of the rest of street and at the same time set the ground rules for entry to their inner sancta.

Not surprisingly, it is also here on Spring Garden Road that mean-spirited merchants attempting to control the public right-of-way agitated

Figure 11 Take Notice: Park Lane Mall, Halifax

Figure 12 Caught in the act: Private security guard patrols Spring Garden Road, Halifax

against the Salvation Army's Soup-Kitchen-on-Wheels and hired private security guards (Figure 12) to harass the panhandlers. Now that the rules of Park Lane and Spring Garden Place rule the street, Spring Garden Road itself is de facto no longer part of the public realm. It is only for those who can afford to be there.

Some time ago, one of our graduate students made a telling point. He said, "We in North America undervalue the public realm. Compared to Europeans, we have little passion or sense of ownership for our public spaces and institutions." I was struck by the directness of his observation. Historically, the public market was always a place of exchange, of goods, services, and ideas. As such, it has been a place of debate and conflict, of community and *civitas*, which is, in the historical sense, not only a place, but a condition, an ideal, and a state of mind. As Allan Gregg stated,

> Creating community, creed, and a common sense of destiny also requires citizen contact. There was a reason the ancient Greeks built theatres and early architects made town squares the centrepiece of their city plans. By strengthening the avenues of cultural distribution, public spaces can be combined with art and ideas to advance citizen interaction and build a stronger sense of civic virtue. Public sponsorship of festivals, reading series, debates, and town-hall meetings can all be used to inveigle individuals out of their rec rooms and into the streets, where citizens will gain a greater feeling of "ownership" of their community and its problems. (Gregg 2007)

We have allowed our streets and parks and public places to be whittled away, and with them their historic roles as arenas for debate, exchange, and encounter. The risks of unwanted encounters that public spaces were said to pose have been reduced in favour of reassuring sameness and comfortable predictability. The public realm has been homogenized. Where historically there was room for all, now who belongs and who does not is not only crystal clear, but policed. It is in this sense that I speak of the impoverishment of the public realm as both a means to and consequence of the criminalization of poverty. In reducing the actual size and complexity of public space we have not only compromised its vitality, we have squeezed the life out of it. In the process we have left little room for the expression of ideas or differences of opinion, and even less for the tolerance of diversity. As Glenn Murray, former mayor of Winnipeg, said at a public forum in Halifax in the spring of 2003, "Our cities have become impoverished and the politics became impoverished, and the citizens disenchanted."

Conclusion

The policies of planners, and the models and drawings of urban and architectural designers, are means by which social and cultural values are given physical form. Therefore, when we ask what this planning policy or that social housing project means, we are acknowledging that what we build is a reflection of who we are and how we think. But the values behind the criminalization of poverty and the privatization of the public realm are not ours in the collective, cultural sense. They are not widely held. They are the values of the relative few who have the wealth and power to make it so. Indeed, by reference to a number of readily available examples, we have revealed how self-serving notions of justice and celebrations of wealth and power have been given shape. Matters of territory are the privilege of political power. Here the tools of the designer are nothing more than instruments of that power and the means by which space is politicized and politics are spatialized. Where the privatization of public space and/or the criminalization of poverty are concerned, there could be no such thing as a benign application of design. It would be a contradiction in terms and, however well-meaning, the designer would be a mere pawn of cultural invasion.

In addition to speaking of the impoverishment of our cities and the disenchantment of their citizens, Mayor Murray spoke optimistically of "building a legacy of hope and skills" and of "asking people to be citizens." These were not empty words. But full citizenship demands a public forum and, as we have shown, ours are in serious jeopardy. We have shown that the impoverishment of the public realm is intimately related to the criminalization of poverty and is both a means to and a consequence of it. That being so, the struggle for the public realm is nothing less than the struggle for democratic control of our streets, parks, and public institutions, and ultimately of public discourse itself. Freedom of access, freedom from being stigmatized, and the freedom for all to enjoy the privileges and responsibilities of citizenship, rest on the outcome of that struggle.

Notes

Photo Credits

All images with the exception of Fig. 7 are the property of the author and have been reproduced here with his permission. Fig. 7 is the property of Dr. Jill Grant and has been reproduced here with her written consent.

1. "A Big Enough Fan," *Da Vinci's Inquest*, Episode 55, directed by Robert Cuffley, Vancouver, BC: Haddock Entertainment.

2. For his ideas on cities see J. Sewell, 2004, *A New City Agenda*, Chicago: Zephyr Press.

Chapter 7

The Penis Police

Regulating, Punishing, and Excluding Single Mothers on Social Assistance

Jeanne Fay

In 2001, Nova Scotia's Employment Support and Income Assistance Act (ESIA 2001) eliminated single motherhood as a discrete rationale for social assistance. The Nova Scotia Family Benefits Act (1977), which created a distinct assistance program for single mothers and persons with disabilities, intended to remove the stigma of receiving aid, was repealed with adoption of the ESIA. Single mothers are now recipients on par with the single, able-bodied, two-parent families and persons with disabilities. This change posed immediate financial consequences for single mothers: an average of 10 percent less income assistance, a higher wage deduction rate, further restricted funding for transportation, dental coverage, and child-care expenses, and the deletion of children's allowances from mothers' monthly allowances. The non-financial aspects were also drastic: monthly income statements were required, post-secondary students became ineligible, and mandatory employment assessments and other programs were implemented with passing reference to unmet child-care needs as employment barriers. Job search requirements were imposed when a mother's youngest child turned one.[1] Eligibility review officers (EROs) were given police-like powers to root out fraud,[2] with the Revenue Recovery Unit established to track down improperly paid assistance.

Like cutbacks to assistance in Mike Harris's Ontario six years earlier, the Nova Scotia changes signaled a post-Canada Assistance Plan retreat from social security for single mothers,[3] and a return to residualist assistance policy characteristic of nineteenth-century poor relief, which (like the ESIA) was designed to push recipients into the workforce.[4] These sorts of neoliberal reforms have heightened the moral regulation and social exclusion of single mothers. Hillyard-Little (1999) suggests that this neoliberal retreat from social provision has compromised single mothers' claim to assistance and diminished their moral authority and citizen status.

I argue that this historical impact of neoliberalism on single mothers should be understood in the context of a more detailed history. I illustrate this by examining a critical state tool in the criminalization of poverty and of single mothers in particular, what is called the man-in-the-house rule (hereafter the rule):

> A regulation of most Canadian provinces, declaring that a woman who lives with a man cannot receive welfare in her own right. The assumption being that she must be dependent on the man. (Drislane and Parkinson 2006)

The rule predates the ESIA, but is retained in it. I first consider the rule's current application. All the data here, unless otherwise specified, is drawn from my practice as a community worker at Dalhousie Legal Aid Service in Halifax (1985–2005), representing hundreds of women on assistance whose benefits were terminated because of the man-in-the-house rule, and conducting information and advocacy sessions for women on assistance across Nova Scotia. I review the history of the rule, from its implicit beginnings in Nova Scotia's Mothers' Allowance Act (1930). This evolution is highlighted through analysis of the history of policy on single mothers, Nova Scotia Legislative Assembly debates, single mothers assistance statistics, front-line practices, Department of Community Services annual reports, and newspaper reports. I discuss the impact of the Family Benefits Act, which was a watershed in Nova Scotia welfare policy because it separated assistance for those not expected to work in the market —persons with disabilities and single mothers — from assistance for those deemed employable, but which also (along with the ESIA replacing it) formally entrenched the rule. I explore briefly how race and class inequities helped frame the exclusion and criminalization enacted through the rule, giving expression to a White, middle-class bias against the common-law arrangements of people in poverty. The chapter concludes by highlighting how such forms of regulation exclude single mothers on assistance from social and political participation and how the individualistic character of Canada's liberal welfare state, beleaguered by neoliberal attacks, produces this kind of moral regulation through assistance programs.

Current Application of the Man-in-the-House Rule

People on assistance who are deemed able to work have long been subjects of suspicion and presumed fraudulent. In my experience, investigations in Nova Scotia occur most often when the provincial Department of Community Services (hereafter the Department) believes someone has not reported income or there is evidence of a man in the house. The term "penis police" signifies the bundle of punitive and coercive regulations, including the man-in-the-house rule, that discipline the sexual and social relations of single mothers. Although under the ESIA and Department regulations both heterosexual and homosexual relations are now illegal,[5] the vast majority of people affected by this rule continue to be women in relationships with men (Fay 1997). The ESIA regulates single mother recipients by requiring the cancellation of assistance in any of the following circumstances: a man and woman represent themselves to others as husband and wife, or the Department believes that they are spouses; a man and a woman separate for the purposes of one or both qualifying for benefits; a woman is allegedly living with a man without disclosing that to the Department; or a woman is unable or unwilling to name the father(s) of her child(ren) and sue for child support.[6] Each of these regulations includes its own sub-set of bureaucratic procedures that effectively criminalize single mothers on assistance (the ESIA *Policy Manual* is 160 pages long). For example, to satisfy Regulation 23(3) of the ESIA, stipulating that a single mother must obtain the information necessary to enforce child support, the Department can subject a woman to exhaustive questions concerning temporary encounters with men that lead to pregnancy. I argued such a case before the Social Assistance Appeal Board (hereafter SAAB) in the late 1980s after the woman contacted Legal Aid when her caseworker terminated her assistance because the woman did not know the name of the father of her child and thus could not seek child support.

In the same way, the man-in-the-house rule subjects women to bureaucratic intimidation and suspicion of fraud. In 1995, Jean Chrétien's finance minister, Paul Martin, began dismantling the Canada Assistance Plan (CAP), which regulated and equalized cost-sharing between the federal and provincial governments. Provinces used the opportunity to reform social assistance to reflect the neoliberal claim that welfare fraud was rampant. As Mosher and Hermer note in their work on Ontario assistance, this claim of widespread cheating has been used to support an array of mechanisms to detect and deter fraud. These include broad consents to the release of personal information, information sharing agreements with a host of state and non-state entities, expanded powers for eligibility review officers, consolidated verification procedures (requiring the ongoing production and verification of documentation), and provincial and local fraud control units (Mosher and Hermer 2005).

These measures entail severe invasions of privacy, loss of personal dignity, and material deprivation, including the terror of having benefits terminated with little warning. In a 2005 case I represented before the SAAB, the woman's building superintendent contacted the local assistance office to complain that her boyfriend was living with her. This led to an exhaustive investigation by an ERO, whose report included information about the woman's living arrangements from past and present neighbours and superintendents, searches of her bank accounts and credit rating, and police reports concerning complaints and counter-complaints of noise and harassment made by the woman and one of her neighbours. This woman and her five-year-old daughter had their assistance terminated on the basis of information from the superintendent and neighbours, yet the financial information reviewed in the ERO report disclosed no financial relationship between the woman and her boyfriend.

As this case demonstrates, assistance regulation invades the lives of recipients in a way seldom experienced by other citizens[7]; it attempts to govern women's intimate circumstances — where she lives and with whom, the paternity of her children, and the source and amount of every aspect of her income and material supports. The agents who enforce these regulations have broad powers to invade privacy and investigate personal matters. Caseworkers interview friends, family, neighbours, landlords, former spouses, and school administrators in a suspected man-in-the-house situation. Department officials have the power to review bank accounts and credit histories, deeds, loans, and mortgages for links with the man in question. Caseworkers may call creditors to find out if the man's name is on utility bills and credit cards, and obtain copies of any court orders pertaining to the individual receiving assistance or their children.[8] Department agents have the right to see recipients' tax returns for previous years.[9] The Department also has the authority to share personal client information with any other state agency, including Family and Children's Services, who have the power to remove children from the woman's care.[10]

The policy directives governing the application of the rule caution caseworkers to be respectful and professional when investigating.[11] The days may be gone when a man's truck parked in front a woman's apartment and reported by a neighbour is enough for assistance to be terminated, but some form of the rule has long been, and continues to be, the bane of single mothers on assistance. Sandy Falkiner, an Ontario single mother who took the Ontario government to court over the rule, confirms this reality: "The road from public humiliation to the court house where the 'spouse in the house rule' met its end was strewn with despair…. How I arrived there was a complicated tale — though no more so than the stories of thousands of other women who find themselves in similar situations not of their own making" (Falkiner-Budgell 2002).[12]

Caseworkers in Nova Scotia have such great latitude in terminating assistance with little or no warning because the regulation contains a "deeming" provision — cohabitation is *deemed* to occur where a man and a woman represent themselves to others as husband and wife, and any relevant evidence may be used to find that cohabitation exists.[13] Sandy Falkiner had her Ontario assistance terminated because she had the father of her children, who did not live with her, baby-sit while she went to work. Women in Nova Scotia are cut off for having a boyfriend who is not the father of their children stay over too many nights a week. At sessions I have conducted across Nova

Scotia since 1985, single mothers frequently ask, "How many nights can my boyfriend stay over?" I tell them there is no fixed number, although dozens of single mothers have reported to me in workshops and information sessions that their case workers quote an unwritten rule setting the maximum number of nights before termination at two to three per week. According to the Department's policies, overnight stays do not, on their own, constitute spousal relations.[14] Public pressure is a factor, however, in the push to punish single mothers on assistance for having a boyfriend. In provinces such as Ontario and Manitoba fraud hot lines have been established.[15] No Nova Scotia line exists, but "complaints can be received from the general public."[16]

The Woman and Abuse Welfare Research Project in Ontario found that living under this kind of surveillance causes single mothers to feel like they are suspected criminals (Mosher et al. 2004). The same problem exists in Nova Scotia. I have represented single mothers whose abusive and/or disgruntled ex-boyfriend or spouse causes assistance to be terminated by alleging that she has been living with him or another man (see also Mosher et al. 2004). Unhappy landlords, family members, and neighbours can do the same (see also Mosher et al. 2004). I have seen caseworkers mistake a cousin, brother, uncle, or son for a man in the house. I have seen the Nova Scotia Department terminate assistance if it finds co-signed loans, mortgages, or leases, and/or a woman's utility bills are in the man's name, even though this may simply reflect the poor financial circumstances of the woman in question. From the need to sign the intrusive Release of Information Authorization Form to interactions with caseworkers, women have told me how they fear the Department.

Adding to the difficulties caused by the inconsistency and breadth of evidence that can be used against single mothers, when the Department cuts off benefits, there is no right to assistance pending an appeal. The woman can appeal the decision and go to a hearing where she can produce evidence that she is not living with a man, but unlike in criminal law, there is no presumption of innocence. Social assistance law presumes single mothers to be ineligible (guilty) until they can prove otherwise. In my experience the consequences of termination are swift and brutal. Without warning the assistance does not arrive, or a letter comes days before bills are due notifying the woman that she has been cut off or that funds are withheld pending investigation. The mother and her children lose a significant portion of their monthly income — the funds to pay the rent and buy groceries. She and her children *may* obtain emergency assistance pending appeal in the form of food vouchers and rent payments if an eviction notice is served.[17]

If a woman accused of fraud does not appeal or loses her appeal, she faces another material consequence: the Department calculates an overpayment for the entire time in which she is alleged to have cohabited. The rule renders single mothers ineligible for all the assistance received during the time of the alleged cohabitation. Some single mothers owe thousands of dollars back to the Department. These overpayments are recovered at the rate of $45 per month when on assistance, or are subject to collection procedures if the woman leaves the program.[18] Collection means a letter from the Revenue Recovery Unit (RRU) stating the amount of the outstanding overpayment, and threatening seizure of Income Tax refunds if there is no response. The RRU requires that overpayments be paid back over a maximum of six years. In the fifty or so cases I have seen since 1998, the women are often in school, with student loans, or working for low wages, or both, and thus have little capacity to make these RRU payments. If women cannot make the payments, their income tax refunds will be sent, upon request of the province, to the RRU. A change made to the federal Income Tax Act s. 154 in 1998 granted provinces this ability.

The man-in-the-house regulation makes social exclusion palpable: "Those who are in receipt of welfare benefits live within the web of surveillance created by these various measures to detect and deter fraud" (Mosher and Hermer 2005: 6). The stories I have heard through my advocacy work exemplify what exclusion sounds, feels, and looks like in daily interaction. One woman on assistance who was involved in an anti-poverty group I worked with said, "People don't care. Everyone is out for themselves. Living on the system makes me afraid to make friends. I'm always looking over my shoulder. I have to hide any support I get" (Fay 1997: 3). At a 1996 Nova Scotia Status of Women meeting with Cape Breton mothers I attended shortly after new eligibility review measures were put into effect, women described caseworkers' tactics interviewing women about whether they had boyfriends. One woman said she was put into a room with no windows and a locked door and badgered by the caseworker to admit she was living with her boyfriend. Another woman said she cried and begged her worker not to cut her off, but he refused because he was convinced her ex-husband was living with her and her children. As Mosher and Hermer have documented in their work on Ontario, and as my decades of Nova Scotia advocacy confirm, women look over their shoulders when they go out in public with a man and monitor who they share information with about their assistance. They are careful about who knows they have a boyfriend and more careful about seeking support from social agencies, including transition houses for battered women, because abusive men threaten to allege that they are living with them (Mosher et al. 2004). This climate of regulation estranges single mothers from the sources of support — landlords and neighbours, their children's teachers, friends and family, and community organizations — that they need the most.

Mothers' Allowance: The Genesis of the Penis Police

Prior to Nova Scotia's adoption of the Mother's Allowance Act in 1930, single mothers were considered paupers if they had no private means of support. The term pauper was not removed from Nova Scotia law until 1954 (Fay 1997). Portraying people as shiftless and morally and physically defective made policy to discipline them politically acceptable. This punitive attitude toward people in poverty can be traced to the British new poor laws (1834), which helped usher in industrial capitalism by legally encoding the principle of "less eligibility." First enacted by the Poor Law Reform Commission of 1834, this "decreed that in Britain, the standard of living provided by the municipality for their dependent poor must be at a less favourable standard than that which the lowest paid labourer could earn for himself and his family" (Guest 1991: 36).

Nova Scotia social assistance programs from 1930–1966 did not stray far from the ideology of the new poor laws. People in poverty were suspect for needing assistance; the causes of poverty were sought in their personalities, behaviours, and attitudes. Several social forces converged just after World War I, however, to modify public attitudes about poverty, making possible the first Nova Scotia experiment in state income assistance. The charity and social reform work of women in the late nineteenth and early twentieth centuries helped to shift the moral ground toward defining widows with small children as worthy of some public assistance (Fingard 1993). Female reformers perceived that family instability, juvenile delinquency, and single mothers living in poverty posed a threat to national security and social order (Strong-Boag 1979). In Manitoba, Saskatchewan, Alberta, British Columbia, and Ontario, where mother's allowance programs were implemented between 1916 and 1920, these fears were coupled with the staggering human losses of the war and a long-standing Anglo-Protestant imperative to reproduce the Canadian (White British) race to convince the public that financial relief for widows was warranted (Dua 1999; Strong-Boag 1979). In Nova Scotia it took the devastating effect of the 1930s economic depression and a coalition of labour representatives and female reformers linked with the local Young Women's Christian Association to tip the political balance in favour of public assistance (Forbes 1993).

The Nova Scotia Mothers' Allowance Act first entitled poor widows to assistance in 1930; however, not every widow in need was deemed eligible. Annual Mothers' Allowance reports from the 1930s bristle with moral language, particularly concerning the distinction between virtuous mothers and women perceived to have fallen into moral delinquencies, or to have low mental and moral qualities, and thus believed unable to provide a proper home for their children (Nova Scotia Minister of Public Works and Mines 1932). The mother worthy of assistance had to be "in every respect a fit, proper and suitable person to have custody and care of her children."[19] Mothers who passed the test were glorified for labouring, struggling, and sacrificing their own health to provide for their children and train them to be useful citizens (Nova Scotia Minister of Public Works and Mines 1931). Ineligible women and their children eked out an existence, perhaps assisted by private charity. Alternatively, child welfare authorities could separate mother and child, or the desperate mother might arrange a private adoption or purchase arrangement for her offspring. Virtuous widows, who were viewed as deserving of public assistance to raise their children, were given a minimal level of monetary support, as well as moral supervision by volunteer home visitors, who encouraged proper housekeeping and childrearing, budgeting, and religious training (Nova Scotia Minister of Public Works and Mines 1931). As well, the Mothers' Allowance Commission called upon the public to assist by transmitting information about families receiving the allowance to the Commission (Nova Scotia Minister of Public Works and Mines 1937). Worthiness implied sexual propriety — in this case, not having sex, as the women were widowed and not remarried. That the public was encouraged to spy on these women signals the stigma and sexual regulation inherent in the Mothers' Allowance Act. Once on public assistance, these women had to start looking over their shoulders, just as single mothers do today.

Unmarried Mothers and the Hierarchy of Motherhood

The struggle over meaning has been crucial in shaping the welfare claims of single mothers and social assistance policy in North America. Initially, for example, the maternalist reformers who fought for assistance programs for mothers at the turn of the twentieth century attempted to increase public sympathy for poor mothers by casting their *children* as needy. The women themselves have always been morally suspect. Reformers did not deem unwed mothers to be worthy of pubic assistance because they did not want to encourage having children out of wedlock, especially among immigrant women (Strong-Boag 1979). This view of maternal poverty created a hierarchy of motherhood with "ladies" (deserving widows and blameless, deserted wives) on the top and "tramps" (single women with babies) on the bottom (Mink 1990: 117).

Nova Scotia assistance statutes since the Mothers' Allowance Act in 1930 have reproduced this hierarchy. Twenty-five years after suitable widows were entitled, wives of disabled husbands became Mothers' Allowance Act beneficiaries in 1954.[20] Wives of prisoners, deserted wives, and common-law widows became entitled in 1956. The creation of the Canada Assistance Plan in 1966 significantly expanded the federal contribution to provincial social services and broadened the definition of persons in need to include "loss of principal family provider."[21] Nova Scotia enacted a new assistance statute in

1966, which entitled unmarried mothers for the first time.[22] Divorced women appeared in the revised provincial Social Assistance Act of 1970, presumably because the liberalization of the federal Divorce Act in the same year meant more divorced women were raising children. In the 1970 Provincial Social Assistance Act, the hierarchy of motherhood was just about complete. Single mothers were listed in descending order of worthiness: widow, deserted wife, husband in sanatorium, husband imprisoned, divorced woman, unmarried mother.[23] Divorced women and unmarried mothers were presumably the least worthy because they were thought responsible for their own situation and therefore were morally suspect. Teen mothers were added to the bottom of this list through changes to the act in 1974.[24] The hierarchy of motherhood encoded in Nova Scotia's assistance legislation over forty-five years reproduces a construction of poor women that slimly rewards propriety and seriously punishes women suspected of having sex out of wedlock.

The major policy shift of including unmarried mothers did not occasion any public debate. The negligible number of women who became entitled — eighty-one in 1967 (see Table 7.1) — may have made their inclusion a non-issue. A Halifax newspaper article in June 1966 suggested that the public was more concerned about men misusing municipal assistance for drink and gambling than with the morality of unmarried mothers (Urquhart 1966: 39). The Nova Scotia Minister of Welfare hinted at another reason for the lack of concern in a second article explaining changes to the act.[25] The only moral issue he addressed was the long-standing concern about the suitability of unmarried mothers to raise children. He asserted that child welfare casework supervision would be extended to these women, signalling that only "fit and proper" mothers would receive assistance (Urquhart 1966: 39). This suggests that as long as single mothers were being supervised, public concern could be appeased.

Within the Department, however, the eligibility of unmarried mothers and divorced wives raised a pressing moral and economic issue: the obligation of fathers to support their children. In all previous assistance legislation, the father had to be deceased or impossible to locate for mother and children to be eligible (Fay 1997). Thus, there was no need to encode the father's obligation to support. Entitling unmarried mothers to assistance in 1966–67 meant that a spousal and child support enforcement provision became part of assistance regulation for the first time (Fay 1997). This new rule made it mandatory for women to prove that the fathers of their children could not or would not pay child support. The Halifax Family Court, which opened in January 1967, has seen hundreds of these women forced to go through the motions of applying to the court for child support from their child's father in order to be granted social assistance (Fay 1997).[26]

The Family Benefits Act

The man-in-the-house rule was explicitly encoded for the first time in a 1975 change to Nova Scotia assistance regulations: "dependent mothers" were formally barred from cohabiting with a man (Fay 1997).[27] This formal inscription of what earlier legislation implied by "suitable, fit and proper to raise children" transformed the man-in-the-house rule from a moral issue to an economic one as well (Fay 1997). It is ironic that this regulation came into effect during International Women's Year, given that it has been a source of such pain, humiliation, and fear for women on social assistance (Mosher et al. 2004).

In 1977 the Liberal provincial government of Gerald Regan introduced the Family Benefits Act and regulations, including the man-in-the-house rule. The act changed Nova Scotia welfare policy by separating those who were not expected to work but were eligible for assistance — persons with disabilities and single mothers — from those deemed employable (the allegedly unworthy poor). This attempt to legally make single mothers deserving did not translate into changed regulations concerning surveillance of their intimate relations with men. The hierarchy of mothers entitled to assistance was transferred to the regulations of the Family Benefits Act, with the rule designed to regulate deserted or divorced wives and unmarried mothers. The Assembly debates during the introduction of the Family Benefits Act articulated the exclusionary thinking that has condemned single mothers to lives of fear and deprivation. The majority of the speeches portrayed only the most worthy recipients: widows with children and wives of men who were disabled.[28] Politicians of the day also expressed uneasiness about the morality of people in poverty. Specifically, they feared that assisting unmarried mothers would undermine the legitimacy of marriage[29] and might encourage couples to collude by presenting themselves as separated in order for the women and children to collect benefits.[30] To allay fears, the obligation to seek and enforce child support and the man-in-the-house rule were included in the regulations.[31]

The dramatic increase in single mothers on assistance in Nova Scotia between 1967 and 1977 (Table 7.1) suggests another source of these fears. During the thirty years between the adoption of the Mothers' Allowance Act in 1930 and its repeal in 1960, the caseload doubled only once, with the addition of wives of disabled husbands in 1942 (Nova Scotia Minister of Public Works and Mines 1943). By 1958, the number of widows and wives of disabled men had decreased to about 1400 and remained constant for the next twenty years (Nova Scotia Department of Public Welfare 1958; Department of Social Services 1973–77). During the same time period (1958–1977), the deserted wives caseload increased by 640 percent. The rates for divorced women and unmarried mothers increased even more. Enumerated sepa-

Table 7.1 Single Mother Caseload 1958–1977

Category	1958	1967	1969	1971	1973	1975	1977
Married widows	1407	1435	1514	1483	1461	1389	1315
Divorced wives	n/a	43	144	198	314	618	855
Deserted wives*	304	495	802	1073	1184	1485	1949
Common-law widows**	42	51	n/a	n/a	n/a	n/a	n/a
Unmarried mothers	n/a	81	207	334	503	964†	1448
Single mother totals	n/a	2105	2667	3088	3462	4456	5567
Percentage of single mothers in social assistance case loads***	n/a	36%	34%	25%	24%	27%	31%

*   The number of deserted wives remained at between 300 and 350 between 1958 and 1966.

**   Common-law widows also remained constant at about fifty until that category was folded into the widow category in 1967.

*** The percentages drop until 1973 because the disability caseload was rising much faster than single mother numbers. By 1975 the disability cases levelled out, while single mother numbers were still rising.

†   In 1974 the restriction that unmarried mothers had to maintain a house of their own was removed. As a result the increase jumped 310 percent from about 150 new cases a year between 1967 and 1973 to an increase of 461 cases between 1973 and 1975. The increase between 1975 and 1977 was slightly larger, at 484.

Source: Fay 1997: 172.

rately in Nova Scotia Department of Social Services annual reports for the first time in 1967, between 1967 and 1977 the caseload for both categories increased nearly 2000 percent, even though single mothers in all categories made up only 31 percent of the total number of people on any assistance.

A Class Analysis of the Man-in-the-House Rule

The rule gives modern expression to middle-class bias against the common-law marital arrangements of people in poverty. It also produces the material deprivation and social exclusion of low-income families, and single mothers specifically. In order for women and children to qualify for benefits, couples are forced to separate. In order to continue benefits, women have to hide relationships with men. Economically marginal heterosexual couples with children in Nova Scotia were prohibited from receiving assistance under the Family Benefits Act. These couples received municipal social assistance, which provided lower monthly entitlements, thus further impoverishing and punishing couples.

The rule excluded and criminalized couples with children in poverty when it was introduced in 1975. According to Agatha Patterson, a welfare rights activist during the late 1960s and early 1970s in Halifax, and a paid staff member of Halifax Welfare Rights from 1972–1993, caseworkers treated married women on assistance with more respect than unmarried ones (Fay 1997). This differential treatment is an example of the hierarchy of mother-hood in operation and represents class bias against women in poverty who have children out of wedlock. According to Patterson, local people in her North End Halifax community made little differentiation between legally married and common-law couples: "People resented the distinction between single mothers and married mothers. 'Mrs.' was a sign of respect [and should have been used by social workers], what did it matter whether [the woman on assistance] was actually married or not? She had children to support" (Fay 1997: 172).[32]

A second class-based difference in the married/unmarried distinction concerned the support of children. The economic reality for north end fami-lies in Halifax sent men outside the area, sometimes outside the province, to find work. When that happened, women would apply for assistance as single mothers if they were not married, or as deserted wives if they were. The community attached no stigma to receiving welfare, because there were children to support. Rather, the stigma came from caseworkers, who labelled community men as "lazy bums who should have taken any job" (Fay 1997: 172). If men returned without work, which many did, assistance rules made it impossible for them to live with their families; they would have to stay somewhere else and visit their wives and children (Fay 1997). Halifax Welfare Rights fought to protect these family relationships in north end Halifax by ensuring that caseworkers did not visit women unannounced and terminate their assistance because there was a man in the house.

Conclusion

Four key conclusions about the social exclusion of single mothers on assistance and the criminalization of poverty emerge from this study of the man-in-the-house rule. First, this rule enshrines in law female dependency on men and the masculine power such dependency engenders, as well as middle-class bias against the common-law relations of people in poverty. Legal marriage is a sign of bourgeois respectability and inclusion. A single mother suspected of living with a man will be excluded from assistance, regardless of her financial need, because of her alleged marriage-like relationship with a man. The state's sexist presumption of financial dependence is "profoundly discriminatory toward women"[33] and enshrines female dependency on men and/or the state. Thus, the rule not only discourages but also criminalizes relations with men out of wedlock, childbearing among single women, and couples in poverty. A woman on benefits "is thus progressively isolated from male contact. Any real chance she may have of establishing long term relations with a man is cut off at the outset by the precipitate assumption of the authorities" (Eberts and Brodsky 1986: 5). The Woman and Abuse Welfare Research Project also documents how men, and abusive men in particular, use the rule to enhance their control over wives and girlfriends (Mosher et al. 2004). The fear having assistance cut off forces some single mothers to stay in abusive relationships: "They are being abused by a partner and... by a system that's supposed to be helping them" (Mosher et al. 2004: 9).

Second, the rule reproduces a sexist hierarchy of motherhood that bases a single mother's social inclusion on where she fits in the predominant definition of maternal suitability. This definition of suitability reflects a standard of sexual propriety in our society: no sex outside of marriage. The rule tests eligibility for assistance not on financial need but on sexual activity. Brenda Thompson, for example, suggests that it makes prostitutes of single mothers on assistance who are having sex with men, since the rules assume that if a woman is having sex with a man, he must be supporting her financially (Thompson 1991). The comparison is apt, as single mothers on assistance are "often stereotyped as 'promiscuous.'"[34]

Third, the rule, and its administration in particular, have reinforced the view of single mothers on assistance as "morally suspect persons, criminals in waiting, poised to abuse a public expenditure and trust" (Mosher and Hermer 2005: 5). In Ontario "a significant percentage of all fraud investigations seek to determine whether a recipient is living with a non-declared 'spouse'" (Mosher et al. 2004: 50). In Nova Scotia, the only ERO investigations that I have encountered are man-in-the-house cases. This application of the rule causes the most exclusion and criminalization of poor single mothers and it has not changed since widows were recognized as (more) worthy of receiving assistance. It catches single mothers in a web of suspicion and surveillance; they feel they are treated as suspected criminals (Mosher et al. 2004). Politicians, and often the general public, characterize welfare fraud as pervasive, but the actual number of convictions is miniscule.[35] As the Woman and Abuse Welfare Research Project notes, "The discourse of 'welfare fraud' now permeates both official and public mindsets to such an extent that social assistance programs have been quite firmly re-located by government as a problem of crime, social order and regulation" (Mosher et al. 2004: 50).

Finally, the loss of the Family Benefits Act, which Hillyard-Little characterizes as disenfranchising "poor single mothers on social assistance," is disheartening but not surprising (Hillyard-Little 1999). As this chapter argues, the social exclusion of single mothers on assistance has been a consistent part of assistance law since the Mothers' Allowance Act in 1930. Nor is the second-class status of people in poverty a new phenomenon. Neoliberal dominance of political discourse and policy making is, however, a potent ideological and practical force in Canada in the early twenty-first century. Morality and individual accountability have always framed the struggle for social security in liberal states such as Canada; moral debates reward success in the market place and punish those not able to compete (Esping-Anderson 1990). Our social assistance programs are designed to humiliate and stigmatize people. Neoliberals believe that "the poor" are suspect for needing assistance, just as their classical-liberal counterparts did in the days of the British new poor laws of 1856, when the principle of "less eligibility" was adopted. The ideological basis of Canada's welfare state has not progressed much beyond that construct. The CAP and the Family Benefits Act were as progressive as our liberal values allowed; single motherhood was recognized as a cause of need, but in order to justify this need, single mothers' dependency and sexuality had to be regulated. Single mothers have long been excluded and pushed to the socio-economic margins by public programs that stigmatize them for their need, fail to provide adequate aid, and scrutinize and criminalize their relations with men.

Notes

1. See Nova Scotia Department of Community Services, 2001, *ESIA On-line Policy Manual*, Policy 7.1.1: Nova Scotia Employability Assessment, <gov.ns.ca/coms/>.

2. Nova Scotia Department of Community Services, 2001, *ESIA On-line Policy Manual*, Policy 11.1.1: Eligibility Review, <gov.ns.ca/coms/>.

3. The Canada Assistance Plan (CAP) was enacted by the federal government in 1966 and repealed in 1997. It required provinces to lessen poverty through the provision of adequate social services to persons in need by category. One of these categories was "loss of principal family provider," which encouraged provinces to add single mothers to those considered in need. Under the CAP most provinces, including Nova Scotia, created a separate program for those not required to look for work actively — single mothers and persons with disabilities. With the repeal of the CAP, provinces no longer have to assist people for these reasons.

4. Steve Hicks provides a basic definition of residualist models of welfare (which researchers most often contrast with universalist or institutional models): the "residual concept of social welfare sees state assistance as temporary, minimal, requiring evidence of need, and available only after all other avenues of help have been exhausted.... The idea was that social welfare organizations should play a residual role to those of the private market and the family. The institutional concept of welfare see[s] social welfare programs as protecting individuals... from the social costs of operating an industrialized capitalist market.... Need is established based on the fact of need, without consideration of the cause of need. The shift to this view occurred in the post-war era." See <http://www.socialpolicy.ca/cush/m3/m3-t7.stm> and the discussion of "less eligibility" and

the poor laws below.

5. *ESIA Regulations*, 2001, Regulation 2(ac)(ii) <gov.ns.ca/coms/legislation.html>.

6. *ESIA Regulations*, 2001, Regulations 10, 15(3), 6 and 23 respectively <gov.ns.ca/coms/legislation.html>.

7. One noteworthy exception is the control the Indian Act exerts over First Nations Peoples. See P. Montour-Angus, 1999, *Journeying Forward: Dreaming First Nations' Independence*, Halifax: Fernwood Publishing.

8. *ESIA Regulations*, 2001, Regulation 5(1) and (2) <gov.ns.ca/coms/legislation.html>.

9. *ESIA On-line Policy*, December 2005, Chapter 9, Revenue Recovery, Section 6 Co-habitation <gov.ns.ca/coms>.

10. *ESIA On-line Policy*, December 2005, Chapter 5, Basic Needs; Section 1, Initial and On-going Eligibility: Conducting an Annual Review <gov.ns.ca/coms>.

11. *ESIA On-line Policy*, December 2005, Chapter 9 Revenue Recovery, Section 6, Co-habitation <gov.ns.ca/coms> July 7, 2006.

12. The Ontario regulation for the man-in-the-house rule has been re-written to conform to the decision in *Falkner*. Sole support parents are still not eligible if they have a social, familial, and financial arrangement consistent with cohabitation. Ontario Disability Support Program Act, 1997, General Regulations, Regulation 1(1) <e-laws.gov.on.ca/html/regs/english/elaws_regs_980222_e.htm>.

13. *ESIA Regulations*, 2001, Regulation 6 <gov.ns.ca/coms/legislation.html>.

14. *ESIA On-line Policy Manual*, 2001, policy 5.2.8 <gov.ns.ca/coms>.

15. The Ontario Ministry of Community and Social Services Welfare Fraud Hot Line is described on-line as "available for the public to report suspected cases of Ontario Works or Ontario Disability Support Program fraud. Callers will be asked for the name and address and, if possible, the phone number of the person who may be cheating. Callers can remain anonymous." Information Niagara <niagara.cioc.ca/details.asp?RSN=5355>.

16. *ESIA On-line Policy Manual*, 2001, policy 11.1.1: Eligibility Review <gov.ns.ca/coms>.

17. There used to be an emergency assistance provision under previous assistance policy. This provision no longer exists under ESIA, but in my experience emergency assistance is sometimes offered at Departmental discretion.

18. *ESIA On-line Policy Manual*, 2001, policy 8.1.2: Recovery from Income <gov.ns.ca/coms>.

19. Mothers' Allowance Act, N.S. 1930, c. 4, s. 5(1)(a).

20. Mothers' Allowance Act, RSNS 1954 c.182, section 4(1)(a).

21. Canada Assistance Plan, SC 1966-67 c.45, s. 1 section 2.

22. Social Assistance Act, SNS 1966, c.13, section 9.

23. Social Assistance Act SNS 1970 c. 16, sections 7(c)(i-vi).

24. An Act to Amend Chapter 16 of the Acts of 1970, the Social Assistance Act, S.N.S. 1974, c. 26.

25. The provincial department responsible for public assistance has changed over the years. Initially, the Mothers' Allowance Act 1930 was under the authority of the Department of Child Welfare (section 1[d]). The act directed the appointment of the Mothers' Allowance Commission (section 1[b]), whose job it

was to supervise home visitors and other administrative functions (section 4). By 1956, the Social Assistance Act SNS 1956, c.7 charged the Minister of Public Welfare with the administration of that act in section 2(c). The Department of Welfare was renamed the Department of Social Services in 1973.

26. The intent of the Social Assistance Regulation Assistance Act 1966 section 10(a)(v) remained in subsequent legislation: Social Assistance Act 1970, regulation 1(g) and the Family Benefits Act regulation 21.

27. Social Assistance Act, 1970, N.S. Reg. 44/75. This set of rules made significant changes to the "Schedule A" regulations. The language became more legalistic. Definitions of cohabit (s. 1[c]), cohabitation (s. 3[4][e]) and spouse (s. 1[l]) also appeared for the first time. The barring of "dependent mothers" from cohabitation was in s. 6(4).

28. Nova Scotia, *Debates,* (Hansard 1977[2]): 1284-1287, 1294, 1298.

29. Nova Scotia, *Debates,* (Hansard 1977[2]): 1284.

30. Nova Scotia, *Debates* (Hansard 1977[2]): 1288, 1298.

31. Nova Scotia, *Debates,* (Hansard 1977[2]): 1322.

32. The north end of Halifax is home to the largest indigenous African Canadian population east of Montreal. It is a racially integrated community with low-income White families and individuals as well as immigrants from many countries. Gentrification has also brought the White middle-class in the last decade. For this history see B. Melles, 2003, "The Relationship Between Policy, Planning and Neighbourhood Change: The Case of the Gottingen Street Neighbourhood, 1950–2000," MA thesis, Dalhousie University; J. Stern, 1993, "Gentrification and Community in the Northend of Halifax: Re-examining the Issues." MA thesis, Technical University of Nova Scotia.

33. Margaret Hillard-Little, affidavit prepared for *Falkiner et al. v. Ontario Minister of Community Services,* (copy in collection of author) paragraph 15.

35. Hillyard-Little, affidavit, paragraph 49.

36. By way of illustration, 0.1%, or 38 of the 38,000 investigations in Ontario in 2001–02, Mosher and Hermer 2005: 6.

Chapter 8

Apprehensive Wives and Intimidated Mothers

Women, Fear of Crime, and the Criminalization of Poverty in Toronto

Amanda Glasbeek

> No one else has the right to intimidate someone else into giving them money…. It's quite intimidating to persons who don't happen to be strong, healthy males.[1]

So said Attorney-General Jim Flaherty, part of the Ontario Conservative Party that won a second-term majority government in 1999 and promised on the campaign trail to "give police the power to crack down on squeegee kids."[2] The resultant Ontario Safe Streets Act (OSSA) effectively criminalized poverty by making "aggressive" panhandling illegal, including squeegeeing and asking for money from a "captive audience."[3] Insightful research already exists on OSSA, including analyses of the discursive devices used to demonize a population of young people whose poverty, defiance, and unruly presence in the public streets made them the bane of private enterprise and a bourgeois moral order (Gordon 2007, 2004; Parnaby 2003; Gingrich 2002; Hermer and Mosher 2002). Despite this, surprisingly little attention has been paid to the ways that women's concerns for safety, and concerns for women's safety, have been mobilized as part of the anti-squeegee campaigns. This chapter explores the intersections between gender, safety, and crime control as these were played out in public debates about squeegee kids in Toronto between 1998 and 2000. Feminist scholars have long been interested in the relationship between gender and perceptions of urban safety, and especially in the effect that women's fear of urban public spaces have on their quality of life. Generally, such scholars argue that women's fear of criminal victimization acts as a form of social control, so that, in order to avoid troublesome encounters, women limit their mobility to certain areas of the city, activities, and times of day (Wekerle and Whitzman 1995; Pain 2001, 1991). These self-imposed limits restrict women's exercise of their broader citizenship rights; as Amy

Caiazza has argued, "for women as a group, a sense of perceived safety is strongly related to involvement in the community, while a lack of perceived safety is linked to disengagement" (Caiazza 2005: 1609). The significance of women's fear of crime for their participation in public processes has also been taken up in criminology, where greater attention is being paid to gender in crime prevention and risk discourses (Shaw and Andrew 2005; Chan and Rigakos 2002; Stanko 1998, 1997). Specifically, feminist criminologists have suggested that crime control and risk management policies and analyses have been overwhelmingly masculinist in orientation, and that women tend to appear as "voiceless objects in the negotiation of our own safety" (Stanko 1998). Margaret Shaw and Caroline Andrew are representative of feminist critics when they conclude that women need to play a greater role in decisions about crime prevention, especially at the local level (Shaw and Andrew 2005). Because women tend to feel more insecure in urban environments than men, and because women are more comfortable talking about these insecurities, these scholars argue that "giving women the lead role [in crime prevention] makes sense in terms of effective community development" (Shaw and Andrew 2005 :305).

But what happens when women's voices about urban safety contribute to the criminalization of poverty? How do women's anxieties about violence in the public sphere — a concern that feminists have struggled to get lawmakers to deal with — become a conduit for a neoliberal agenda that includes the coercive regulation of the poor? In what ways do discourses about gendered fears of public dangers work alongside the classed nature of urban neoliberalism? An analysis of the debates that lead to the passage of the OSSA suggests that the struggle for safety is more complicated than it may at first appear. Drawing on articles and letters to the editor from Toronto newspapers and legislative debates prior to passage of the Safe Streets Act, this chapter shows how women's concerns for urban safety were often appropriated and positioned as oppositional to, and more important than, the needs of poor people eking out a living in the streets.

The chapter is divided into four sections. First, I provide a brief overview of the Ontario Safe Streets Act. Second, I analyze men's concerns for women's safety to show how a particular gender order built on passive femininity and protective masculinity was produced through appropriations of women's concerns for safety. I next explore the more complex ways that women articulated their own safety concerns in the context of squeegeeing. I conclude by arguing that feminists must not allow neoliberal governments to implicate women's desire for safety in their law-and-order responses to visible poverty in urban spaces.

The Ontario Safe Streets Act, 2000

Jim Flaherty, the Ontario Conservative government's attorney general, introduced Bill 8 into the Legislative Assembly on November 2, 1999 claiming that it fulfilled his party's "commitment to take action about behaviour that jeopardizes the safe use of the streets."[4] The bill received third reading by December 7, 1999, and on January 31, 2000, the Ontario Safe Streets Act came into effect. Most significantly for the purposes of this chapter, the act created new provincial offences for what it named "aggressive solicitation," which included "obstructing the path of the person solicited" (s. 2(3)(2)), "continuing to solicit a person in a persistent manner" (s. 2(3)(6)), and the solicitation of a "captive audience," which included persons at an automated teller machine, a pay telephone or public toilet, a taxi or public transit stop, and "while on a roadway… a person who is in or on a stopped, standing or parked vehicle" (s. 3[2]). Although technically a province-wide regulation, the OSSA in fact targeted street people in urban centres, mainly in Toronto. In particular, the Ontario Safe Streets Act was largely aimed at eliminating squeegee kids, who earned money by washing windshields while cars were stopped at downtown intersections.

By the act's passage in December 1999, Torontonians had been debating the issue of squeegee kids for almost four years. The anti-squeegee discourses, however, reached a peak in the summers of 1998 and 1999 as a new hostility toward street youth emerged. This hostility likened squeegee kids to "pests" and "thugs" in what Patrick Parnaby has called a "disaster rhetoric" (Parnaby 2003). Toronto mayor Mel Lastman captured this sentiment when he proclaimed: "This is a major problem in the city…. This is a menace and there's disaster waiting to happen on our streets. There's people being hurt, there's people who could be hurt, there's people who could be killed and you don't think that's a disaster?"[5] The Safe Streets Act was offered as a remedy to this pending "disaster."

A range of critical analyses of the Ontario Safe Streets Act have deconstructed the class-based meaning of safety that took shape through the debates leading up to, and the implementation of, the act (Gordon 2007, 2004; Parnaby 2003; Gingrich 2002; Hermer and Mosher 2002). Simply put, the people presumed to be in need of protection were middle-class and elite citizens while the potential danger to their urban mobility was embodied in the visible poor population of Toronto. This concept of safety contained a perverse irony. Although most squeegee kids were able to ply their trade without incident, to the extent that danger and violence were features of squeegeeing, the victim was most likely to be a squeegeer. In one particularly egregious instance, a twenty-six-year-old squeegeer was beaten and threatened with a gun by an irate driver at Yonge and Richmond Streets.[6] Examples of violent encounters such as this, however, seemed to do little to transform anti-squeegeers' opinions of the criminality of street youth. The insistence on perceiving squeegeeing as a public danger was most evident in the case of a squeegee kid who, too slow to leave an intersection at the light change, was run over by a truck and hospitalized with broken legs and fractures in his back.[7] Despite his injuries, he was criminally charged with "obstructing traffic"! More generally, as Stephen Gaetz has demonstrated, "the experience of inadequate access to shelter and housing, limited employment opportunities, weak social capital, and restricted access to public space" meant that street youth were disproportionately more likely to be crime victims than other Torontonians (Gaetz 2004: 424). If anyone was in need of legislative protection to ensure their safety, it was socially excluded youth. Their safety, however, was not what the Ontario Safe Streets Act was designed to provide.

To the contrary, the proponents of the OSSA, both within the Conservative government and in the general population, waged a form of class warfare of which the Safe Streets Act was a crucial part.[8] The act is consistent with broader neoliberal strategies of undermining welfare provisions and social citizenship rights, privileging a "market morality" (Gingrich 2002: 163) and the "unleashing of zero tolerance initiatives and insidious discourses aiming to reimage cities within a vernacular of renaissance" (Coleman 2004: 23). The OSSA effected what Sue Ruddick terms a "metamorphosis of civic life" (Ruddick 2002: 55) by transforming public space, once celebrated as a site for democratic engagements, into a privatized, class-based, commodified urban zone (Kipfer and Keil 2002: 227–64; Keil 2002: 578–601). In this neoliberal vision of urban life, street people, panhandlers, and squeegeers become a public nuisance and a barrier to commerce rather than citizens with a claim on public space equal to that of the more affluent.

Some scholars argue convincingly that the Ontario Safe Streets Act is, for all intents and purposes, a return to the old status offence of vagrancy. As Todd Gordon asserts, the provisions of the OSSA that make it an offence to beg within certain spaces, obstruct passers-by, and engage in "aggressive solicitation" all echo the original provisions of the 1892 Criminal Code vagrancy section (Gordon 2004). For this reason, legal scholars have suggested that the act should be declared unconstitutional because it oversteps the jurisdiction of the provincial government, which cannot enact criminal statutes (Esmonde 2002; Schneiderman 2002) To this end, thirteen defendants charged under the OSSA challenged the constitutionality of the act, but this challenge was defeated and the act upheld (Esmonde 2002).

Although it survived this constitutional challenge, the OSSA reproduces the spirit of the old vagrancy statutes, which were similarly designed to punish the able-bodied poor for not living within the established market economy (Gordon 2007). Clearly, the OSSA is a class-based piece of legislation enacted to protect middle-class and elite consumers from contact with the (apparently) unseemly bodies of the poverty-stricken, whose very poverty is a result of the neoliberal strategies pursued by the act's proponents in the first place.[9] The following analysis builds upon these insights about neoliberalism, class, the criminalization of poverty, and commodified urban space. What remains to be discussed is the ways in which gender discourses were also part of the construction of safety in this context. Although I rely heavily on print media sources in the discussion that follows, this is not a content analysis of media coverage about squeegee kids in general. Patrick Parnaby has conducted such an analysis and, as he demonstrates, gender was not the only, or even a central line of argument in the construction of the debates about regulating Toronto's squeegee population (Parnaby 2003). Thus, this analysis is not as concerned with the frequency with which gender entered into the debates as it is with how, and with what significance, gender played a role in the criminalization of poverty through the Ontario Safe Streets Act, and what that can tell us further about the broader project of neoliberal constructions of citizenship, safety, and urban space.

Protective Men and Victimized Women: Men's Concerns for Female Safety

Gender played a useful role in the anti-squeegee discourses. The intimidation associated with being approached by young people and/or panhandlers in the streets was transformed into a politically salient form of victimization largely through gender. As Luann Gingrich points out, "since it was not unlawful to solicit before this act, there must be something differentiating the 'law-abiding citizen' from the 'offender'" (Gingrich 2002: 158). To constitute soliciting as unlawful, the Ontario Safe Streets Act focused not only on acts that were deemed to be intrinsically harmful, such as asking for money from a "captive audience," but also on acts that were considered aggressive. Section 2(1) of the Act defined "aggressive" solicitation as asking passers-by for money in "a manner that is likely to cause a reasonable person to be concerned for his or her safety or security." In other words, the manner of solicitation was an offence depending on its reception by the person being solicited. To clearly work out this process of differentiation between law abiding and unlawful behaviour, it was necessary for the Conservative government to create a sense that the (non-poor) citizenry was victimized through intimidation.

As a result, throughout these debates, there was an often-repeated refrain, especially from Conservative Members of Provincial Parliament (MPP), that women were especially prone to intimidation and, thus, victimization. One MPP asked, "Do I feel apprehensive when I'm approached by a squeegee person or an aggressive panhandler? I may not. But I can assure you my daughter does; I can assure you my mother does; I can assure you your wives do."[10]

In these invocations, women were sometimes represented as a group, but more often as familially defined sub-groups, such as elderly women, young mothers with children, and wives and daughters. For example, MPP Frank Mazzilli captured the Conservative gender politics when he announced: "These people [panhandlers] target the most defenceless members of our community: the elderly, mothers with young children.... This is wrong."[11] MPP Bart Maves drew a vivid picture of female intimidation for his colleagues in the legislature:

> Picture an 18-year old here in Toronto going out to meet their friends on a school night or on a Friday night. They stop at an automatic teller by themselves... and they turn around and there are three or four — or two or three — I don't care how many — people who just corner them and start to solicit them.... She can't say, "I don't have any money." They know she does. But you folks on that side of the aisle [the Opposition] think it's OK that those people corner her and solicit her for money? I don't think it's OK.[12]

In this portrait of vicitimization, MPP Maves slips easily from a generic eighteen-year-old at a bank machine to a frightened girl threatened by menacing strangers. This gendered representation of urban danger likely resonated with his colleagues and supporters because it fit within a broader pattern identified by Kristen Day, whose survey of men's understanding of women's fears shows that men perceive such fearfulness "in terms of women's weakness and small stature, or women's physical inferiority to men" (Day 2001:109–27). Such explanations, however, mask the degree to which fear and vulnerability are socially constructed, especially through gendered tropes of innocence imperiled, as in MPP Maves' imagined scenario. Conservative MPP Wayne Wettlaufer offered his reasons for supporting the OSSA by drawing on similar tropes: "[The police] are very concerned about squeegeeing and the problems it poses for the people, the older people particularly, the senior citizens, women, mothers with children in their cars. They're very concerned about that."[13] By invoking the police, Wettlaufer further implied that the "problems" experienced by vulnerable populations required a law-and-order solution.

To round out this picture of a cityscape in which women were continuously terrorized by intimidating strangers, squeegeers were routinely portrayed as male. This was so despite the fact that it has been estimated that roughly one-third of squeegee kids were young women (O'Grady and Green 2003). Newspaper columns and letters to the editor consistently attempted to ingrain the idea of intimidating squeegee kids by drawing upon gender-based "recipe knowledge of established deviant types" (O'Reilly and Fleming 2001). A *Toronto Sun* columnist's anecdotal introduction to the "problem" of squeegeeing characterizes this tendency:

> Not long ago, I saw a woman pull up to a red light and this strange-looking, filthy, smelly creature approached her car. I watched as she, anticipating his request, rolled up her window. But it was too late. After washing her windshield he was right there with his hand out.... The next thing I saw was this woman, clearly frightened, reaching for her purse and handing over the cash.[14]

The maleness of squeegee kids, in this example, was indistinguishable from the portrayal of squeegeeing as a quasi-criminal activity. Correspondingly, femaleness here stands in for victimization, a marker for the social harm caused by squeegeeing.

In the context of debate over the Ontario Safe Streets Act, male politicians and journalists were not the only ones to view women as passive victims in need of rescue. Other men, in letters to the editor, expressed similar ideas about female vulnerability and the necessity of offering masculine protection. Writing to the *Toronto Star*, one man angrily reported: "My wife has endured a torrent of abuse from... squeegees at these busy intersections for waving them off or for not providing a large enough tip."[15] Similarly, the *Star*'s Doug Bartholomew insisted, "Squeegee people are not harmless. Recently, when I asked a squeegee man not to touch my car, he attempted to assault me, and I had to roll up the windows and lock the door to keep him at bay. He stood outside the window spewing obscenities until the light changed. Most women I know are intimidated by squeegee people."[16] Clearly finding their experiences with squeegeers unsettling, these men preferred to express concern for women rather than for themselves.

As Patrick Parnaby has pointed out, "By conflating both fear and vulnerability with femininity, eliminating squeegee-kids became not just a matter of crime control, but a matter of chivalrous obligation."[17] Chivalry decrees that a good man is a vigilant man who keeps watch over the safety of his family, and whose very goodness is affirmed by the presence of some predatory danger "lurking outside the warm familial walls" (Young 2003: 4). Thus, good masculinity is defined as "that associated with the position of the male head of household as a protector of the family and, by extension, with masculine leaders and risk takers as protectors of a population" (Young 2003: 3). The image of a protective male figure defending his family against aggressive intruders emerged as a dominant theme in men's claims about gendered safety and the necessity of the Safe Streets Act, rhetoric that allowed men to assert their authority over urban space. If public space was masculine terrain, then women, as the ones being protected, were removed from active citizenship and instead became the objects of it. MPP Gerry Martiniuk drove this point home as he completed his speech: "The Safe Streets Act is saying to everyone: We want our streets back. We are entitled to have our streets back, where our wives and mothers and children can walk the streets without fear, without apprehension and in safety."[18] Nor was he the only MPP to distinguish between women and "the public." MPP Gill reinforced this separation: "[The general public has] shared their concerns about the difficulty that some of our mothers, our sisters, our friends, our spouses are facing."[19] Toronto's ever-blunt Mayor Mel Lastman was also of this view: "It [squeegeeing] has got to stop. Women are petrified. Women are scared. Adults are scared."[20] Separated from the public, from government, and even from adulthood, women became both objects of governance and a reason for governing. The governing public, meanwhile, was presented as staunchly male.

From this self-appointed position, men, and especially those in the Conservative Party, congratulated themselves on their good deeds in offering protection to their subordinates. Brendan Crawley, spokesperson for the Attorney General's office, explained to the press that "it's a priority of the government and the ministry to allow Ontarians, particularly women, to feel safe and not be harassed on the city streets."[21] Similarly, MPP Martiniuk answered his own rhetorical question with paternalistic satisfaction: "Why do we need this bill? Bill 8, the Safe Streets Act, 1999, is only one element of our government's broad effort to make our towns and cities safer places to live and raise a family."[22] He was echoed in these sentiments by MPP Galt at the bill's third reading, who took the opportunity to remind the legislature of women's vulnerability: "Often these [women] are the people who are targeted by our panhandlers because they believe they are indeed a soft touch and easily frightened away. This really reinforces the need for this particular bill."[23]

These political constructions of men as chivalrous protectors and of women as blameless victims intimidated by menacingly rootless male squeegeers clearly drew upon, dramatized, and reinforced women's fears of male violence in public spaces. Even more, in the discourses about the Ontario Safe Streets Act, we can see an appropriation of not just women's, but feminist concerns about male harassment, intimidation, and violence. In these examples, the basic feminist observation that women's fear of male violence acts as a form of social control because it limits women's civic engagements and mobility in public spaces is being used to bolster the logic of law and order. This form of appropriation was most apparent in a speech made on December 7, 1999, by the Conservative Member for Northumberland, Mr. Galt:

> It's time we gave back to people the right to go out at night and feel comfortable. That happens in one of my communities, Cobourg,

where they stage "Take Back the Night." It's a candlelight march that occurs every year.... I think it's very appropriate that that should happen, particularly as we look at the recent anniversary of the Montreal massacre.... Women should have the comfort of going out at night and feeling safe on the streets and not have the kind of threat that seems to be out there at this point in time. Men take that for granted at any time. You know, I really wonder why the opposition isn't jumping up and down and screaming about this gender imbalance.[24]

The identification of women's fear of victimization operates here not as a feminist critique of male dominance but as a means by which to cement the politically necessary link between subjective experiences of panhandling and the kind of street activity that was to become punishable under the Ontario Safe Streets Act. A masculinist understanding of women's urban safety became a standard by which the activities of the poor were to be deemed criminal.

"Speaking on a Personal Level": Women's Concerns for Women's Safety

Although men comprised a clear majority of those making public claims about women's vulnerability — in large part, no doubt, because MPPs and media spokespeople tend to be men — women invoked similar themes when they voiced support for anti-squeegee legislation (Lee 2000). Conservative MPP Julia Munroe expressed her sympathies, as a woman, with women who felt intimidated by street youth and squeegee kids: "Mothers with children and seniors are particularly vulnerable to harassment from aggressive pan-handlers.... Speaking on a personal level, I can tell you, as a woman driving from time to time alone, I certainly recognize the fear that people have in having someone approach their car, at night particularly."[25] In her submission to the Standing Committee on Justice and Social Policy's review of Bill 8, Margaret Knowles, of the Yonge-Bloor-Bay Business Association, was clear about who she thought was being victimized:

> There are women who are working in these businesses [at Bloor and Avenue] who, when leaving a night shift, are afraid to leave. They are not afraid of homeless people or poor people; they're afraid of people who threaten and intimidate. I'm sorry, but I've stood and watched squeegeers at Yonge and Bloor, and who do they pick on? Mainly they pick on women, who never say no because they are intimidated and they give them money.[26]

Knowles effectively clarified the process of "differentiation" necessary to distinguish law-breakers from law-abiders. As she was careful to point out, it was not poverty or homelessness per se that troubled women workers; more specifically, they were made uncomfortable by homeless persons they found threatening and intimidating. Women like Margaret Knowles positioned themselves as the litmus test in making this differentiation.

In addition to framing women's anxieties as central to the determination of "aggressive" solicitation, Knowles' portrayal of women as people "who never say no" to requests for money from street youth reveals something about the role that gender plays in neoliberalism more generally. In particular, Knowles' view highlights the significance of gendered understandings of compassion, and of the role of gendered compassion, within broader restructuring programs. As feminist political economists point out, the retrenchment of the welfare state has led to a greater reliance on privatized caring labour as families, rather than the state, become "responsible for caring for each other and their other immediate relatives" (Luxton 1997). Because women are disproportionately responsible for such labour, in effect the withdrawal of the state from social reproduction depends upon women's unpaid caring work as a key resource through which needs will or will not be met (Bezanson 2006; Cameron 2006).

At the same time that the dismantling of the welfare state elevates women's "labours of love" (Luxton 1997) to the status of social policy, women's presumed compassion, at least in the instance of squeegeers, was presented as a problematic quality from which they were to be protected. In this way, the gendered dimensions of the anti-squeegee debates illuminate neoliberal assumptions about the legitimate uses of women's ostensibly greater compassion or, at least, greater reluctance to turn their backs on those asking for help. In the name of women's protection, the Safe Streets Act policed women's caring by limiting it to families and to the private rather than the public sphere.

In light of such tensions, it is not surprising to find that many women had a more complex, and sometimes ambiguous, relationship to urban anxieties such as those surrounding squeegeeing. An examination of interviews with women recounted in daily newspapers, and letters to the editors of those papers, demonstrates that there were Toronto women who were afraid of squeegeers. Most commonly, they expressed themselves in terms that identified their concerns about the potential violence of unwanted encounters with strange young men. In a letter to the editor, one woman linked her complaint about squeegee kids directly to the ways that they undermined her sense of urban safety: "As a woman driving alone in a car in Toronto, I not only feel uncomfortable, intimidated and harassed by squeegee kids, they terrify me."[27] Sandy Scagnol, a Queen Street West storeowner, drew on a similar theme in her disapproval of squeegee activity: "There is accosting going on out there…. I mean, say you're a woman in a car, and you have someone with 52 nails stuck in their face coming at you waving a stick… what do you expect?"[28] In another letter, the writer offered her own experience as proof of the violation contained in the act of squeegeeing: "I'm constantly harassed by a squeegee person. The other day, while in the centre lane, stopping for a light at the corner of Bloor and Yonge, one of them appeared from nowhere and startled me by thumping his squeegee down on my windshield…. When I asked him to stop, he became abusive."[29] The imagery of young men with piercings and nails appearing from out of nowhere to thump on windshields, waving sticks and yelling obscenities, speaks volumes about women's fear of public violence. Such actions are treated as prima facie intimidating for women because women are expected to be, and often are, frightened of strange young men in public.

These kinds of claims by women seem to reinforce Elizabeth Stanko's observation that women speak of their general apprehensions about violence in terms of violence committed in public by strangers because "public 'crime' talk about safety for women… privileges the danger of the public" (1997: 490). Such crime frames provide women opposed to squeegeeing with a ready narrative through which to articulate their opposition. Such expressions of fear also seem to betray a set of class anxieties lurking just below the surface, as taken up below.

At the same time, however, women spoke about their urban anxieties in ways that transcended simple dichotomies between public and private fears. In part, this duality was endemic to squeegeeing itself: "squeegee kids' use of public space involved a simultaneous violation of what is generally assumed to be *private* space," namely the car (Parnaby 2003: 301, emphasis in original). Moreover, as feminist geographer Carol Sanger (2001) reminds us, the car has meant different things for woman and men. In particular, while the car has given women more autonomy and mobility, it has also been adapted as a tool of household technology, thereby extending women's sphere of domesticity. In this sense, the idea of women being approached by squeegeers becomes akin to a domestic invasion. *Toronto Sun* columnist Heather Bird captured this theme in her argument against squeegee kids:

> My street was a quiet one with a safe feel…. Until recently late night strolls were possible without undue stress. That has changed recently due to too many sightings of midnight intruders…. The squeegee kids, tolerable when they were contained to small numbers and certain intersections in the downtown core, are menacing as large groups of squeegee men are invading residential neighbourhoods.[30]

In this example, the line between a fear of squeegeers approaching cars in public space and a sense of violated security within the privacy of domestic space is blurred.

Also blurred in such examples is the line between gender and class anxieties. In shifting squeegeers from daytime to night, from the downtown core to residential streets, and from adolescence to threatening masculine adulthood, the *Sun* columnist seems as alarmed about the potential trespasses against her property and a sense of middle-class propriety as she does about her physical safety as a woman. Some women made little effort to disguise their class anxieties. For example, Carolyn Cleland, described by *Toronto Sun* columnist Sue-Ann Levy as a "classy, blue-eyed blonde with upswept hair," complained to a City Council meeting that she had been blocked by a panhandler on her way out to a restaurant for dinner: "Why are we subjected to this? I feel like people are extorting me."[31] Clearly, Cleland's privileged social status reinforced her assumption that she had a right to move about and spend her disposable wealth as she pleased without being confronted by the poverty-stricken (whom, she implied, had no such mobility rights). This sense of entitlement to city spaces and the prioritization of urban streets as sites of private leisure rather than economic survival was echoed by another woman at the Council meeting, who declared: "I'm entitled as a citizen to walk down the street without someone pushing in my face," adding that being confronted by beggars was "really very frightening."[32] Both women's insistence that they had the right not to be "subjected" to the demands of the poor are indicative of the ways in which "privileged identities themselves become markers of difference that contribute to a feeling of potentially being 'targeted' (Kern 2005).

Perhaps it is not surprising, then, that despite neither woman being recorded as having experienced a gender-specific fear of panhandling, Councillor Denzil Minnan-Wong completed the process of rendering their markers of social privilege invisible by responding that he "did not like *women* feeling uncomfortable" (*Toronto Sun*, July 16, 1998: 16). The entire exchange in City Council, and its coverage in the news, thus served to rewrite class anxieties as gendered discomfort. Images of "women clutching their purses in fear of the 'beasts in the gutter'" displaced class politics with gender rhetoric, such that the very presence of poor people in the Toronto streets appeared to be less a problem of the poor than it was constitutive of middle-class female victimization.[33]

Such constructed binaries between class and gender interests did not mesh with the experiences of all Torontonians. There were women who publicly resisted these presentations of themselves as either uniformly defenceless or politically arrayed against street youth and panhandlers. In a letter to the *Globe and Mail*, Helen Hansen insisted: "As frequent road users, my family and I have never felt a physical threat from any squeegee person or beggar."[34] Other women resisted the presumed vulnerability of older women. In her letter to the *Star*, Eleanor O'Connor asserted: "As a 58-year-old woman, I have never felt threatened or intimidated by those who beg outside my local bank… nor outside the liquor store, and I am often amazed at their patience and politeness."[35] When the *Toronto Star* ran a telephone survey asking, "Should the provincial government change the law to make it easier to get squeegee kids off our streets?" one unidentified woman's response hit a similarly gender- and age-specific note: "I'm a 67 year old woman who drives alone and I never feel threatened by these young people."[36]

These women spoke out precisely because they refused to allow what they saw as a targeted campaign against the poor to be conducted on their behalf. In so doing, they also displayed what might be called, in this context, a resistant compassion, through which they reclaimed a broader, non-familial, public community whose needs were to be taken into account. For some women, this resistant compassion stemmed from recognition of the class disparities between those in need of aid and those in a position to provide it. For example, one letter writer pointed out the clear material differences between those in cars and those eking out a living on the street: "As a young woman who drives in this city, I have never felt threatened or scared by a squeegee kid. How much of a threat can they be? You're in a powerful, lockable, thousand-pound machine; they're wielding a wet stick with rubber on the end."[37] This view of the dynamics of squeegeeing simultaneously subverted the masculinist assumption that women's fear is rooted in physical weakness and pointed out the significance of access to material resources as key to a sense of security.

The feminist *Toronto Star* columnist Michele Landsberg made a political point of women's resistance to the OSSA, suggesting that all the apparent concern for women was a "whitewash… you fellas might be shaking in your boots, but I've never yet met or heard from a woman who was 'petrified' of squeegees. In fact, reading the letters to the editors and listening to the phone-in shows, I can confidently say that it's mostly men who are bitterly squeegee-phobic."[38] Landsberg may have overstated the case. Even if many women were neither as passive nor as intimidated by squeegeers as some men (and some women) supposed they were, clearly there were women for whom squeegee kids were a source of anxiety. This anxiety did not need to manifest as hostility to be a palpable force in the squeegee debates. As one woman explained: "I'm a middle aged woman who has to drive downtown alone tonight and I'm filled with angst at the thought of some scruff approaching my car, even if he is a poor guy trying to earn a buck."[39] That this woman, and others, felt forced to choose between a sense of urban security as a woman and the well-being of poor people on the streets of the city illustrates the central dilemma created by the mobilization of gendered discourses about urban safety.

Conclusion: Feminism, Safety, and the Criminalization of Poverty

> Chivalry is a poor substitute for justice.... It is like the paper lace around the bonbon box — we could get along without it. (McClung 1972: 42)

The safety promised by the Safe Streets Act involved a clear act of division intended to render some citizens and uses of public space safe from other citizens and from what was constituted as illegitimate use of that space. Most research to date on the act demonstrates the ways in which safety was a tool used to discipline the poor and to narrow participation and citizenship rights in the public domain to law-abiding, tax-paying, middle-class consumers. As illustrated here, there is reason to consider the complex gender meanings of safety as well, if we are to understand and resist the coercive regulation of the poor.

Feminist scholars argue that women's sense of urban safety is "a reflection of gendered power structures" (Koskela 1997: 303). The more equal a society, the less likely women are to feel unsafe or intimidated by fears of violence. It is all the more notable then that the appropriation of feminist demands for safety evident here occurred in a context in which women are being made less secure. At the same time that Conservative voices used women's insecurity as a basis for criminalizing the poor, they also engaged in a systematic attack on welfare, unions, the minimum wage, affordable childcare, employment and pay equity, legal aid, and services for abused women and children (Kitchen 1997; Little 2003). Policies such as these make a mockery of Conservative claims that they wanted to create a "safe" environment for the province's women. As the Ontario Association of Interval and Transition Houses observed: "All of the cuts together create an environment that, in effect, revictimizes abused women and reinforces, or rewards, male violence" (Ontario Association of Interval and Transition Houses 1998: 37).

The claim that women are apprehensive about public violence was clearly more useful to those interested in criminalizing poverty than it was to women seeking urban safety. Moreover, men's loud voices about women's victimization and need for protection ultimately rendered women as subordinates in need of rescue by chivalrous men. The mobilization of women's fears and the rationale of women's safety as a discourse in the anti-squeegee debates exacerbated, rather than alleviated, the gender imbalance that gives rise to women's fears in the first place. Rather than address women's fears, the use of gendered anti-squeegee discourses created what Murray Lee has called "fearing subjects" (Lee 2001: 471). For Lee, fear of crime is socially produced and is not independent of our attempts to identify it, study it, and govern based upon it. In this framework, "fearing subjects" are "both the imagined objects of governable regulation... and also the subjects of disciplinary analysis" (Lee 2001: 471). In other words, fear is not simply something that people have; rather, people are deemed fearful and thus become objects that can be governed, as well as a reason for governing.

This examination of the anti-squeegee debates suggests that fearing subjects are also gendered. Women's fear became both the object, and the subject, of regulating visible poverty in urban spaces. Through such presentations of women as "fearing subjects," women were portrayed, sometimes by themselves, as "the unproblematic category of Woman... *she* is white, middle class... *a victim*, helpless" (Stanko 1998: 483, emphasis in original). Thus, the mobilization of gendered discourses in the anti-squeegee debates was "performative of respectable femininity," in which "good" women separated themselves from "dangerous" populations and spaces (Stanko1997: 481). Viewing women as victimized and intimidated allowed men to assert themselves as women's natural protectors. These hierarchical gendered relations became part of the working of the state. Normative gender ideals were not only a tool in producing "safe" streets but, further, the Safe Streets Act was constitutive of a new kind of gender order in which feminized citizenship was subordinated to a masculinized and authoritarian security state.

The ways in which gender was mobilized to substantiate anti-squeegee discourses means that we must ask not only why women's concerns about urban safety are often marginalized, but also, why some concerns get taken up as legitimate. It is troubling that, in the discourses about securing "safe" streets in Toronto, women's fear of crime was appropriated to bolster a law-and-order agenda that is inimical to feminist concerns. As Dianne Martin has argued in a slightly different context, the criminalization of social problems often produces "good" women victims who have few options but to participate in "'reforms' that strengthen the coercive power of the state.... This position [as crime victims] means that women are silenced as allies to those constructed as criminal" (Martin 2002). Viewing the Safe Streets Act through a gendered lens adds to the analysis, illustrating not only how gender is a tool by which to divide the "safe" from the "unsafe" but, further, how women as a group are divided from the poor. For feminists, an important task must be to resist such appropriations and divisions, and to reclaim the concept of safety, so that economic and gender security cannot be pitted against one another.

Notes

1. Attorney General Jim Flaherty, 1999, quoted in *Globe and Mail*, September 1: 10A.
2. Ontario Progressive Conservative Caucus, 1994, *New Directions: A Blueprint for Justice and Community Safety in Ontario*, vol. 3, Toronto: Queen's Park Printer.

3. *Statutes of Ontario*, 1999, c. 8.
4. Ontario Legislative Assembly, 1999, *Debates*, November 2.
5. Mel Lastman, 1998, quoted in *Toronto Star*, July 30: 3B.
6. *Toronto Sun*, 1998, July 15: 30.
7. *Toronto Star*, 2000, March 1: 5B.
8   See 1998, "Premier Declares War on Squeegee Kids" *Toronto Sun*, July 22: 1.
9. National Anti-Poverty Organization, 1999, "Short-Changed on Human Rights: A NAPO Position Paper on Anti-Panhandling By-Laws" <www.napo-onap. ca/docs/panhandling-en.pdf>.
10. Gerry Martiniuk, 1999, Ontario Legislative Assembly, *Debates*, November 16.
11. Frank Mazzilli, 1999, Ontario Legislative Assembly, *Debates*, November 15.
12. Bart Maves, 1999, Ontario Legislative Assembly, *Debates*, November 19.
13. Wayne Wettlaufer, 1999, Ontario Legislative Assembly, *Debates*, November 15.
14. 1999, *Toronto Sun*, July 30: 17.
15. 1998, *Toronto Star*, August 11: 15A.
16. 1998, *Toronto Star*, February 24: 21A
17. Parnaby, "Disaster through Dirty Windshields," 297.
18. Martiniuk, 1999, Ontario Legislative Assembly, *Debates*, November 17.
19. Gill, 1999, Ontario Legislative Assembly, *Debates*, December 7.
20. Mel Lastman, 1999, quoted in *Globe and Mail*, October 22: 9A.
21. Brendan Crawley, 1998, quoted in *Toronto Star*, July 25: 4A.
22. Martiniuk, 1999, Ontario Legislative Assembly, *Debates*, November 16.
23. Galt, 1999, Ontario Legislative Assembly, *Debates*, December 7.
24. Galt, 1999, Ontario Legislative Assembly, *Debates*, December 7.
25. Julia Munroe, 1999, Ontario Legislative Assembly, *Debates*, November 16.
26. Margaret Knowles, 1999, testimony, *Ontario Standing Committee on Justice and Social Policy*, November 29.
27. 1999, *Toronto Star*, September 27: 15A.
28. Sandy Scagnol, 1998, quoted in *Toronto Star*, May 31: 6A.
29. 1998, *Toronto Star*, June 23: 21A.
30. Heather Bird, 1998, "Squeegee Editorial," *Toronto Sun*, July 19: 3.
31. Carolyn Cleland, 1998, quoted in *Toronto Sun*, July 15: 16.
32. "Witness Testimony," *Meeting of the Toronto City Council*.
33. 1998, *Toronto Sun*, June 28: 33.
34. Helen Hansen, 1999, quoted in *Globe and Mail*, July 29: 14A.
35. Eleanor O'Connor, 1998, quoted in *Toronto Star*, July 23: 21A.
36. 1998, *Toronto Star*, July 30: 2B.
37. 2000, *Toronto Star*, February 13: 12A.
38. Michele Landsberg, 1999, Squeegee editorial, *Toronto Star*, October 31: 2A.
39. 1998, *Toronto Star*, July 30: 2B.

Chapter 9

It is Not a Crime

Amy Collins

There's one thing I'd like to say about poverty: it is NOT a crime. But if it isn't, why are so many of us treated as criminals for simply trying to survive? There's a lot of issues surrounding poverty that I think need to be looked at a little more closely. Our number one problem is that the same people who tell us so rudely to get a job are the ones who will not hire us — nobody hires when your résumé says no fixed address.

But nobody ever asks how you got there in the first place. There are a lot of reasons people end up homeless. Parents. Lack of work. Poor health. Eviction. Drugs and alcohol.

That's another problem. So many of us are seen drinking that it's automatically assumed that's what got you there. Most people on the street don't want to be there. They're on the street because their parents beat or molested them or simply kicked them out. Others are evicted, or there are other reasons. But drugs are on the street and a lot of people get so depressed that they resort to drugs and alcohol, which keeps them on the street. We need more outreach programs to help deal with addiction and depression.

That money put into keeping us in jail would be better spent on programs that help us help ourselves, such as ID clinics. Money could also be spent on affordable housing, financial support, and community programs.

Poor people do sometimes commit crimes but that wouldn't be needed if we had the support we need to get up on our own two feet. This can start with people simply looking at us as regular human beings who happen to be in a tight spot.

Poverty is not a crime: it's a means of survival.

Chapter 10

Street Kids as Delinquents, Menaces, and Criminals

The Criminalization of Poverty in Canada and Guatemala

Jeff Karabanow

Much of the current academic literature about street youth has conceptualized this diverse population as exploited, stigmatized, and in need of support and care[1] (Green 1998; Karabanow 2004a; Karabanow et al. 2000; Panter-Brick and Smith 2000). The majority of government approaches to street youth emphasize correctional and/or rehabilitative dimensions, which tend to both blame the individuals involved for their own situation and identify the population in homogenous terms that label the entire population as delinquent or a threat to society, and attempt to remove them from society in order to fix their pathologies (see Americas Watch and Physicians for Human Rights 1991; Bhanji 2004; Ortiz-de-Carrizosa and Poertner 1992; Alianza 1995; Karabanow 2003; Lusk 1989). Nation state policies in the northern and southern hemispheres concerning young people on the street have become increasingly punishing. In numerous venues, governments have directed state social control agents to clean up the streets and make street living less viable (Amnesty International 2006; Bhanji 2004; Earls and Carlson 1999; Human Rights Watch 1997; Lave 1995; O'Grady and Greene 2003; Strathcona Research Group 2005).

This chapter discusses the plight of young street people as they attempt to survive in public environments. The discussion is informed by numerous studies by the author and colleagues in Canada and Guatemala. The analysis is shaped by in-depth interviews with over 300 street youth and 100 service providers in both countries that explore the ways in which young people enter street life, survive on the street, and for some, exit street culture.[2] Emphasis is placed on the experiences of young people vis-à-vis police forces, government policies, and interaction with the public. Findings suggest a disturbing trend in Canada and Guatemala of governments and civil society understanding street youth as menaces in need of punishment and correction. Accounts of police and public citizen harassment and violence towards street youth are commonplace in both countries. Horrific accounts of torture and murder by police and/or para-military forces in Guatemala signal the extreme means by which governments attempt to eradicate poverty — and send a cautionary lesson to the north about criminalizing those who are marginalized, poor, and visible in public spaces.

Exploring the Issue

It's a humid Tuesday morning and I'm walking to work along a loud, busy, and diesel smoke-filled Guatemala City street artery when a colleague approaches and asks whether I could come with him to identify another young body which has turned up at the local morgue. I've been working with a street youth organization in the city for several months now and sadly, nothing surprises me much any more. Rumor has it that this body is of a young street boy who was brutally attacked and killed by para-military forces the night before. There's talk that the boy was sniffing glue in one of the many alleyways which make up the downtown market area of Guatemala City's Zone One. If the evidence supports these hypotheses, it will be another case example of the brutality inflicted upon street youth in the City by members of the nation state. What a sad place.[3]

My field notes from Guatemala document alarming violations of the human rights of marginalized and poor young people living on the street (Karabanow 2004a). By no means is this something new. Non-governmental organizations (NGOs) such as Human Rights Watch, Casa Alianza, Canadian Centre for International Research and Cooperation, and Amnesty International have meticulously documented such horrific cases for several decades (Alianza 1995; Human Rights Watch 1997). Throughout Latin America, nation state actors, agents of social control, and a variety of other social groups generally perceive street youth as menaces and garbage. Street cleansing has taken the form of imprisoning young people, placing them into closed-unit correctional compounds, forcing them into child welfare institutions, or worse, torture and death. The notorious 1993 case of a death squad of off-duty police officers executing eight street youth as they slept on the streets of downtown Rio de Janeiro illustrates such a worst case scenario. Underlying the spectrum of treatment toward street youth populations in Latin America is the feeling that these young people are dregs of society to be feared and controlled (Birch 2000; Ortiz-de-Carrizosa and Poertner 1992; Godoy 1999; Karabanow 2003; Lave 1995; Lusk 1989). As the population of young people on the street grows, so do beliefs that street youth are menaces in need of correction. A neoliberal political agenda increasingly influential throughout the globe has shaped tougher actions towards those deemed delinquent. Para-military death squads (*grupos de exterminio*) are not new to Latin America and indicate the extreme way in which some nation states (or agents of social control such as para-military) address poverty and marginalization. In this manner social cleansings of squatter environments within the urban cores of numerous Latin American countries have been undertaken. Fixing the problem tends to be equated with eradicating the person.

In Canada, neoliberal political agendas have shaped a more subtle correctional approach to street youth. While death squads and torture experiences are unheard of in Canada, there has been a growing attack on the country's most marginalized and impoverished populations. Neoliberal market frameworks of the past decades have shaped Canada's dismantling of a national safety net to support its citizens. Our welfare state has been stripped of provisions like affordable and supportive housing units, alternative educational structures, remotely adequate social assistance payments, and funding to grassroots NGOs working with street populations (Campfens 1997; Karabanow 2000; Olsen 2002; Teeple 1995). Underlying these attacks has been the adoption of more conservative perspectives on and approaches to homelessness. Public space ordinances in Ontario and British Columbia (such as each province's Safe Streets Act) are illustrative of regulations on the behaviour of homeless people on the street and tougher penalties for those found to be in violation of such scriptures. Moneymaking street activities such as panhandling and squeegeeing have been the focus of these ordinances. Recent Canadian analyses have suggested that the unintended consequences of such ordinances include street youth reverting to illegal activities (such as prostitution and drug selling) in order to survive on the street (Karabanow et al. 2005; O'Grady and Greene 2003). There is also clear evidence that because of these policies young people are living in more dangerous environments and increasingly relying upon meagre social assistance allowances (O'Grady and Greene 2003; Strathcona Research Group 2005).

The implicit functioning of such ordinances is to regulate and contain the behaviours of street populations, thus shaping in public consciousness a greater interweaving of homelessness with notions of criminality (Karabanow 2004a). A recent study of public perception of homeless youth in Halifax found that 70 percent of randomly sampled citizens viewed youth homelessness as a major problem getting worse over the past few years (Karabanow 2004b). In 2005, Halifax City Council voted in favour of asking the provincial government to enact "safe streets" legislation in order to, as one city councillor argued, "protect residents" from those who panhandle and squeegee (Fraser 2005). While official support for public space regulation adopts the guise of providing security to citizens in public spaces (see McNeil in this volume), the day-to-day realities involve more aggressive targeting of those deemed non-citizens. As such, "safe streets" acts can be interpreted as overt and covert attempts to criminalize those who have no choice but to make the street their temporary home (Gaetz 2004; O'Grady and Greene 2003).

Inclusion and Exclusion

Inclusionary and exclusionary dimensions shape street youth culture. Young people living on the street spend most of their day-to-day existence on survival mechanisms — locating food, shelter, employment, clothing, and security (Green 1998; Karabanow 2004a; Karabanow et al. 2005; McCarthy 1990; Panter-Brick and Smith 2000; Webber 1991). Much of their identity and status vis-à-vis the more privileged segments of society is made up of exclusionary components. A young Guatemalan boy articulated this idea: "nobody cares about street kids... we're garbage to non-street people." By definition of their situation, the majority of street youth are socially excluded in terms of their lack of adequate housing, their location outside the formal employment market and educational systems, their lack of social and economic capital, their age and inexperience, and their poverty and marginalization (Gaetz 2004). As one Guatemalan girl pointedly explained: "I would love a job, I would love to go to school, but I am a street kid." Street youth tend to be situated outside of mainstream culture, social institutions, and civil society (Karabanow 2004a; Karabanow et al. 2005).

In-depth interviews with over 100 street youth across Canada in 2005 shed light upon the interrelation between marginalization, poverty and social exclusion (Karabanow et al. 2005). The following comments eloquently describe young people's experiences of non-citizenship:

> I stayed on the streets and slept in the dumpster and it was really gross and dirty and didn't make me feel so well. I felt unwanted, unloved.

> You have to sleep in alleys and bank facilities and down at the waterfront or underneath the bridge or something. It's really sad. It's really depressing.

> I didn't really fit anywhere. I didn't know where I was going... I was just ready to get a box and sleep in the woods.

> Out here [on the street] you don't feel human — you feel like an animal.

Concerning street engagement, evidence points to young people's experiences with family conflict, poverty, and child welfare failures. Physical, sexual, and emotional abuse within the family and/or child welfare environment provide the most significant factors for entering the street. Despite such past traumatic experiences, young people demonstrate resilience and creativity through daily survival activities, from bin-diving (seeking food from garbage bins) to flying signs (displaying one's situation on cardboard signs to solicit help) to squatting (using abandoned buildings for shelter) and squeegeeing (cleaning car windshields for money) (Green 1998; Karabanow 2003; Karabanow 2004a; Karabanow 2004b; Kufeldt and Nimmo 1987; Morrissette and McIntyre 1989; Webber 1991).

However, such activities place already visible street youth further under the gaze of non-poor citizens and social control agents (such as police officers, security guards, and, in Latin America, para-military groups). Within the web of social exclusion, street youth are forced to live out their private lives in public domains. Many young people across Canada describe encounters with bystanders and police officers as often demeaning and abusive:

> I've sat on the streets and bawled my eyes out panhandling. 'Cause you get to the point where you don't want to be there and you're so hungry… and people walk by and no one gives you anything except dirty looks and mean comments.

> I got robbed by two crack-heads before, they picked me up and slammed me down and stole my stuff.

> I was sleeping in the park one day — and it's not like I was sleeping on a park bench or where anyone could see me, I was way off in the back corner, curled up in a sleeping bag — and I got woken up to a cop kicking me in the head, like full-on kicking me in the head.... He ruptured my eardrum and I'm half-deaf because of it.

Recent investigations have documented that an already tense relationship between street youth and police has become more distressed in recent years, especially with the rise of neoliberal politics (Gaetz 2004; Green 1998; Karabanow 2004a; McCarthy 1990; O'Grady and Green 2003; Webber 1991).

Street life presents difficult experiences for its inhabitants, not only in terms of the significant risks associated directly with being homeless but also in terms of interactions with mainstream culture. Street life is physically, emotionally, mentally, and spiritually unhealthy (Ensign 1998; Ensign and Bell 2004; Karabanow et al. in press). Layered upon this harsh experience is the condemnation, surveillance and control, lack of empathy and, at times, brutality levelled against those without homes. As a Guatemalan psychologist explained, "Guatemala is a military state and that permeates to all levels of society. People walking in the market… see these dirty street kids, they want something done so these kids won't steal or hurt them." For the majority of street youth, social exclusion is experienced externally (not having a home to go to) and internally (feeling marginalized by the treatment of others).

Less documented in the literature is the important finding that street life presents inclusionary processes at work within homeless youth cultures. First, the majority of young people indicate that their current street status is healthier and safer than where they have come from. This point is telling of the traumatic experiences facing young people prior to street engagement. Second, there is evidence that street life acts as a form of community to young people — a symbolic space where one can feel accepted, cared for, and even protected (Karabanow 2003). While street communities are often fraught with episodes of violence and exploitation by other street people, the police, and the public, they also provide inclusionary places for some young street people (Karabanow 2004a; Karabanow et al. 2005). Third, there is evidence that street youth support structures established in street youth territories within downtown cores (drop-in services, youth shelters, employment offices, health clinics, and outreach projects) help to build a sense of community among homeless populations (Karabanow 2004a; Karabanow et al. 2005).

These services often represent community spaces for marginalized young people and play significant roles in their development of identity and a sense of place. Street and youth services commonly take on a surrogate family role for street youth. Moreover, while the street is conceived of as public for most citizens, it has a private connotation for those who spend considerable time within its environment (Gaetz 2004; O'Grady and Green 2003). Street youth regularly manage personal and private activities (such as taking a nap or needing to relieve oneself) in the public domain. As such, the way in which nation state and private social control activity targets street youth is a direct attack on the private lives of these young people. Street youth are vulnerable to negative intervention primarily because of how overt their presence is to bystanders and law enforcement officials. While there is some evidence that street life represents a hidden culture that includes illegal activities, all of these youths' daily lives have increasingly come under surveillance and regulation, simply because they are forced to live their private lives within public spaces.

Building a Culture of Hope, Resisting Social Exclusion

Street youth are a traumatized population dealing with past and present hardships and abuses (Earls and Carlson 1999; Green 1998; Karabanow 2004a; Panter-Brick and Smith 2000). The identity of street youth is often shaped by external environments and actors. Harsher interventions by police forces and demeaning and disrespectful interactions in public spaces cause street youth to be seen as menaces, criminals, and garbage. Such experiences further alienate and exclude an already marginalized group of young people. As one young Montreal girl noted, "You just feel like shit, like dirt, like the way everybody around you treats you." However, there is evidence that presenting respectful and immediate support for street youth can foster street disengagement and increased wellness (Karabanow and Clement N.d.). Creating spaces where young people feel supported represents a culture of hope within an increasingly unsympathetic global environment (Karabanow 2003).

There are numerous case examples of NGOs building supportive and caring communities for street youth. From my research in Canada and Guatemala, the majority of street youth NGOs provide immediate and helpful resources such as food, clothing, showers, and short-term shelter space. In addition, many support centres advocate with and/or on the behalf of street youth in order to infuse a more sympathetic understanding of the population into government bodies and/or civil society. According to young people, such organizations also attempt to address structural issues such as affordable and safe housing and adequate employment opportunities. Moreover, these NGOs act as brokers between street youth and formal institutions such as schools and government bureaucracies. Many youth services also support young people's exit from street life and movements toward mainstream living (such as returning to school, reconciliation with family, and/or locating housing and employment). Recent academic investigations (Karabanow 2004a; Karabanow et al. 2005) have showcased the significant and diverse work of NGOs to support street youth populations in Vancouver, Calgary, Ottawa, Toronto, Montreal, Halifax, and Guatemala.[4] While each of these organizations provides distinct services within unique philosophical structures, they all maintain a strong commitment to and respect for the suffering and agency of street youth. Individual counselling, group mutual aid collectives, consciousness-raising and empowering projects, social action initiatives, and the adoption of strong broker-enabler-partisan roles for street youth advocates or street youth themselves (Karabanow 2003) make up holistic and powerful means to provide cultures of hope within seemingly hopeless situations.

Conclusion

Given the global restructuring of economic, political, and social infrastructures, increasing populations of those left behind are treated, not as victims of environmental forces but rather as pathological entities in need of surveillance, rehabilitation, and correction. Street youth are a marginalized population both economically and socially, and are understood as public nuisances, or worse, criminals that warrant increased control and punishment. Such a perception lacks any understanding of the root causes of homelessness or acknowledgement of street youths' current survival struggles. Calls for tougher enforcement and punishment of this population further marginalize and stigmatize street youth. Models of intervention that provide safe and supportive communities and address structural issues such as housing and employment not only provide effective alternatives to current responses by government and civil society, but also shed light on meaningful and respectful ways to engage marginalized and alienated young people.

Notes

1. See "Zone One: A Case Study of Street Kids in Guatemala City," produced by Jeff Karabanow et al., 1997, film documentary project; Karabanow 2004b; Karabanow et al. 2005.
2. Three studies inform this paper: "Zone One," J. Karabanow et al. — this project involved the development of a film documentary eliciting the voices of 120 street youth and forty service providers concerning the plight of street youth in Guatemala; Karabanow 2004b — this study looked at the experiences of living on the street for seventy youth in Halifax and the perceptions of 221 random sampled Halifax citizens towards homeless youth. Qualitative and quantitative analyses were used; Karabanow et al. 2005 — this qualitative study involved in-depth interviews with 128 youth and fifty service providers in Halifax, Montreal, Ottawa, Toronto, Calgary, and Vancouver concerning street disengagement.
3. Karabanow, 1996, "Field Notes," (17 April, 1996).
4. Examples of such organizations include Vancouver's Downtown Eastside Youth Action Society, Calgary's Backdoor and Exit Outreach, Ottawa's Operation Go Home, Toronto's Covenant House, Street Outreach Services, Evergreen, and The Meeting Place, Montreal's Le Bon Dieu Dans La Rue and Le Roc, Halifax's ARK Outreach and Phoenix Youth Services, and Guatemala's Casa Alianza and CEDIC.

Chapter 11

Young and Feared

Greg X

Being on the street definitely attracts more attention from police and when you're homeless this police attention is rarely a good thing. In my case, I don't think run-ins with the law ever benefit me or my well-being.

Twice in my earlier life I was returned by the authorities to homes across country that I was not even welcome in anymore. The reason for this is that the law says a person is not physically able to evolve until the age the law has set for a young adult to live unsupervised!

Another injustice is the random view that "every homeless is guilty, let's charge them all." It's funny how many times it's either happened to me or other street kids I know. What they do is round up a few and charge everyone with one offence, like one count of theft. I call it the "you rat or you suffer" charge. The strangest part of that is, why does it take four street kids to mastermind the supposed theft of a pack of cigarettes?

Then there is the civilian with a home and a steady job who spits insults and saliva at us when accompanied by friends or is mute and deaf and walks by us fast when alone.

Another thing is public intoxication. It seems that if me and other street kids just smell of an alcoholic beverage it's considered impairment and can be punished in many ways, mainly removal from the street to a small cage for a few hours, usually with no food. That gets a little aggravating when you're actually sober on a night near the end of the month, when you need to pay rent.

But if you're anyone else out drinking you can do one of two things to keep you out of the tank: one is to drive home, and two is to go homeless hunting with some buds to show your manhood! Go ahead, man, just chase them no good bums out of town. Don't worry, they don't have feelings, and most important, they just don't belong here. But we do remember. That's one thing that civilians or cops can't steal from us.

We've all been beat down countless times, sometimes for nothing more than a friendly "hello," a wrong answer, or being in the wrong place at the wrong time. And then we're still expected to carry a smile and a conversation when asked a question.

I know other street kids who have had possessions stolen. I myself had all my gear and clothing thrown out because of a two-week stay in jail. No matter how filthy they say my belongings were, it was everything I owned. But who was I to challenge their authority? So I just started collecting gear again with caution!

There are a lot of other situations in which cops and others decide the homeless should be punished. The last thing I'm going to mention is panhandling. If it is not on privately owned land, or if no anti-loitering or -solicitation signs are present, and if it is not aggressive to anyone I don't see why we should be punished or looked down on for asking for money! Isn't it better then having to watch me eat garbage out of the dumpster while you're out dining with your family or friends? What did you say? "Get a job!" Get me a place to stay and I will work. Who wants to stay at a shelter when the only privacy they offer is maybe sometimes in the washroom? And it's a breeding ground for bugs (body lice, scabies, etc.). I'm not looking forward to catching T.B. from the something like seven out of ten of the homeless who have it there!

Chapter 12

Homeless in Halifax

The Criminal Justice System Takes Aim at the Poor

Claire McNeil

In 2002, the Halifax Regional Police Department implemented aggressive new charging strategies aimed at silencing and removing poor youth from public spaces. Without public announcement, consultation, or comment, the force conducted regular surveillance at intersections in order to ticket young people offering to clean windshields at intersections. In a city where, by 2001, welfare had reached its lowest level in twenty years (National Council on Welfare 2005: 45), where the mayor declared the critical shortage of afford- able housing a "national disaster" (Federation of Canadian Municipalities n.d.), and where the rate of violent crime was the highest among the thirty largest police forces in Canada,[1] the Halifax Regional Police Department focused on criminalizing the activity of panhandling, setting their sights on "squeegee kids."[2]

The legal basis for these charges against the youth was twofold: a vintage municipal by-law regulating the use of signs,[3] and a very old but never previ- ously enforced section of the Nova Scotia Motor Vehicle Act (MVA), restricting the use of the streets by pedestrians.[4] Although the laws themselves made no mention of panhandling or soliciting, the charging policy, according to police briefing notes, targeted homeless youth engaged in panhandling. In this chapter I plot the development of these policing tactics and how they further marginalize street-involved youth within the city and the legal process, by effectively rendering it illegal to panhandle at intersections.

Several youth fought back in the courts through the simple act of pleading not guilty. This chapter examines the consequences of the charging policy and subsequent state prosecution of the youth. It reviews the municipality's involvement in these attempts to regulate homeless youth in Halifax through police powers. As the lawyer involved in their legal battle, I trace the pro- cedural hurdles these youth faced and the challenges presented in linking their experience of disadvantage and discrimination, to the constitutional protection of freedom of speech and equality rights.[5]

Background: Criminal Code Vagrancy Offences

As far back as 1892, the Canadian Criminal Code criminalized people in poverty by punishing vagrancy as a criminal offence. Rather than criminalizing specific offences, vagrancy laws criminalized "loose, idle or disorderly persons" and the status of being unemployed in a public place. A 1917 court decision justified these provisions as an effort to "curb the movements of the morally unclean."[6] Beggars, prostitutes, and petty criminals were all deemed vagrants, and the offence of vagrancy included loitering on a highway or begging (except if certified by a member of the clergy).[7]

By the 1950s and 1960s forms of moral regulation increasingly conflicted with more contemporary definitions of the scope of the criminal law and criminal responsibility.[8] By 1972, the vagrancy sections of the Criminal Code were substantially amended and restricted to persons living off the avails of crime. These sections were later expanded to include convicted sex offenders and others found loitering in public parks and other places.[9] By 2000, the Ontario Court of Appeal accepted that "a status offence contravenes fundamental justice" under section 7 of the Canadian Charter of Rights and Freedoms.[10]

Provincially, the Nova Scotia legislature also took aim at "loitering" as early as 1941. This offence was based on the 1892 criminal offence of vagrancy and defined loitering as "to lie or lurk in any highway, yard or other place in the town and not give a satisfactory account of himself [*sic*]." The provincial legislation limited the use of public space and gave police the power to arrest and detain those charged.[11]

In 1980, three accused, convicted of loitering under the Nova Scotia Towns Act, challenged their convictions on the basis that the provincial law was in "pith and substance" criminal (i.e., federal) law, and thus outside the scope of provincial jurisdiction. The Nova Scotia Court of Appeal upheld the convictions under the act, concluding that the section was aimed at the regulation of vehicular and pedestrian traffic on the streets and thus fell within provincial powers.[12] The act was repealed in 1998 as a result of municipal, and the provincial legislation against loitering was lost in the process. Ontario's controversial legislation regulating panhandling, the Safe Streets Act, was the subject of a 2001 court challenge based on a similar argument — that the provincial government strayed into federal jurisdiction, thus offending the constitutional division of powers — and met with similar results as the Ontario courts ruled that the provincial statute fell within the provincial power to regulate roads.[13]

Targeting "Squeegee Kids"

By 2000, the phenomenon of young people washing car windows at intersections for change had begun to attract the attention of the media across

Canada. By 2002, the Halifax Regional Police Department geared up for a full-fledged campaign to deal with a group of young people the police department dubbed "squeegee kids." These actions mirrored those of other municipalities and police forces in Toronto, Winnipeg, Calgary, and Vancouver (Collins and Blomley 2001). The police brass assigned a special Problem Solving Unit of officers to conduct a six-week review of the problem through a high-profile police presence. This involved staking out targeted intersections with marked police vehicles during peak traffic times. The special unit questioned young people engaged in panhandling, developed a list of names of those involved, issued warnings, and charged individuals by issuing summary offence tickets.[14]

As a result of the development of legal restrictions on offences dealing with vagrancy and loitering, legal advisors to the Halifax Regional Municipality (HRM) were forced to look elsewhere to find an offence that would afford the police the power to arrest, detain, and charge young people cleaning windshields at intersections. The police derived their authority first from a little-known section of the provincial MVA, which provides that "Where sidewalks are provided it shall be unlawful for any pedestrians to walk along and upon an adjacent highway."[15] Although no charges had previously been laid under this section, it became the main tool used by the police in their campaign. A municipal by-law regulating the use of signs was also employed. Displaying a sign without a permit could lead to fines in excess of $300, but the city provided no procedure to obtain a permit for a handheld sign.[16]

From April to June 2002, three Halifax officers gathered information and used these tools to undertake a six-week sweep that found twenty-one windshield cleaners operating at six intersections on the Halifax peninsula. All the cleaners were young, and the officers concluded that most were of no fixed address. Only two of the twenty-one youth identified were from Nova Scotia, and the officers noted: "it appears that these people are travellers and just go from place to place." The official police reports concerning squeegee kids also categorized panhandlers as individuals with addictions, disabilities, and mental illness, and as people "who have dropped out from society and do not wish to follow rules or work to support themselves" (Beazley 2002).

The motivation of the police in their campaign against squeegee kids remains uncertain. Media reports in 2000 and 2001 referenced the issue of panhandling on Spring Garden Road and called for increased security, including requests by local business for surveillance cameras in the busy shopping area. Local media coverage made no reference to the Halifax phenomenon of squeegee kids until October 2002, when the media reported on a police report submitted to City Council (Moar 2002: 3). Even before City Council requested and received a police report on panhandling and squeegeeing at intersections in October 2002, significant police resources had been assigned to the issue. Police attention to this problem coincided with political preparations and security arrangements by the police department and the provincial and federal governments for an international meeting of the Group of Eight finance ministers, held in Halifax on June 14 and 15, 2002, and continued during the peak summer tourism months for the next three years. The Halifax campaign against squeegee kids also paralleled the activities of police forces in other large Canadian cities.

It is not clear that ordinary members of the public provided the impetus for this crackdown on street-involved youth. In his October 2002 report to City Council, Deputy Police Chief Frank Beazley noted that "police continually run into... the reluctance of members of the public to formally complain and go to court" (Moar 2002; Beazley 2002). Without a complainant or a witness willing to testify, the police were unable to build a case. The police report touches briefly on the reasons for this reluctance, including the possibility that its own policing strategies with respect to panhandling lacked public support. In commenting on negative public feedback to aggressive police tactics towards panhandlers in Calgary, the Halifax Deputy Chief noted that "our officers have received similar feedback from members of the public when dealing with the panhandlers, everything from dirty looks and comments on their disapproval of the police action to actually passing money to the panhandlers when they are being dealt with." An October 2002 op-ed in the Halifax *Chronicle Herald* decried the police charging strategy (Hunter 2002: B2; Beazley 2002). In November 2002 the *Herald* reported a link between the increase in panhandling and the lack of affordable housing in the city (Power 2002: A3). In addition to concerns about negative public reaction to their crackdown on squeegee kids, the police reported reservations about the effectiveness of fines as a deterrent, noting to City Council that the offenders were transient and unlikely to show up in court or to have a vehicle or driver's license, renewal of which is often used as leverage in the fine collection process.

Beazley's report to City Council thus identified weaknesses in the police strategy to prosecute panhandlers. However, the larger social problems underlying the squeegeeing and panhandling debate, such as the accused's inability to pay fines due to poverty, were not addressed. Nor was the link drawn by Council members between youth squeegeeing and the critical shortage of affordable housing that Council members' own staff had identified as a key component in the rise of homelessness (Federation of Canadian Municipalities n.d.). The inadequacy of local welfare rates and minimum wage incomes became particularly critical in 2001, when Nova Scotia welfare rates were cut by an average of 10 percent. This exacerbated the fact that by 2000 the welfare rate for a single unemployable person in Halifax had already dropped by almost 40 percent in constant dollars from the previous decade (National Council on Welfare 2006). At the same time, real estate prices in these years jumped dramatically and rents followed suit. Yet City Council, having received the police department's report on squeegeeing youth, continued to focus on criminalization as a response to squeegeeing and panhandling.

The allocation of police resources to targeting squeegee kids was raised in the police report to Council, when Deputy Chief Beazley concluded with the questions: "How big is the problem, what priority should we put on it, and what resources should we devote to it?" (Beazley 2002). The police strategy required taking officers away from other activities at a cost to taxpayers. Estimates of the hours of policing and legal services allocated to the issue have never been made public and the charging policy against homeless youth remained in place for a further three years. It ended only after a provincial court found that the section was unconstitutionally broad and dismissed charges based on a lack of evidence that the activities of the youth had obstructed traffic.

The Charging Strategy

In early June 2002, prior to the G-8 meeting, Halifax Regional Police officers were briefed on the charging strategy and the options available to them to address panhandling and squeegeeing at intersections. The police strategists noted that after issuing four summary offence tickets against the same individual, the police had the power to arrest and detain the suspect. Despite the relatively few number of youths involved (twenty-one in May 2002 according to the police briefing memo), the police began issuing tickets for offences under the MVA and the municipal by-law regulating the use of signs. Thirty-nine charges were laid under the MVA and an equal number under the signs by-law, often resulting from the same incident. Most of these charges were laid from May to September 2002 (twenty-eight out of a total of thirty-six charges for the year). Police officers issued multiple tickets in most cases and placed particular intersections in the city under surveillance. The charges and tickets issued pursuant to these legal provisions, often combined for maximum effect, led to a sudden spike in police activity at intersections in Halifax. The charges laid resulted in thousands of dollars of fines levied against youth who were homeless and in most cases without jobs, social assistance, or any other means of support.[17] Imposing fines — in some cases of over $300 for a single infraction — on individuals who were without resources had the effect in many cases of pushing youth out of Halifax, and the region, to avoid being punished for failure to pay the fine.

Reaction to Police Pressure

One of the few sources of support for homeless youth in Halifax was the staff at Ark Outreach, a drop-in centre for street-involved youth. The Ark's Dorothy Patterson was one of the first in the community to identify the impact of the new charging policy on youth. Those charged felt persecuted and deprived of their ability to provide for themselves. The fines and threat of incarceration added to the stress of already difficult circumstances. The police even seized the youths' buckets and sponges. The police crackdown and high-profile police presence meant that even those not charged felt the chill. While it may not have stopped the activity — which is clear since young people were charged repeatedly — the charging strategy did create an urgent situation.

As youth faced a flood of summary offence tickets, Ark Outreach investigated possible responses with the legal community. Legal services for persons charged with criminal offences in Nova Scotia are provided through provincial legal aid offices, based on financial and case type eligibility. Given their extreme poverty, financial eligibility was not an issue; however, as a result of the relatively minor nature of the charges, legal representation through Nova Scotia Legal Aid was limited. Access to criminal legal aid in Nova Scotia depends on the seriousness of the charge and is restricted to charges that are likely to result in incarceration. Instead, community workers from Ark Outreach turned to Dalhousie Legal Aid Service. Rather than failing to show up in court, as the police had probably predicted, the youth and volunteer student representatives from the Dalhousie Pro Bono Law Students chapter began turning out en masse to contest the tickets and the charges through the simple act of pleading not guilty. Youth targeted by the police entered over twenty not guilty pleas between August and September 2002.

Lengthy delays ensued in these cases as a result of court backlogs, and trial dates were not scheduled until the winter and spring of 2003. Other realities intervened in the legal struggle. Many of the youth moved away, seeing little by way of local supports and services to meet their needs, and facing the oncoming winter months. If part of the police strategy was to push the "travellers" — as the police dubbed them — to move on, it was successful. One by one, as the charges came up for trial, youth were tried in their absence and fines levied. By June 2003, only one individual remained in the area to contest the charges. He faced multiple charges under the Signs Ordinance and the MVA. Police delays in evidence disclosure resulted in postponement of his trial date. The by-law and MVA charges were placed in separate courts with different prosecutors, further complicating the defence. Police continued to lay charges. Twenty-two charges were laid in the spring and summer of 2003 under both the MVA and the by-law, and twenty-nine charges under the MVA followed in the first six months of 2004.

Freedom of Expression and the By-law Charges

Tickets issued under the city's signs by-law penalized young people for publicly displaying a sign without a permit.[18] The signs held by young people at city intersections typically communicated messages concerning their individual circumstances, including homelessness, hunger, and sometimes desire for a job. The defence challenge rested on an assertion that the by-law infringed the constitutional right to freedom of speech under section 2(b) of the Canadian Charter.[19] Courts have interpreted the constitutional protection of freedom of expression to include public expression of meaning necessary for participation in the community. The defence needed to prove that the signs were an important means of communication and that the charges deprived youth of their only viable means of public expression given the defendant's lack of financial resources. The defence also needed to show that this use of signs was an example of participation in the community, which was important to the youth's self-fulfillment.

By June 2004, days before the sole remaining trial was due to begin, negotiations between the HRM legal services department and defence counsel resulted in a public agreement by HRM to withdraw all outstanding summary offence tickets and charges under the city by-law, and to change police policy in this regard. On June 9, 2004, a police memorandum was sent out advising all officers that they would "not be able to proceed charges under section 44 of *by-law* S300," but reminding officers that charges could still be laid under section 127(2) of the MVA. The advantage to the defendant of this plea bargain and agreement was that his charges were dropped and other young people would benefit from the change in policy. The advantage to the crown was that the courts did not have the opportunity to rule on the constitutional validity of by-law S-300, a law that appears on its face to be constitutionally flawed.

This victory, while celebrated by youth involved in the struggle to survive on the street, was partial at best. Apparently concerned with the impact of visible street youth on tourism, police continued to target youth at intersections through the summer of 2004 using charges under the MVA. The remaining trial dealing with the MVA charges still had not taken place.

Discriminatory Enforcement and the Principles of Fundamental Justice

The issue of the legality of squeegeeing in Halifax finally came to a head in the trial of *R. v. McCluskey*.[20] The narrow legal issue was whether Mr. McCluskey had violated s. 127(2) of the MVA, which makes it an offence to walk "along or upon" a roadway. The larger legal matter at stake can be found in the defence notice filed under the Constitutional Questions Act which alleged violations of two sections of the Canadian Charter of

Rights and Freedoms. The first violation alleged, under section seven of the Charter, was that the MVA law deprived the defendant of his right to liberty and security of the person by imposing criminal sanctions and the risk of imprisonment based on a law that was vague and overbroad, contrary to the principles of fundamental justice. The second violation alleged was a breach of the defendant's equality rights under section fifteen, in particular his right to equal treatment under the law, as a result of the selective police enforcement of that law and their targeting of a disadvantaged group.

The trial commenced in the first week of September 2004, coincidentally the day after the Shinerama campaign. This charitable campaign involves Halifax university students approaching vehicles at city intersections with signs and buckets for donations. Despite thousands of students plying intersections throughout the day, no charges were laid against Shinerama participants. The only apparent distinction between activities of the squeegee kids and their more fortunate university counterparts lay in their social condition and economic status. The "war on the poor" was graphically highlighted.[21]

The trial began in Provincial Court with the city calling its star witness, the arresting officer, who dropped a bombshell when he admitted that he was not sure that the defendant was the individual he had ticketed. Given that in a criminal proceeding the burden rests on the prosecution to prove the offence beyond a reasonable doubt, and that identification of the accused is a vital component of every charge, the police witness torpedoed the prosecution's case. The officer also testified that he had received no reports of citizen complaints, but laid the charge against the defendant based on the directive from his superiors after conducting his own surveillance of the intersection and seeing the defendant step onto the street at a red light in order to approach stopped vehicles. He admitted there was no obstruction of traffic or aggressive behaviour by the defendant.[22]

Given that the prosecution failed to prove a vital element of the offence, the defence was faced with a dilemma: make a motion for a directed verdict that would result in a dismissal of the charges before the court, or proceed with the case by calling evidence from the defendant, during which he would be subject to cross examination and no doubt forced to make an admission of guilt. The defendant would need to put his head in the noose, figuratively speaking, in order to pursue his goal of putting an end to the charging strategy under the MVA. After waiting two years for his day in court, the defendant chose to proceed.[23]

The defence called further police witnesses to establish the existence of an explicit police policy targeting squeegee kids, and an expert on homeless youth culture, researcher Dr. Jeff Karabanow, to address the status of those targeted by the police. Karabanow's research with street-involved youth in Halifax allowed him to testify concerning their social disadvantage and vulnerability. His evidence was vital in establishing that the poverty experienced by street youth was a ground of discrimination protected under section fifteen, the equality rights provision of the Charter. Much of the ensuing defence evidence focused on establishing the basis for an equality rights violation by showing that the charging strategy imposed a burden on a disadvantaged group, thus undermining their human dignity.

Karabanow testified concerning the social condition of Halifax "street-involved youth." His research findings stood in stark contrast to the assumptions relied upon by the police. For example, contrary to police expectations concerning the role played in youth homelessness by psychiatric illnesses and addictions, Karabanow testified that most youth end up on the street as a result of poverty and the lack of social supports for families. Many young people on the streets have experience with the child welfare system and have been bounced from foster placements and group homes before leaving for the streets. He testified as to the nature of panhandling as an activity of subsistence for homeless youth, and the heavy toll such a lifestyle places on the physical and emotional health of the youth involved. While addictions and depression were not uncommon, he identified these problems as the by-product rather than the cause of living on the street. In most cases, he testified, youth are escaping from situations, not running toward the street. In some respects the expert evidence agreed with the police findings: the youth involved lived in extreme poverty, had no homes to go to, and travelled widely. Karabanow concluded that one of the contributing factors to the transience of the population was the youth's experience of local police harassment and mistreatment.[24] The defence established that the youth charged experienced many of the same disadvantages as those enumerated, in terms of stereotyping, lack of political clout, and longstanding economic disadvantage, thus supporting its argument that the youth formed an analogous group protected by the equality rights guarantee of the Charter.

Anna Hunter of the Halifax Coalition Against Poverty took the stand to testify about the police treatment of university students in the Shinerama campaign the previous morning. She noted that the students had approached motorists at intersections to solicit funds, and on one occasion even appeared to successfully solicit a police van. The police witnesses confirmed that they do not lay charges against individuals soliciting funds in a manner identical to the poor and homeless when the funds are for charitable causes.

The defendant, Mr. McCluskey, also took the stand, testifying as to his circumstances at the time of the offence and the impact of the charges upon him. Originally from New Brunswick, he arrived in Halifax only weeks before being charged and was living in abandoned buildings and lots. He had his dog with him for companionship and protection while living on the streets. Because of his attachment to his dog, he was denied entrance to the local shelters, a common problem for homeless youth (Karabanow 2004). Without an address, he was told he was ineligible for income assistance.[25] Thus he found himself cleaning windshields in order to survive. He testified that, at twenty years of age, he had no family or friends in the city except other youth he met on the streets. He was offered odd jobs as a labourer, but because he lived on the street he was plagued by health problems such as bronchitis and pneumonia.[26]

The Court's Decision

The defence presented two main arguments against the charges. The first was that in selectively targeting a disadvantaged group with criminal sanctions the police violated the defendant's equality rights under section fifteen of the Charter. The evidence established that the defendant was a member of a disadvantaged group based on his youth and social condition. The police admitted that they had targeted this group for criminal sanctions. The legal argument was that, regardless of whether the police intended to discriminate, the effect of their charging policy was to impose a burden upon an already disadvantaged group. This result was tantamount to discrimination and thus unlawful under the constitution.

The second defence argument was that the law, which prevented pedestrians from walking "upon or along a roadway," was vague and overly broad, and thus contrary to section seven of the Charter, which provides that individuals cannot be deprived of the life, liberty, or security of the person unless this is in accordance with the "principles of fundamental justice." Following a well-trod route that has led in other cases to Supreme Court of Canada decisions dealing with overly broad or vague laws,[27] the defence argued that the wide ambit of section 127(2) of the MVA made it impossible for a pedestrian to know when they were in jeopardy of being charged. The section was in fact so broad that stepping off the curb for any reason — other than crossing the street — placed a pedestrian at risk of being charged.

On February 4, 2005, Provincial Court Judge Michael Sherar released his decision. He dismissed the charges against Mr. McCluskey and ruled that section 127(2) of the MVA relied upon by the police was overly broad, and thus contrary to "the principles of fundamental justice" and section seven of the Charter.[28] The judge's ruling referred to defence evidence concerning the discriminatory impact of the charging policy and the disadvantaged position of street-involved youth, including Karabanow's testimony. However, ultimately the Judge found it unnecessary to make a determination of the equality rights claim under section fifteen of the Charter against the police department in its enforcement of the law.

The court held that the provincial MVA infringed on the liberty of pedestrians in a "disproportionate and arbitrary way." In discussing the charging strategy the court found:

> Discretion to apply punitive sanctions, especially the deprivation of a citizen's liberty ought to be most narrowly constrained. The exercise of such discretion without reasonable and purposeful parameters can result in arbitrary or capricious actions. Such inappropriate use of discretion can lead to abuse of process which in turn can bring the administration of justice into disrepute.[29]

In its conclusion, the court drew back from sweeping statements concerning the constitutionality of police action against street-involved youth, and determined that in order for charges to be proven, the police required evidence that the pedestrian endangered, hindered, or obstructed the safety of other pedestrians or vehicles.[30] The result was an almost immediate halt in the charging activities against youth at intersections. In unreported decisions, other Provincial Court judges following the same reasoning dismissed remaining charges based on the prosecution's inability to prove obstruction.

Aftermath

While these legal skirmishes yielded positive results for homeless youth, city officials continued to advocate the criminalization of those who depend on access to public spaces. In June 2005, the City Council passed a resolution encouraging the province to adopt legislation similar to Ontario's Safe Streets Act in order to restrict panhandling.[31] In the leadup to that year's tourist season, minutes from a May 2006 meeting of the Board of Police Commissioners reflect a renewed push toward such legislation, noting that while the previous Minister of Justice determined that he would not proceed on this front, the new Minister of Justice should be lobbied to reconsider introducing provincial legislation along these lines.[32]

By late 2007 legislators pushed again for a criminalizing measure to target squeegeeing in Halifax, and in early 2008 the Nova Scotia Motor Vehicle Act was amended to make it illegal to "stop or approach a motor vehicle for the purpose of offering, selling or providing any commodity or service or soliciting the driver or any other person in the vehicle." At the time of writing, it is not yet clear how or if this new law will be applied or challenged (Nova Scotia Department of Justice 2007).[33]

Notes

1. Violent offences include homicide to attempted murder, assault, sexual assault, robbery, and abduction. M. Wallace, 2002, *Juristat: Crime Statistics in Canada*, Ottawa: Canadian Centre for Justice Statistics.
2. The Halifax Regional Police Department internal memoranda used the well-known term "squeegee kids" to refer to young people soliciting change from

motorists by cleaning windshields at intersections in Halifax. Halifax Regional Department, Internal Memoranda, 2000.

3. "Respecting Signs, Billboards, and Advertising Structures," City of Halifax Ordinance Number 166, 1978: "No person shall display a sign without a permit, unless it falls within an exception defined under the ordinance."

4. "Where sidewalks are provided it shall be unlawful for any pedestrian to walk along and upon an adjacent highway," Motor Vehicle Act c. 293, as amended, R.S.N.S. 1989 s. 127(2).

5. The author was the supervising lawyer involved with the resulting court cases and the community file through Dalhousie Legal Aid Service, a community clinic that provides legal aid to persons who cannot otherwise afford the services of a lawyer. As a teaching clinic, third-year law students and other student volunteers are actively involved in working with clients.

6. See *R. v. Jackson*, [1917]40 O.L.R. 173, O.J. no. 71, at para 63.

7. *R. v. Jackson*, [1917]40 O.L.R. 173, O.J. no. 71, note 8, at para. 67.

8. Throughout the 1950s and 1960s, offences related to homosexuality and prostitution came under increasing scrutiny. Sexual activity between consenting adults in private spaces was decriminalized in Canada in 1968; prostitution as an offence remained on the books until it was repealed by the Canadian Parliament in 1972. While privacy rights advocates succeeded in getting the state out of the bedrooms of the nation, in the terminology of Pierre Elliott Trudeau, the battle over the policing of the poor in public spaces, and particularly the debate over panhandling, continues to be fought on a number of legal fronts at the municipal, provincial, and federal levels. See Collins and Blomley 2001; Esmonde 2002; R. Brewer, 2005, "Deconstructing the Panhandling Norms: Federated Anti-Poverty Groups of B.C. v. Vancouver (City) and Western Print Media," *Review of Current Law and Law Reform* 10.

9. *Criminal Code*, R.S.C. s. 179.

10. *R. v. Budreo* ((2000)142 C.C.C. 3d, 225 Ontario Court of Appeal), para 24. The court went on to find that the "peace bond" provisions at issue in the case did not create offences because they were not punitive but preventative. As a result, the Court upheld the provisions, concluding that they did not create status offences.

11. Towns Act, R.S.N.S. 1967, c. 309, s.209(1).

12. See *R. v. Jarvis et. al.*, (N.S.J. No. 543, NSCAAD 1980). Conversely, in *R. v. Beaver* ((1984) 66 N.S.R. 2d, 419 NSSCTD), affirmed on appeal ((1985) 67 NSR 2d 281 NSCA), the court found that the provincial Attorney General had intruded into the federal criminal law jurisdiction and dismissed the government claim for an injunction against thirty-four women alleged to be working the streets as prostitutes.

13. See *R. v. Banks* (2001) 55 O.R. 3d 374 Ontario Court of Justice, upheld on appeal (2005) 248 DLR 4th 118 Ontario Supreme Court of Justice.

14. Halifax Regional Police, "Exhibit 1, Operational Plan" *Halifax Regional Police Problem Solving* (Halifax: Halifax Regional Police, 2004). Filed September 8, 2004 in *R. v. McCluskey* (NSPC 2, (2005) 230 N.S.R. 2d 171 N.S. Provincial Court).

15. Motor Vehicle Act, R.S.N.S. 1989, c. 293 s 127[2].

16. Halifax Regional Municipality City By-Law s-300; see also the pre-amalgama-

tion *Signs Ordinance*, 1978, Ordinance 166, City of Halifax, as amended.

17. See *R. v. Jackson*, (1917), at para 63; *R. v. McCluskey* (2005) at para 19.

18. See Note 5 Motor Vehicle Act, 1989.

19. Canadian Charter of Rights and Freedoms, Part I Constitution Act 1982, Schedule B to Canada Act, c. 11.

20. See *R. v. McCluskey* (2005).

21. See *R. v. McCluskey* (2005), at para. 13.

22. See *R. v. McCluskey* (2005), at para. 5 and 6.

23. See *R. v. McCluskey* (2005), at para. 1–3.

24. See *R. v. McCluskey* (2005), at para 18–19.

25. At the time, social assistance policy required that applicants establish residency through an address, which could include a homeless shelter.

26. See *R. v. McCluskey* (2005), at para. 7.

27. See *R. v. Heywood* (S.C.J. No. 101 SCC; 3 S.C.R. 761 1994); *R. v. Demers* (S.C.C. No. 43 SCC; 2 S.C.R. 489 2004).

28. Canadian Charter of Rights and Freedoms, Part I Constitution Act 1982, Schedule B to Canada Act, c. 11.

29. See *R. v. McCluskey* (2005), at para. 27.

30. See *R. v. McCluskey* (2005), at para. 34.

31. Halifax Regional Council, Peter Kelly et al., *Halifax Regional Council Minutes* (June 14, 2005) <http://www.halifax.ca/council/documents/c050614.pdf>.

32. Board of Police Commissioners, *Board of Police Commissioners Minutes* (8 May 2006), http://www.halifax.ca/boardscom/bpc/documents/060508.pdf.

33. Nova Scotia Department of Justice, *Safer Streets and Communities, Report to the Minister of Justice* (Nova Scotia Department of Justice, May 2007) <http://www.gov.ns.ca/just/minister/documents/moj_safestreets_report_1.pdf>. In this report to the Minister of Justice, following public consultation concerning crime prevention in Nova Scotia, neither panhandling, squeegeeing, nor begging are identified as issues of public concern. For Bill 7 (2008), an amendment to the Nova Scotia Motor Vehicle Act, see Chapter 293, Section 173A (1) at <gov.ns.ca/legislature/legc/bills/60th_2nd/1st_read/b007.htm>.

Chapter 13

Squat the City, Rock the Courts

Challenging the Criminal Marginalization of Anti-Poverty Activism in Canada

Lisa M. Freeman

On September 27, 2004, five anti-poverty activists entered a criminal court in Ottawa to defend their political action and to challenge the criminal charges that were brought against them as a result of these acts in *R. v. Ackerley et al.*[1] Two years earlier the five accused, along with seventeen other people, squatted in an abandoned building on Gilmour Street in downtown Ottawa. During their trial the accused went beyond arguing the technicalities of the criminal charges brought against them. From their perspective as anti-poverty activists, they directly questioned whether the act of squatting should be defined and prosecuted as a criminal activity during a major housing crisis, challenging liberal conceptions of the proper place of and for politics in the courtroom.[2] Consequently, their trial reveals ways in which activists, specifically squatters, have resisted the criminalization of both poverty and anti-poverty activism in Canada.[3]

The trial of the Gilmour Street squatters raises significant questions about the relationship between activism and law. Does the criminalization of anti-poverty activism and the political techniques used to combat poverty (such as urban squatting) substantially demobilize political resistance? Can activists find space for political resistance within the criminal courts of Canada? In this chapter I address these questions by analyzing the experiences of the accused in *R. v. Ackerley et al.* I argue that activists, as demonstrated in the case, move beyond a simplistic understanding of a binary opposition between radical activism and liberal legal procedure and reform (Sheldrick 2004). I demonstrate how the Gilmour Street squatters confronted the boundaries of liberal conceptions of legal victory and the proper place of political activism in the courts.[4]

The chapter begins by contextualizing the actions of Ottawa's Gilmour Street squatters in a broader history of squatting, social movements, and the law, and then situates *R. v. Ackerley et al.* within the context of the eviction of the squat at 246 Gilmour. The remaining sections of the chapter uncover the social significance of *R. v. Ackerley et al.* by highlighting how the squatters represented themselves in court, interacted with legal actors during the trial, and how their legal strategy stretched the boundaries of the criminal courts. In many ways the analysis of *R. v. Ackerley et al.* is intended to provide a glimmer of hope in the fight against the criminalization of poverty.

Squatting: A People's History

Public and political squats in Europe gained attention through their affiliations with autonomous and anarchist social movements in the late 1960s, 1970s, and 1980s. Italy had approximately twenty thousand documented squatters between 1969 and 1975, while towards the end of 1980 in Zurich, Switzerland, "more than eleven hundred youth faced criminal charges" for squatting with "more than sixty confrontations with the police and over twenty-five hundred arrests." There were an estimated six or seven thousand squatted houses in Amsterdam in the spring of 1980, and squatters there had a strong influence on urban planning.[5] Denmark's Christina squat in 1970 occupied a fifty-four acre site with over 175 buildings in Copenhagen, which represented one of the largest squatter settlements in Europe (Gimson 1980). Meanwhile several German squats were associated with the radical Autonomen movement and the fall of the Berlin wall. Berlin's squatter movement controlled approximately 165 houses at its peak in the late 1970s, and by 1980 formed a squatters' council (Katsiaficas 1997). European social and legal struggles over squats continue today; police eviction of a squat in Copenhagen on March 3, 2007, resulted in lengthy police confrontations, with anarchist squatters from around Europe joining the protest, resulting in over five hundred arrests (Olsen 2007).

Police evictions, governmental responses, and legislation regulating squatter's title vary significantly between European countries. For example, under the 2003 provisions of Adverse Possession in the United Kingdom, a squatter needs to possess the land for ten years with few other restrictions before they are allowed to apply for Adverse Possession rights. If the landowner does not reply to or challenge this request within three months, the squatter is then entitled to be registered as the new landowner (*Radclifees LaBrasseur* May 12, 2004). In the Netherlands a building can be squatted legally if it has been unoccupied for a minimum of one year. The criminal charges of break and enter are applicable only if the police catch the squatters entering the building. If the squatters are simply found living in the building and the police did not intervene during the initial stages of the occupation, a formal eviction notice and legal action are required to evict the squatters (Wiegand 2004).

Unfortunately, Canadian laws around adverse possession are far stricter than European laws and are virtually impossible for Canadian squatters to put into practice. Although each province and territory uses its own land holdings system, the majority of Canadian public and private land is subsumed under the Torrens system of land titles, which primarily prohibits squatter's title (Ziff 2000). Under this system, to acquire public (or crown) land in Canada, a squatter must openly remain on the land for sixty years. For privately held land, the statutory period is ten years (Ziff 2000). The combination of restrictive property law and a lack of squatter's title makes squatting in Canada difficult and dangerous. Squats are viewed as illegal, and occupants are vulnerable to arrest. Continual conflict with the criminal justice system is a reality for Canadian squatters.

Due to the legal landscape, most squats in Canada occur covertly, making it difficult to document a comprehensive history of squatting and squatters' rights in Canada. Over the past ten years however, the steady presence of public and politicized urban squatting in grassroots anti-poverty movements has drawn attention to the plight of squatters and the related social problems surrounding affordable housing (Katsiaficas 1997; Gimson 1980). From Montreal's Overdale squat (2001), the Infirmary squat in Halifax (2002), Toronto's Pope squat (2002), and Victoria's Pandora Street squat (2002) to Peterborough's Water Street squat (2003), Vancouver's Woodward's squat (2003), and Toronto's Gatekeeper's squat (2003), Jarvis Street squat (2004) and Women Against Poverty Collective squat (2007), occupations of abandoned properties have created temporary shelter and ignited heated debate on the lack of affordable housing. Most of these squat actions have occurred as part of a mass rally or protest and have involved squatter demands on and/ or attempts to negotiate with municipal governments. The actions have also tended to cumulate in police-led evictions, multiple arrests, criminal charges, and occasionally trials (Arsenault 2003; Patriquin 2001; Levine 2002).[6]

Public squats in Canada are perceived by the media, mainstream anti-poverty groups, and housing agencies as a marginal tactic used by a few radical activists; however, these squats have received a significant amount of media attention and community support. While most Canadian squats have been short-lived, with some lasting for only a few hours and the longest enduring three months, these actions have resulted in identifiable if limited achievements.[7] In Montreal, Toronto, and Vancouver these achievements have included the establishment of temporary deals with the government consisting of the reconnection of electricity, the promise of city council discussions focused on alternative housing projects, and monetary support. In the case of Montreal's Overdale squat, the squatters moved to a city-owned abandoned building with advice and approval from the municipal government, intending to create long-term affordable housing, only to be evicted in a police-led operation shortly thereafter, allegedly due to a breach of contract (MacAfee 2001: 03). Attempts to negotiate long-term housing settlements with municipal governments have generally been unsuccessful.

With a history of limited and inconsistent municipal support, the majority of Canadian squatters are cautious of any negotiations and collaboration with politicians. Still, these squats are not as marginal and socially unsupported as the reported municipal responses suggest.

Recent public squats have relied heavily on moral and financial support from an extended community of social work agencies, shelters, unions, neighbours, and individual city councillors. In many instances, union support has been invaluable. For example, during the Ontario Coalition Against Poverty's Pope squat, the Canadian Autoworkers Union pledged $50,000 to help renovate the building. Several national unions donated money and supplies to Ottawa's Gilmour Street squatters, and lent support even after the squatters were evicted (*Canadian Press Newswire* 2001). John Baglow, then president of the Public Service Alliance of Canada, was a supportive witness for the squatters in court.[8] While limited in scope, these examples suggest that squatting has the potential to be a unifying strategy among social justice groups in the fight against poverty and its criminalization.

Even as a potentially unifying force, political squats are unfortunately only a temporary tactic in the present struggle against poverty in Canada. A relatively uniform state response consisting of regular police surveillance, lack of municipal government support, and brutal police-led evictions and arrests has criminalized and marginalized squatters, making it difficult to create permanent housing from public squats (Lamble and Freeman 2004). However, from Halifax to Vancouver, lessons learned from evictions are informally shared amongst anti-poverty organizers and squatters. Knowledge of policing tactics during evictions, failed and successful negotiations with landlords and municipal governments, and legal defence strategies (including the effectiveness of Charter arguments), build an on-the-ground archive of accessible information for anti-poverty activists working together in the fight against the criminalization of poverty.

246 Gilmour Street, Ottawa

The criminalization of urban squatting may appear to push the efforts of anti-poverty activism out of the public eye, but the case of the Gilmour Street squat reveals that when people challenge the criminal marginalization of such direct actions, the space for political resistance may also be redefined. When the Gilmour Street building was occupied on June 28, 2002, during a mass demonstration against the economic summit of the Group of Eight nations,[9] it was the first public squat that Ottawa had witnessed in approximately forty years. The action received substantial community and media attention, and the activists pursued an innovative defence strategy in their criminal trial. These factors make the Gilmour Street squat significant in its implications for future squats, legal challenges, and anti-poverty organizing in Canada.

The abandoned, privately owned house at 246 Gilmour Street was located in a trendy section of the Centretown neighbourhood, a few city blocks away from Parliament Hill. Shortly after the occupation began, the squatters presented a list of demands to city officials, and through media interviews they posed the central question: why would a house remain un-used and neglected for seven years despite the city's shortage of affordable housing? According to defendant Dan Sawyer, the Gilmour Street squat "reignited a debate about poverty… during one of the worst housing crises the city had seen."[10] The squat garnered substantial support from neighbours, community activist groups, national unions, affordable housing and tenant support organizations, and a local city councillor. Daily newspaper articles and letters to the editors indicate that both skeptical and supportive Ottawa residents and municipal politicians perceived the Gilmour Street squat as a novel political action. The actual occupation lasted only seven days and the squatters' interactions with municipal government officials — who acted as negotiators for the mayor — and police enforcement were predictably inef-fective and full of empty promises.

The police response was excessive. The deployment of various gas sub-stances and the use of force during the eviction of the Gilmour Street squat were reminiscent of earlier police responses to politicized squats in Montreal and Toronto (*Ottawa Citizen* 2002). According to defendant Mandy Hiscocks:

> The way the police arrested people was pretty typical of a squat action. Coming in strong when they decide to arrest, forcing people out. Other squats in Toronto that has been what has happened. This arrest was [at a] different level, because it was really brutal. The police were a little more armed. A guy with a machine gun, I don't think that is very common in a political operation to evict people from an empty building. A battery arm may be common, smashing the house. It seemed over the top.[11]

The six-hour eviction process involved multiple city vehicles, including fire engines, city buses, and paramedic vans (Freeman and Lamble 2004). In addition to a police force armed with the "regular weapons [as well as] a MP-5 machine gun, rubber bullets and… a gas gun," a battering ram was used to breach several window frames on the third floor of the house in order to deploy the gas substances.[12] The entire city block surrounding 246 Gilmour Street, including several other privately owned properties, was cordoned off by crime scene tape, and supporters were forced to keep away.

Upon their arrest the squatters were held in police custody for thirty-six hours. They were released despite their refusal to sign the original bail conditions, which included a curfew, a clause forbidding the defendants from associating with each other, a ban on all participation in political activity, and a restriction barring them from being within 500 metres of 246 Gilmour Street.[13] The ban on political activity and the non-association clause are fairly standard bail conditions for activists charged by the police in Ontario, but the curfew and geographical restrictions placed on these squatters went beyond this scope.[14]

Each of the twenty-two squatters was initially charged with break and enter with intention to commit mischief, three counts of mischief over $5,000, and obstruction of a peace officer.[15] Over the two years of administrative court proceedings, fifteen of the squatters opted to make a deal with the crown prosecutor and obtained court diversions instructing them each to complete forty hours of community service in lieu of standing trial. The criminal trial of five remaining squat defendants (*R. v. Ackerley et al.*) ensued from September 27 to October 22, 2004. Ultimately, the jury did not find the squatters guilty of a single criminal offence. A couple of months after this verdict was announced, the crown declared a mistrial instead of opting for a retrial. The squatters declared victory.

On Trial

While it is not unusual for activists to appear before a criminal court, the level of cooperation between activists and legal actors varies. Some activists refuse to acknowledge hierarchical authority in the courtroom, by refusing to stand when the judge enters the room, for example, and primarily use the courtroom as a stage to vocalize their political dissent. Others actively engage with the court system, using the law as a tool for achieving their political goals. The approach taken by the Gilmour Street squatters strategically deviated from these two approaches; the squat defendants did not openly dismiss the hierarchical organization of the courts, nor did they wholeheartedly embrace the law as a tool for progressive social change. The squatters were skeptical of modifying their politics to fit within the technical arguments of criminal law, yet at the same time recognized the importance of fighting the criminalization of squatting. For them, going to court was not a choice. However, deciding to work *with* the courts was.

In choosing to actively fight the criminalization of squatting in court, the Gilmour Street squat defendants did more than avoid a conviction or act according to a particular type of politics. They challenged the liberal separation of politics and law in the courtroom and redefined what constitutes a legal victory. Participating in a criminal trial hardly necessitates radical politics or a comprehensive strategy for social change, but the Gilmour Street squatters utilized their position as accused to fight the further criminalization of anti-poverty activism. They expanded the scope for political resistance by inserting political claims and social context into the proceedings of a criminal trial, by refusing to abandon their grassroots politics, and by defending themselves along these lines without the aid of legal counsel.

On the surface, *R. v. Ackerley et al.* proceeded like any other criminal trial. Crown prosecutor David Elhadad began with an opening statement describing the details of the occupation of 246 Gilmour Street, the interactions between the squatters and the property owners, and the criminal charges. The self-represented accused prepared for trial, followed court procedures assiduously, deployed their knowledge of applicable case law, and predominantly conducted their case in a manner respectful of court decorum; they submitted factums, wrote opening and closing arguments, examined and cross-examined witnesses, participated in jury selection, and utilized the traditional defences of necessity and colour of right.[16] During the six weeks of trial, interactions between the squatters, the judge, and the crown appeared to be professional, cordial, and mutually respectful.[17]

In his arguments and closing statement, Elhadad stuck to the technicalities of the criminal charges and relied heavily on video evidence supplied by the Ottawa police. He went through painstakingly detailed accounts of minute damages to the inside of the building, the particulars of the real estate transactions before and after the squat, and highlighted the whereabouts and arrests of each accused. The crown emphasized that the squatters committed mischief by damaging the building, "rendering the property so that the owner could not use it, preventing him from lawfully using and enjoying his property," and refusing to leave the premises.[18] Elhadad also made it clear that it was not his job to "bring to the forefront social issues and decide that those are more important than dealing with the law."[19] The crown representative also voiced his perspective on squatting an abandoned house by stating, "you do not take property which belongs to other people simply to promote your social cause."[20] In contrast to the squatter's defence, the crown's case did not budge from a strictly legal perspective and adhered to the norms of private property ownership.

The squatters' defence strategy made the social context of the housing crisis in Ottawa the basis for their legal arguments. They did not deny that they had entered the house or even that they modified parts of the property. They made it clear that the occupation of the house was a direct response to the housing crisis in Ottawa and should therefore not be viewed as criminal activity. The defendants used the courtroom strategically. Even though the accused never took the stand themselves, the witnesses they called, the content of their opening and closing statements, and their overall approach all demonstrated how politics were relevant to this trial.

Witnesses called to the stand included John Baglow, neighbour to the Gilmour Street residence and then-president of the Public Service Alliance of Canada, and housing advocate Robert MacDonald. Both men commented on the social consequences of the local housing crisis on the stand:

When this squat took place, it managed to put the whole issue of homelessness on the front burner, to attract attention to it, to attract debate, to attract interest broadly across the region in the problem [of homelessness]. I would have to say [the squatters] were more effective than any means that I have employed personally or that my union has employed up to that time.

I think what the squatters did was manage to put that agenda and turn it into a very high profile issue in a way that a lot of the agencies who actually work [on] homelessness on a daily basis were not able to do. I mean, they made an impact; there's no doubt about that.[21]

The witnesses for the defence helped shape the political relevance of this trial. They linked the Gilmour squat to broader campaigns for the rights of the poor and re-affirmed the role of local anti-poverty organizing in Ottawa.

The closing arguments of the defence, presented in turn by each of the accused, similarly emphasized the political significance of the squat by highlighting its community support and the non-criminal intentions behind it. The defendants framed the political necessity of this squat with reference to the traditional legal defences of necessity and colour of right. Defendant Rachelle Sauvé, in her section of the closing arguments, applied the defence of necessity to the squat by asking the jury the following:

Was there really a choice? Were [we] really wrong to act? Could we have protected the right to housing without taking shelter and occupying it? In the reality and extremity of a housing crisis, where people in the city needed housing immediately, while buildings sat abandoned, a decision needed to be made.[22]

Occasionally Justice MacKinnon reprimanded the accused for bringing political claims not directly related to the evidence into their legal arguments. For the most part, however, the squatters were able to integrate the political grounds of the squat within their case. Justice McKinnon's instructions for the jury regarding the defences of colour of right and of necessity highlighted the extent to which the squatters had successfully made the social context of homelessness and the criminalization of poverty the grounding for this trial. In his closing remarks to the jury Justice McKinnon emphasized how the jury could substantiate both the defence of colour of right and necessity when he stated: "In this instance, the accused's honest belief must be that each of them had a right to the property which is the subject matter of the charge," and "here you will evaluate whether homelessness in Ottawa had become a situation so desperate and the peril of the homeless so pressing that it cried out for the actions taken by the accused."[23]

The jury's inability to make a decision on the charge of break and enter with intent to commit mischief illustrates the extent to which the defendants' emphasis on the squat's political context affected the outcome of *R. v. Ackerley et al.* By submitting pamphlets, witness testimonies, and videotape evidence, the defendants emphasized that the intention of the squat was to create permanent housing, not to commit the crime of mischief.[24] The squatters challenged the legal notion that there is no place for politics in a court of law by incorporating the political motivation and social context of the squat within their legal arguments. Their physical presence in and approach to the trial challenged individualistic liberal conceptions of the role of activism in court. Most of the squatters remained apprehensive about working within the confines of the legal system. Consequently they organized their case in a collective manner resembling the politics that they used to organize the squat. According to defendant Mandy Hiscocks:

> We brought politics into the courtroom in how we were organized. When we had ten people with no lawyers, we [still] worked by consensus. The court had to adjust their own process to accommodate us. The judges didn't really mind it as an effective way for a lot of people to represent themselves… stop, huddle, take discussion outside. Then one person would speak for everyone. Highly abnormal for the courts [but it] ran smoothly. Judges were really tolerant of that, all the way through to the end. A big shift they had to make, [it] worked really well.[25]

This consensus-based, collective approach to the act of self-representation enabled the squatters to conduct their case in a manner consistent with their politics as they navigated their way through the regimented aspects of trial.

In fact, skeptics of self-representation on both sides of the legal system viewed the actions of the defendants in a positive light. On the last day of trial, Justice MacKinnon thanked the accused for the "responsible way they acted in their defence" and for the respect they showed the court.[26] After the trial, several of the defendants commented on how proud they were of their achievements in court and referred to the experience as empowering, remarking that it was "one of the more worthwhile activist projects" they had been involved in. They approached the task of self-representation as part of a broader political struggle, and thus were successful in more than their immediate, personal objectives of not being convicted.

The squatters' grassroots politics may not have been as visible in court as they were during the occupation at 246 Gilmour Street, but they were present nonetheless. The decision to represent themselves in court enabled them to structure their defence in the current political context of the state of affordable housing and poverty in Canada. This led to the establishment of what I term non-legal (but legally produced) social precedents. In this way, *R v. Ackerley et al.* is a noteworthy case: it reveals how the legal apparatus does not always extinguish grassroots politics through arrests and criminal trials.

Moving On

From a strict case law perspective, nothing new was gained from the trial of *R. v. Ackerley et al.* A new formal legal precedent concerning the criminality of squatting was not established, alternative uses for traditional defences were not created and (due to the nature of Canadian jury trials), a written legal reasoning for the decision was not produced. If we measure political resistance only in a strict legal framework, and within a definition of effectiveness along those lines, the full meanings attached to political acts such as fighting the criminal marginalization of squatting and anti-poverty activism in Canada are obscured. From this limited perspective, perhaps law does demobilize anti-poverty activism. But fighting the criminalization of political actions, like urban squatting, does more than challenge legal discourse and criminal court procedure.

The case of the Gilmour Street squat is significant beyond narrowly defined legal goals. An informal social precedent was established through the trial that altered how those acting against poverty can form and sustain resistance. Broader positive social change could occur as a result of this precedent because other activists and the public at large have observed how it is possible for activists to fight their charges in court and win. Ottawa-based civil liberties lawyer Yavar Hameed has noted that, by going to trial, self-representing, and not being convicted, the squatters set a social precedent that extended beyond the immediate needs of the squatters.[27] Recognizing the social precedent set by *R. v. Ackerley* contributes to future anti-poverty organizing efforts, reveals how the courts may react to self-represented accused, and redefines the interaction between the legal system and political activism.

Specific gains in social precedent established through *R. v. Ackerley* can lead to the possible development of new resources for self-represented accused. With recently revised eligibility restrictions for Ontario legal aid support, many poor people have difficulty accessing the criminal courts.[28] Any new resources for self-represented accused gained from *R. v. Ackerley* may present a useful tool and framework for future unrepresented accused in Ontario courts. During pre-trial motions the squatters presented an argument outlining why they (as self-represented accused) deserved financial support from Legal Aid Ontario.[29] Even though the legal aid documentation and testimony clearly indicated that a trial judge did not have the authority to grant the squatters' request, the presiding judge suggested that the crown appeal to the Attorney General for a set sum of money in order to ensure a fair trial. In the end, the Attorney General's office supplied financial support for the basic costs of trial, including daily court transcripts, photocopies, and other court-related costs, amounting to over $1,000.[30]

While the allocation of this money was a victory for these defendants, it did not establish any formal legal precedent. The crown clearly indicated that the circumstances of *R. v. Ackerley* were exceptional and that future self-represented accused may not receive the same funding.[31] Despite the lack of a formal legal precedent, though, this victory may have established two social precedents. First, Justice McKinnon and followers of the trial gained awareness about the ineligibility of self-represented accused for legal aid. Second, the case law used by the squatters to ask for financial support may provide an unofficial guideline and motivation for other defendants.[32] The knowledge produced through this specific situation has the potential to be disseminated by personal connections, internet list-serves, and news articles throughout the extended network of anti-poverty activists in Ontario.[33]

The defendants also illustrated how grassroots activists can interact with the criminal courts without demobilizing their politics. Nonetheless, despite the positive verdict, compliments from the judge, and the generally positive experience of the trial, most of the defendants remained critical and wary of political activism in the context of the legal system. Days after the trial ended, two defendants in particular continued to vocalize their apprehension about using the courts as a venue for political activism. In a comparison with the political challenges posed by the Gilmour squat action itself, Dan Sawyer commented: "Court is different. In court we were not calling [political powers] into legitimacy."[34] He concluded that court should be "one of the packages of last resort [and] not part of a comprehensive strategy" for activism.[35] Similarly, defendant Mandy Hiscocks remarked:

> Once I thought that the best way to make social change was to get arrested, change the law. Law is not a good place to make social change but people are going to end up there if they are trying to make social change. Might as well get something out of it. I think you can affect change in the court, not through the laws. Trial shouldn't be the goal of activism.[36]

This critical attitude toward achieving justice through the legal system strengthened the defendants' political convictions and actions in court. As a result, they were meticulous and thorough in making decisions that would coincide with their political values. The defendants did not view the criminal courts as a harbinger for change and thus they defined their victories beyond the confines of traditional legal discourse. A criminal trial was expected to challenge the defendants' anarchist politics and the gains that they made in court were conscious and deliberate. This willingness to engage with the courts while remaining skeptical of them reveals an astute recognition of and resistance to the ways in which the law effectively demobilizes political activism.

Even though the accused in *R v. Ackerley et al.* successfully navigated their way through trial procedures and established several social precedents, the courts are still inaccessible to most people, and are thus not necessarily the best venue for promoting social change. Nonetheless, while numerous legally defined gains may not have resulted, the occupation of 246 Gilmour Street and the accompanying trial highlight how one political action can influence social understandings of urban poverty and of activist engagement against it, both outside and within the criminal courts.

Conclusion

Challenging the criminalization of anti-poverty political actions like squatting is important, but going to court should not always be the goal of activism. In the case of urban squatting, fighting the criminal marginalization of direct actions for housing is necessary. The criminality of squatting an abandoned house during a housing crisis should be challenged. Even though this social precedent is not binding in a strictly defined legal way, it has the potential to foster social change.

Activist engagement with the criminal courts does not fit in dichotomous categories. Criminal prosecution does not necessarily demobilize political activism, nor do activists consistently ascribe to liberal notions of individualized rights that inhere in the criminal justice system. The Gilmour Street squatters balanced on a tenuous political line. They did not dismiss the law altogether or make a mockery of the hierarchy of the criminal courts, but neither did they idealize the courts as the holy grail of justice. The Gilmour Street squat defendants worked within the court when necessary and transferred to their trial the grassroots politics that they had cultivated during their squat.

The Gilmour Street defendants pushed the boundaries of liberal definitions of legal process and victory and made a space for political activism in the criminal courts. By weaving the social context of poverty, homelessness, and affordable housing into legal arguments and procedure, the defendants consistently kept their politics at the forefront of this trial. The criminality of squatting and anti-poverty activism was questioned and a legally defined acquittal was not the only victory achieved.

Five anti-poverty activists represented themselves in court and were not convicted of an indictable criminal offence. Through media interviews, magazine articles, and other public forums these activists engaged significant segments of community from Ottawa and beyond — including but not limited to national union presidents and workers, representatives of the mayor's office, and prominent city councillors — in a public debate on housing and homelessness that was not present before the squat and trial. The squatters also set a social precedent for future anti-poverty political actions in Canada.

The trial of the Gilmour Street squatters gives hope and leads us to seriously reconsider how we view the victories resulting from political activism, both in the streets and the courts. Progressive social change may not be bundled in a neat package. As seen in the case of the Gilmour Street squatters, social gains can easily be lost within traditional legal discourse and procedures. When we push beyond established categories, however, a space for political resistance can be made. Challenging the criminality of squatting and of anti-poverty activism in court is a necessary part of, but not the only tool in, the fight against the criminalization of poverty.

Notes

1. *R. v. Ackerley et al.* (Ottawa Sup. CT.J. Crim-div October 21, 2004).
2. *R. v. Ackerley et al.* (October 21, 2004).
3. For stories about other Canadian squats see S. Hemingway, 1997, "6 in Protest Get Bail and a Warning," *Toronto Star*, April 21; T. Clardige, 1998, "Abandoned Building's Squatters Use Charter to Fight Charges," *Globe and Mail*, October 29; C. Dunphy, 2000, "Squatters Told to Get Out — Unsigned Notice Says Owner Must 'Secure' Tent City," *Toronto Star*, December 15; I. Peritz, 2001, "Montreal Police Evict Squatters, Stun Gun Used Against One of Seven Facing Charges After Confrontation," *Globe and Mail*, October 4; W. Imnen and J. Rusk, 2002, "Toronto's Tent City Sealed Off, Squatters Ejected," *Globe and Mail*, September 25; Unknown author, 2002, "Building Called Fire Hazard, Squatters Forced to Leave [Parkdale Pope squat]," *Globe and Mail*, November 2; D. Girard, 2002, "Fighting for a Home — Vancouver's Squatters Try to turn Need for Refuge Into a Cause," *Toronto Star*, Oct 5; B. Gray, 2004, "It was the Wrong Squat; Cops Chuck Out Protestors at Old Police Headquarters," *Toronto Sun*, November 14; L. Freeman and S. Lamble, 2004, "Squatting and the City," *Canadian Dimension* 38, 6 (November–December).
4. This chapter is based on ethnographic research including interviews with the Gilmour Street squatters, Ottawa-based lawyers, participant observation, and an analysis of court transcripts. The research was completed for my M.A. thesis, L. Freeman, 2005, "The Legal Geography of Urban Squatting: The Case of Ottawa's Gilmour Street Squatters," Carleton University. My personal experience with the Gilmour Street squat case informs this chapter — being arrested at the squat, defending myself and representing others at administrative trials, conducting community service instead of being prosecuted through a trial, supporting the squatters during their trial, and writing magazine articles about the squat, as well as casual correspondence with other Canadian squatters and anti-poverty activists.
5. See P. Conradi, 2004, "Tenants from Hell with the Law on their Side," *(London) Sunday Times*, April 18; Katsiaficas 1997.
6. *R. v. Clarke* (O.J. No. 5259 1998). Montreal's Overdale squat began with a march

of 500 people, Toronto's Pope squat was led by a march of 1,000 anti-poverty demonstrators, and Ottawa's Gilmour Street squat was part of an anti-Group of Eight rally of approximately 3,500 demonstrators. On the G-8 see note 9 below.

7. Vancouver's Woodward's squat and Toronto's Pope squat both lasted approximately three months, whereas Ottawa's Gilmour Street squat and Peterborough's Water Street squat lasted a week. Many other squats have lasted mere hours. Toronto's most recent squat (June 2007), conducted by members of the Women Against Poverty Collective, was evicted approximately six hours after it was publicly acknowledged.

8. *R. v. Ackerley et al.* (October 21, 2004).

9. The Group of Eight (G-8) is a political forum where government leaders gather to discuss global economic issues. G-8 member countries are Canada, France, Germany, Italy, Japan, Russia, the United Kingdom, and the United States. For more information on the G-8, refer to the Halifax Initiatives report: "The G8, Globalization and Human Security: A Resource Package and Facilitator's Guide," *Halifax Initiative*, available at <halifaxinitiative.org>. For articles critical of the G-8 refer to S. Hodkinson, 2005, "Inside the Murky World of the UK's Make Poverty History Campaign," *Znet*, available at <zmag.org/content/showarticle.cfm?ItemID=8181>; M. Jarman, 2005, "G8 Climate," *Znet*, available at <zmag.org/content/showarticle.cfm?ItemID=8188>; G. Monbiot, 2005, "The Man Who Betrayed the Poor," *Znet*, available at <zmag.org/content/showarticle.cfm?ItemID=8685>.

10. Dan Sawyer, interviewed by author, December 14, 2004.

11. Mandy Hiscocks, interviewed by author, tape recording, December 2, 2004.

12. *R. v. Ackerley et al.* (October 21, 2004).

13. *R. v. Ackerley et al.* (October 21, 2004), Official Disclosure of Evidence (2002).

14. Law student and Peterborough Coalition Against Poverty activist Nitti Simmonds informed me that in her experience working with anti-poverty groups across Ontario, non-association clauses and bans on political activity are common bail conditions when activists affiliated with anti-poverty groups are arrested. Bail conditions are seldom recorded in the media, thus records of activist bail conditions are informally acknowledged within activist networks. Nitti Simmonds, telephone interview by author, February 2007.

15. *R. v. Ackerley et al.* (October 21, 2004), Official Disclosure of Evidence (2002).

16. *R. v. Ackerley et al.* (October 21, 2004).

17. Field notes, observed by author, September 28–October 12, 2004.

18. *R. v. Ackerley et al.* (October 21, 2004).

19. *R. v. Ackerley et al.* (October 21, 2004).

20. *R. v. Ackerley et al.* (October 21, 2004).

21. *R. v. Ackerley et al.* (October 21, 2004).

22. Rachelle Sauvé, interviewed by author, tape recording, December 2, 2004. In his charge to the Jury, J. McKinnon described colour of right as "a honest belief in a state of facts which, if it existed, would be a lawful justification or excuse for a person's conduct." According to J. McKinnon, the defence of necessity "recognizes that a liberal and humane criminal law cannot require strict obedience to laws in genuine emergencies where normal human instincts, whether of self-preservation or helping others, overwhelmingly inspired disobedience" and "is only available

to those whose wrongful acts are committed under pressure which no reasonable person could withstand." *R. v. Ackerley et al.* (October 21, 2004). For more information on colour of right see: *R. v. Howson* (1966). On the defence of necessity see *R. v. Latimer* (1 S.C.R. 3, 193 D.L.R. (4th) 577, 2001 SCC1 [2001].

23. *R. v. Ackerley et al.* (October 21, 2004).
24. Field notes, September 28–October 12, 2004.
25. Hiscocks interview, December 2, 2004.
26. Field notes, September 28–October 12, 2004.
27. Yavar Hameed, interviewed by author, tape recording, January 7, 2005.
28. Information on the increase of self-represented accused in Ottawa's criminal court is based on casual observations with legal actors and defendants conducted during research from September 28–October 12, 2004.
29. Hiscocks interview, December 2, 2004.
30. *R. v. Ackerley et al.* (October 21, 2004).
31. *R. v. Ackerley et al.* (October 21, 2004).
32. According to self-represented accused Dan Sawyer, there was not any case law used for this decision. The squat defendants were asking for money for disbursements (photocopies, etc.) and were not asking to be paid for their labour. A legal aid lawyer attended court and (with the squatters present) the presiding judge asked if Legal Aid Ontario would be comfortable with allocating money to the accused. The legal aid lawyer answered in the affirmative and the crown representative disbursed the funds to the squatters many months after the trial. This decision, according to Sawyer, may be the only case law where self-represented accused were allocated money to mount a defence. Sawyer interview, December 14, 2004.
33. Discussions and announcements were posted on activist list-serves and web-based news sources: *A-Infos: Anarchist News Service* <www.ainfos.ca>; *Thunder Bay Indy Media* <http://thunderbay.indymedia.org/>; "Montreal Activist Arrest and Trial Calendar (2000–2005)" <http://www.ainfos.ca/05/jan/ainfos00363.html>, <www.cmaq.net>, and <www.infoshop.org>. Information about the trial was also disseminated through informal publications such as Mandy Hiscocks, "Stunning Legal Victory for Ottawa Squatters," *Critical Times* 2, 3 (CUPE 3903, York University Faculty Association, CUPE 1281 Grad Students Association, 2004); Mandy Hiscocks and Amy Miller, "In the Streets and in the Courts: How the Seven-Year Squat Fought and Won," *The Rabble-Rouser's Guide to Surviving Law School: A Disorientation Handbook McGill Radical Law Committee* (McGill Radical Law Community, 2006).
34. Dan Sawyer interview, December 14, 2004.
35. Dan Sawyer interview, December 14, 2004.
36. Hiscocks interview, December 2, 2004.

Chapter 14

On the Streets There's No Forgetting Your Body

Jeff Shantz

On the streets there's no forgetting your body. Its hunger gnaws at you constantly. Tired bones offer regular reminders that pavement makes a rotten mattress. Skin burns from the heat of sun and the lash of wind. The wet cold of rain… the entire body shivers from the marrow outward. My homeless body is the low-end site of biopolitics. It is the low-rent district in which postmodern struggles are engaged. The street is the prime example of what Mary Louise Pratt (1991) calls a "contact zone," those spaces in which cultures meet, clash, and wrestle with each other. Despite the postmodern emphasis on playful encounter, these contacts are quite often brutal and vicious. Poor people are subjected to ongoing violence simply because of the poverty that we embody:

> "Those cheaters on welfare are useless,"
> the young man says. "The best thing
> to do is set up a machine gun
> at Hastings and Main
> and open fire.
> They're gonna die anyway, so it
> might as well be sooner as later." (Cameron 1998)

Sandy Cameron's poem expresses a view that I have overheard many times from allegedly respectable citizens: I am not worthy of living. My body is expendable. My body is viewed as garbage. In a popular series of ads for a Toronto radio station a homeless person is depicted sitting on a garbage can; emblazoned on the photo is the word "PEST." A middle-class tourist is overheard to say about those of us who rest outside his hotel: "The kindest thing would be to get them all drunk and just put them to sleep. Nobody would know the difference. Nobody knows them. They'd never be missed." Graffiti screaming, "Kill the poor" has shown up around town over the last few years.

The threatened violence is too often played out for real. There has been an increase recently in the number of physical attacks on homeless people by neo-Nazi gangs. We are reminded of the vulnerability of our bodies when a friend is killed while sleeping in a park or dies from the winter nights or her body turns up in an alley near the streets where she worked. Not long ago a self-styled street vigilante physically attacked me, screaming that he was "cleaning the garbage off the streets." The intersection of inferiorized subject positions in his thinking was clear as he identified me as a "faggot," and my partner as a "whore," by virtue of our being on the streets. As Jean Swanson suggests, "The poor in Canada are not yet being murdered by government bullets, although some of them are being murdered when they try to supplement inadequate welfare rates with prostitution" (Swanson 2001: 104). Swanson also points out that "the contempt, the lies, the innuendo, and the stereotypes of the media and the politicians are the first manipulating steps to the hatred that must be necessary before killing seems acceptable" (Swanson 2001: 104–105).

My body, when it is living on the streets, is painfully exposed. I have no shelter and few defences. Our life expectancy in Canada is six and a half years shorter than for wealthier, housed people. My body simply stands less of a chance of being around than the likely reader of this book. Mine is an ephemeral body, even in the mortal human terms of life expectancy, a concept that exists for others with the time to sit around and worry about it. This is naked life. As Giorgio Agamben (2000) notes in his discussion of naked life, we are the ones whose lives are considered worthless. We are the exception to the human subject of modern sovereignty. We are the lives (and there are many, including indigenous people and non-status immigrants) who are deemed not part of the citizenry (Agamben 2000). Being labelled criminals, deviants, thugs, and pests, as homeless people too often are, erases my humanity; it places me in the realm of the post-human. I was human once, but that was before I allegedly chose to abandon civil society and its work ethic and become the despised "street youth," the mere echo of a person. Naked life: a condition of violence.

These politics of exclusion remove our poor bodies from civil society and the realm of citizenship. Governments do not invite us to take part in discussions on issues that affect our lives. Poor people do not fill the comfortable chairs at summits on living and working opportunities. We are not asked to tell our own stories. We are treated as objects rather than subjects. We do not design the experiment, and we are not invited to present the findings: "Poor people have as much control over government experiments or think-tank theorizing about their future as lab rats have in a cancer experiment" (Swanson 2001: 77–78). bell hooks notes that while it is now fashionable to talk about overcoming racism and sexism, class remains "the uncool subject" that makes people tense. Despite being such a pressing issue class is not talked about in a society in which the poor have no public voice; breaking this silence is crucial. As hooks notes, however, "we are afraid to have a dialogue about class even though the ever widening gap between rich and poor has already set the stage for ongoing and sustained class warfare" (hooks 2004: 5).

Toronto's homeless have suffered years of vicious attacks by various levels of government, and 2005 was no exception. On February 1, 2005, Toronto City Council voted to accept a proposal to ban homeless people from sleeping in Nathan Phillips Square. The amendment to by-law 1994-0784 says, "no person can camp in the square" (which includes sleeping in the square during the day or night, whether or not a tent or temporary abode of any kind is used). Council went further and decided to extend the ban to all city property. This move to ban homeless people from sleeping in public spaces is part of a City Staff Report "From the Street into Homes: A Strategy to Assist Homeless Persons to Find Permanent Housing" (Staff Report of the City of Toronto 2005). In discussing "ways to address street homelessness" the report suggests "enhanced legal and legislative frameworks and more enforcement of current provincial laws and city by-laws." The report also "recommends that the Toronto Police Service be requested to participate in the work of the Street Outreach Steering Committee." Behind the report's velvet language of "outreach" one finds the iron fist of the Toronto Police. This is an open invitation for more attacks by police on homeless people. In 2005 this offered little more than an excuse to expand already bloated Toronto Police budgets, and these have expanded steadily in recent years, even in the face of the recent recession. By 2009, at around $855 million the Police budget gobbles up 25 percent of Toronto's net operating budget.[1]

These policies are a throwback to the brutal days of former mayor Mel Lastman, who engaged in an open campaign of class war against poor and homeless people (whom he labelled "thugs"). In 1999, with much fanfare and plenty of snarling, spitting, and gnashing of teeth, Lastman and City Council launched a Community Action Policing (CAP) program backed by $2 million in public funds. The following year the city found another $1 million in a supposedly tight budget. Following the model of Rudolph Giuliani's rampage in New York City, the money was spent to pay police overtime to harass, intimidate, and threaten poor people in targeted areas of the city. Each year the police have kept up their campaign into the fall. After that they hope Mother Nature will put in the overtime for them. As the inspector in charge of the operation stated at its launch: "The best crime-fighting tool we have is minus 30 in February" (Barber 1999: A10). Having no home is now a crime. Given that homeless people have frozen to death on the streets of Toronto it would appear that capital punishment is practised in Canada after all, but only if your crime is poverty. The then provincial Tory government, with much prodding from Lastman and his allies on Toronto City Council, changed the Ontario

Highway Act to define squeegeeing and "aggressive" panhandling as illegal. The Safe Streets Act makes it illegal to "cause a reasonable person to be concerned for his or her safety or security" (whatever that might be).[2] This law has given police, local vigilantes, and business improvement associations great leeway to continue or expand their harassment of the poor and homeless.

The Toronto Council's 2005 "From the Streets into Homes Report" recommended that this brutal legislation be enforced more systematically (Staff Report of the City of Toronto 2005). Many Torontonians had hoped for more under the new council headed by the supposedly progressive Mayor David Miller, elected in late 2003. Unfortunately, the current council is showing that, like the one before, it favours criminalizing homeless people rather than developing real solutions such as affordable housing. The year after he was elected mayor, Miller's office sent bulldozers under the Bathurst Street bridge to destroy the homes of a community of teenaged street youth (Ontario Coalition Against Poverty 2004).

This attack was accompanied by a heightened police presence on the streets. The corners of Queen and Spadina and Queen and Bathurst were hardest hit, where police harassed, ticketed, and arrested homeless people who access services in these areas. In addition, ticketing and arrests under legislation such as the Safe Streets Act was stepped up. Young people have found themselves in jail for minor infractions and released on stringent bail conditions: they are not to possess cups and cleaning equipment, and are prohibited access to parts of the city. Along with the mass ticketing, police have used pepper spray to awaken youth sleeping on the streets. The city also revitalized a "Park Ambassador" program to harass homeless people in city parks; along with their efforts to drive squeegeers out of the city, the police were busy chasing homeless people out of so-called public parks. Poverty is okay, just keep it out of sight. A vicious crackdown has been in effect for some time now. Police routinely ticket us for anything, be it trespassing, loitering, or littering. Likewise some store owners verbally or physically attack panhandlers or get the police to do it for them. Police claim that they are not trying to rid the city of homeless kids when they ticket squeegeers, just trying to keep people from stepping into the roadway. So far, however, there has been little demonizing rhetoric or harassment related to the jaywalking scourge by those who are not poor.[3]

It is important to consider this ongoing history of Toronto's preference for criminalizing homeless people rather than addressing the root social and economic causes of homelessness, such as lack of affordable housing, and social services, and access to living wage jobs. Council's actions serve to distort as criminal conditions that are fundamentally social and economic. People sleep at City Hall because the shelters are full and conditions in many are dreadful. People are forced to sleep outside because there is not enough affordable housing. By removing the homeless from Nathan Phillips Square, politicians hoped to remove a major political embarrassment from under their noses. They also sent a message to every police officer, city official, and narrow-minded vigilante in Toronto that it is open season on the homeless.

While Community Action Policing was touted as the "best and latest thinking on community-based policing" (Barber 1999: A10) none of this is new. These are the same tactics the bosses have hit us with for centuries (they called them "poor laws" in sixteenth-century England). The names change but the intentions remain the same. Along with programs like work-fare and the reduction in or elimination of social services, criminalization is about driving the poor, unemployed, and homeless into wage slavery or death. Serve capital or go away! In case this point is missed the soft police in social services launched a "Squeegee Work Youth Mobilization" program to teach squeegeers to get jobs repairing bikes ($250,000 from city council and $395,000 from the federal government). What was not reported was that this program was a complement to Community Action Policing, with police involved in its implementation and decision-making.[4] Despite the great career prospects for bike repairers, the city Commissioner of Community and Social Services has admitted the program faces some obstacles: "The challenge is this is a group of kids that does not fit into the system. They are very wary of any kind of authority — police, schools and even social agen-cies" (Elliott and Immen 1999: A9). *Globe and Mail* July 27, 1999: A9). The nerve of some people's kids.

Despite the images conjured up by names like vagabond, drifter, or hobo, being homeless is an experience of bodily and spatial confinement: "Poor bashing is being told you aren't free to go where you choose" (Swanson 2001: 19). More and more, poor bodies are constrained bodies. We cannot avoid each other's bodies the way middle-class suburbanites can. Our notions of property and privacy are vastly different from those who have plenty of liv-ing space. In hostels and shelters our bodies are crammed together in small spaces under conditions that do not even meet United Nations guidelines for refugee camps. Going to shelters can leave us beaten up, having our few belongings stolen, or contracting tuberculosis, supposedly a disease of the past that is rampant in contemporary shelters. Ironically, given our immobility, our bodies are time travellers picking up ancient illnesses that the rest of the population only reads about in history books.

The ticket to mobility is the capacity to spend. As hooks notes, "No matter your class, no matter your race, if you have access to credit, to cash, every store is open to you" (hooks 2004: 82). If you lack the possibility of being a consumer, all doors are slammed in your face. Nowhere is this clearer than in the criminalization of poverty, when the body ends up in cells and courtrooms. Our bodies are public sites of struggle, matters of great contest.

My poor body is beaten by police and would-be vigilantes "cleaning up the streets," insulted by professionals, and dragged into courts; it endures days in welfare and legal aid offices.

Still, my body is also a site of strength, standing in solidarity, withstanding blows. When you have lived on the streets and dealt with various abuses the body becomes resilient. To survive I struggle over perceptions of my body and the meanings attached to it. Opposing poor-bashing is a good way to confront the internalized messages of shame and blame over our situation. This opposition can stop the bashers, deconstruct the messages about poverty and its causes, and provide a starting point for organizing with other poor people to fight poverty. Part of that struggle involves recounting our stories, providing glimpses into the many "contact zones" — the streets, struggles, and courts — in which our bodies live. Sometimes telling our stories, raising our voices enough to be heard beyond the streets, requires a good old-fashioned bread riot. We are hungry, let us eat. We are weary, let us rest.

Notes

1   "This is an increase of 4 percent over the 2008 police net budget, which was a 5 percent increase over the 2007 budget, which was a 4.5 percent increase over the 2006 figure." The 2009 budget "is about 30 per cent more than the 2004 net budget of $677 million." See Toronto Police Accountability Coalition, "Toronto Police Accountability Bulletin No. 46, March 26, 2009," available at <tpac.ca/show_bulletin.cfm?id=135>.

2   Ontario Safe Streets Act, 1999, c. 8, s. 2 (1).

3   For more recent developments around the criminalization of the poor see also OCAP's bulletins at <update.ocap.ca/housing>.

4   See J. Shantz, n.d., "Attacks on the poor and homeless continue, resistance builds class war in Ontario." A-Info is a multi-lingual news service by, for, and about anarchists at <ainfos.ca/01/dec/ainfos00018.html>.

References

Adam, B., U. Beck, and J. Van Loon. 2000. *The Risk Society and Beyond: Critical Issues for Social Theory*. London: Sage.

Agamben, G. 2000. *Means Without End: Notes on Politics*. Minneapolis: University of Minnesota Press.

Alberta Family and Social Services. 1999. *Annual Report, 1998/99*. Edmonton: Alberta Family and Social Services.

_____. 1996. *Annual Report, 1995/96*. Edmonton: Alberta Family and Social Services.

_____. 1995. *Annual Report, 1994/95*. Edmonton: Alberta Family and Social Services.

_____. 1989 *Report on the Eligibility and Benefit Verification Project and Related Initiatives*. Edmonton: Alberta Family and Social Services, Income Support Branch.

_____. 1988. *Briefing Notes: Evaluation of Fraud and Error Initiatives*. Edmonton: Alberta Family and Social Services, Income Support Branch.

Alberta Human Resources and Employment. 2005. *HR&E Full-Time Equivalents, Staffing, 1993/94 to 2004/05*. Edmonton: Alberta Human Resources and Employment.

Alberta Social Services and Community Health. 1979. *Summary of Findings: Final Report of the Welfare Ineligibility Study: Fraud and Error in the Public Assistance Program*. Edmonton: Alberta Social Services and Community Health.

Alianza, C. 1995. *Torture of Guatemalan Street Children: Report to the U.N. Committee Against Torture, 1990–1995*. Costa Rica: Covenant House.

Americas Watch and Physicians for Human Rights. 1991. *Guatemala: Getting Away with Murder: An Americas Watch and Physicians for Human Rights Report*. New York: Human Rights Watch.

Amnesty International. 2006. "Amnesty International Report on Guatemala." Available at <web.amnesty.org/report2006/gtm-summary-eng>.

Arsenault, C. 2003. "From Street to Squat in Halifax." *Canadian Dimension* 37, 1.

Aylward, C. 1999. *Canadian Critical Race Theory: Racism and the Law*. Halifax: Fernwood Publishing.

Azmier, J., and R. Roach. 1997. *Welfare Reform in Alberta: A Survey of Former Recipients*. Calgary: Canada West Foundation.

Bailey, I. 1997. "Guards Ask Panhandlers to Move: At Least Four Neighbourhood Business Groups, Including Gastown and Chinatown, Have Hired Their Own Security Guards after Losing Patence with Street People They Say Are Bad for Business." *Vancouver Sun*, December 22.

Balakrishnan, T., and K. Selvanthan. 1990. "Ethnic Residential Segregation in Metropolitan Canada." In Hilli, Trovato, and Driedger (eds.), *Ethnic Demography*. Ottawa: Carleton University Press.

Barber. 1999. *Globe and Mail*, July 26: A10.

Barry, A., T. Osborne, and N. Rose. 1996. *Foucault and Political Reason: Liberalism, Neo-liberalism and Rationalities of Government*. Chicago: University of Chicago Press.

Bauman, Z. 2004. "Living (Occasionally Dying) Together in an Urban World." In

S. Graham (ed.), *Cities, War and Terrorism*. Malden, MA: Blackwell.

Beazley, F. 2002. "Information Report." Halifax: Halifax Regional Police Department.

Beck, U., and E. Beck-Gernsheim. 2002. *Individualization*. London: Sage.

Berti, M. 2007. "Handcuffed Access: Homelessness and the Justice System." Paper presented at the Association of American Geographers Annual Meeting, San Francisco.

Bezanson, Kate. 2006. *Gender, the State and Social Reproduction: Household Insecurity in Neo-liberal Times*. Toronto: University of Toronto Press.

Bhanji, Z. 2004. "From Programs to Policy Responses: A Study of Interventions with Street Children in Nairobi, Kenya." M.A. thesis, Dalhousie University.

Birch, A. 2000. "Guatemala's Street Children: Forging Survival Paths." *Development* 43, 1.

Black, J., and Y. Stanford. 2005. "When Henry and Martha Are Poor: The Poverty of Alberta's Social Assistance Programs." In T. Harrison (ed.), *The Return of the Trojan Horse: Alberta and the New World (Dis)Order*. Montreal: Black Rose.

Black Action Defence Committee. 2001. "End The Shootings."

Boessenkool, K. 1997. *Back to Work: Learning From the Alberta Welfare Experiment*. Toronto: C.D. Howe Institute.

Bonefeld, W. 1993. *The Recomposition of the British State During the 1980s*. Dartmouth, UK: Aldershot.

Bortich, H., and J. Hagan. 1987. "Crime and Changing Forms of Class Control: Policing Public Order in 'Toronto the Good', 1859–1955." *Social Forces* 66, 2.

Boyd, N. 1988. *The Last Dance: Murder in Canada*. Toronto: Prentice Hall Canada.

Brenner, N., and N. Theodore. 2002. *Spaces of Neoliberalism: Urban Restructuring in North America and Western Europe*. Boston: Blackwell Publishers.

Brodeur, J., with G. Ouellet. 2004. "What Is a Crime? A Secular Answer." In Law Commission of Canada, *What Is a Crime? Defining Criminal Conduct in Contemporary Society*. Vancouver: University of British Columbia Press.

Brown, E., and S. Herbert. 2006. "Conceptions of Space and Crime in the Contemporary Neoliberal City." *Antipode* 38, 4.

Brown, W. 2003. "Neo-liberalism and the End of Liberal Democracy." *Theory and Event* 7, 1.

Brunson, R., and J. Miller. 2006. "Gender, Race, and Urban Policing: The Experience of African American Youths." *Gender and Society* 20, 4.

Burchell, G., et al. 1991. *The Foucault Effect*. Chicago: University of Chicago Press.

Caiazza, A. 2005. "Don't Bowl at Night: Gender, Safety, and Civic Participation." *Signs: Journal of Women in Culture and Society* 30, 2: 1608.

Cameron, Barbara. 2006. "Social Reproduction and Canadian Federalism." In Kate Bezanson and Meg Luxton (eds.), *Social Reproduction: Feminist Political Economy Challenges Neo-liberalism*. Montreal and Kingston: McGill-Queen's University Press.

Cameron, S. 1998. *Downtown Eastside Poems*. Second edition. Vancouver: Lazara Press.

Campeau, G. 2004. *From UI To EI: Waging War on the Welfare State*. Trans. Richard Howard. Vancouver: University of British Columbia Press.

Campfens, H. 1997. *Community Development Around the World: Practice, Theory, Research,*

Training. Toronto: University of Toronto Press

Canada West Foundation. 1998. *Red Ink IV: Back from the Brink?* Calgary: Canada West Foundation.

Canadian Press Newswire. 2001. "Community Alliances Ready to Renovate Pope Squat." November 11.

Chan, W., and G. Rikagos. 2002. "Risk, Crime and Gender." *British Journal of Criminology* 42, 4: 43–61.

City of Vancouver. 2001. "Administrative Report: Panhandling by-Law. From the City Manager to Vancouver City Council."

_____. 1998. "Administrative Report: Panhandling: From the City Manager to the Standing Committee on Planning and Environment."

Clark, W. 1989. "Residential Segregation in American Cities: Common Ground and Differences in Interpretation." *Population Research and Policy Review* 8.

Colebourn, A. 1997. "Homeless Problem Makes Mess of Park: Police Called in to Deal with Overcrowding." *Vancouver Province*, August 20.

Coleman, R. 2004. "Images from a Neoliberal City: The State, Surveillance and Social Control," *Critical Criminology* 12, 1: 23.

Collins, D., and N. Blomley. 2001. "Private Needs and Public Space: Politics, Poverty and Anti-Panhandling By-laws in Canadian Cities." In Law Commission of Canada (eds.), *Legal Dimensions*. Ottawa: Law Commission of Canada.

Comack, E., and G. Balfour. 2004. *The Power to Criminalize: Violence, Inequality and the Law*. Halifax: Fernwood Publishing.

Comaroff, J., and J.L. Comaroff. 2001. *Millennial Capitalism and the Culture of Neoliberalism*. Durham: Duke University Press.

Committee to Stop Targeted Policing. 2000. *Who's the Target?* Toronto: Committee to Stop Targeted Policing.

Cranford, C., and L. Vosko. 2006. "Conceptualizing Precarious Employment: Mapping Wage Work Across Social Location and Occupational Context." In L. Vosko (ed.), *Precarious Employment: Understanding Labour Market Insecurity in Canada*. Montreal/Kingston: McGill-Queen's University Press.

da Silva, A. 1992. *Earnings of Immigrants: A Comparative Analysis*. Ottawa: Economic Council of Canada.

de Wolff, A. 2000. *Breaking the Myth of Flexible Work*. Toronto: Contingent Workers Project.

Davidson, Kolin. 2000. Defendant's Book of Affidavits. *R. v. David Banks et al.*, par. 17.

Davis, M. 1992. *City of Quartz: Excavating the Future of Los Angeles*. New York: Vintage.

Day, Kristen. 2001. "Constructing Masculinist and Women's Fear in Public Space in Irvine, California." *Gender, Place and Culture* 8, 2: 109–27.

Drislane, R., and G. Parkinson. 2006. *Online Dictionary of the Social Sciences*. Available at <bitbucket.icaap.org/dict.pl> July 10.

Dua, E. 1999. "Beyond Diversity: Exploring the Ways in Which the Discourse of Race has Shaped the Institution of the Nuclear Family." In E. Dua and A. Robertson (eds.), *Scratching the Surface: Canadian Anti-Racist Feminist*. Toronto: Women's Press.

Duggan, L. 2003. *The Twilight of Equality? Neoliberalism, Cultural Politics, and the Attack on Democracy*. Boston: Beacon Press.

Dye, Thomas (ed.). 1998. *Understanding Public Policy*. Toronto: Prentice Hall.

Earls, F., and M. Carlson. 1999. "Children at the Margins of Society: Research and Practice." In M. Raffaelli and R. Larson (eds.), *Homeless and Working Youth Around the World: Exploring Developmental Issues*. San Francisco: Jossey-Bass Publishers.

Eberts, M., and G. Brodsky. 1986. *LEAF Litigation, Year One*. Toronto: LEAF.

Ellickson, R. 2001. "Controlling Chronic Misconduct in City Spaces: Of Panhandlers, Skid Rows, and Public-space Zoning." In N. Blomley, D. Delaney, and R. Ford (eds.), *The Legal Geographies Reader*. Oxford: Blackwell Publishers.

Elliott and Immen. 1999. *Globe and Mail*, July 27: A9.

Elton, D., J. Sieert, J. Azmier, and R. Roach. 1997. *Where Are They Now? Assessing the Impact of Welfare Reform on Former Recipients, 1993–1996*. Calgary: Canada West Foundation.

Ensign, J. 1998. "Health Issues of Homeless Youth." *Journal of Social Distress and the Homeless* 7, 3.

Ensign, J., and M. Bell. 2004. "Illness Experiences of Homeless Youth." *Qualitative Health Research* 14, 9.

Ericson, R., and K. Haggerty. 1997. *Policing the Risk Society*. Toronto: University of Toronto Press.

Esmonde, J. 2002. "Criminalizing Poverty: The Criminal Law Power and the Safe Streets Act." *Journal of Law and Social Policy* 17.

_____. 1999. "Neoliberalism, Youth Poverty and Washing Windshields: An Ethnographic Study of Squeegeeing in Toronto." M.A. thesis, York University.

Esping-Anderson, G. 1990. *The Three Worlds of Welfare Capitalism*. Princeton: Princeton University Press.

Falkiner-Budgell, S. 2002. "Busting Welfare: I took the Tories' spouse-in-the-house law to court and won." *Now Magazine*, Online Edition, June 6–12.

Fay, J. 1997. "From Welfare Bum to Single Mum: The Political Construction of Single Mothers on Social Assistance in Nova Scotia 1966–77." Master's thesis, Dalhousie University School of Social Work.

Feagin, J. 1975. *Subordinating the Poor: Welfare and American Beliefs*. Englewood, NJ: Prentice Hall.

Federation of Canadian Municipalities. n.d. *National Affordable Housing Strategy*. Available at <fcm.ca/english/documents/afford.html>.

Fingard, J. 1993. "The 1880s: Paradoxes of Progress." In E.R. Forbes and D.A. Muise (eds.), *The Atlantic Provinces in Confederation*. Toronto: University of Toronto Press.

Fischer, B. 2000. "Community Policing: A Study of Local Policing, Order and Control." PhD diss., University of Toronto.

Flanagan, G. 2005. "Not Just About Money: Provincial Budgets and Political Ideology." In T. Harrison (ed.), *The Return of the Trojan Horse: Alberta and the New World (Dis)Order*. Montreal: Black Rose.

Fleury, D. 2007. *A Study of Poverty and Working Poverty among Recent Immigrants to Canada*. Human Resources and Social Development Canada.

Fong, E. 1997. "A Systemic Approach to Racial Residential Segregation." *Social Science Research* 26.

Fong, E., and M. Gulia. 1999. "Differences in Neighbourhood Qualities among Racial and Ethnic Groups in Canada." *Sociology Inquiry* 69, 4.

_____. 1996. "The Attainment of Neighbourhood Qualities among British, Chinese, and Black Immigrants in Toronto and Vancouver." *Research in Community Sociology* 6.

Fong, E., and K. Shibuya. 2000. "The Spatial Separation of the Poor in Canadian Cities." *Demography* 37, 4.

Forbes, E.R. 1993. "The 1930s: Depression and Retrenchment." In E.R. Forbes and D.A. Muise (eds.), *The Atlantic Provinces in Confederation*. Toronto: University of Toronto Press.

Foucault, M. 1978. *Discipline and Punish: The Birth of the Prison*. Trans. Alan Sheridan. New York: Pantheon.

Fox, B., and P. Sugiman. 1999. "Flexible Work, Flexible Workers: The Restructuring of Clerical Work in the Large Telecommunications Company." *Studies in Political Economy* 60.

Fraser, A. 2005. "Homeless Advocate Bounced from City Council Meeting." *Chronicle-Herald*, June 15 <www.herald.ns.ca/stories/2005/06/15/f132.raw.html>.

Fraser, N., and L. Gordon. 1994. "A Genealogy of Dependency: Tracing a Keyword of the U.S. Welfare State." *Signs: Journal of Women in Culture and Society* 21.

Freeman, L., and S. Lamble. 2004. "Squatting and the City." *Canadian Dimension* 38, 6.

Fudge, J., and H. Glasbeek. 2003. "Civil Disobedience, Civil Liberties, and Civil Resistance: Law's Role and Limits." *Osgoode Hall Law Journal* 41: 2, 3.

Gaetz, S. 2004. "Safe Streets for Whom? Homeless Youth, Social Exclusion, and Criminal Victimization." *Canadian Journal of Criminology and Criminal Justice* 46, 4.

Galabuzi, G. 2007. "The Pathologies of Blackness, Brownness and Muslim Identity within the Context of National Security and Community Safety Regime in Early 21st C Canada." Paper presented at the RACE conference Toronto.

_____. 2006. *Canada's Economic Apartheid: The Social Exclusion of Racialized Groups in Canada's New Century*. Toronto: Canadian Scholars' Press.

_____. 2004. "Racializing the Division of Labour: Neo-liberal Restructuring and the Economic Segregation of Canada's Racialized Groups." In J. Stanford and L. Vosko (eds.), *Challenging the Market: The Struggle to Regulate Work and Income*. Montreal/Kingston: McGill-Queens University Press.

_____. 2001. *Canada's Creeping Economic Apartheid: The Economic Segregation and Social Marginalization of Racialized Groups*. Toronto: Centre for Social Justice.

_____. 1987. "Community Policing: Towards the Local Police State?" In P. Scraton (ed.), *Law, Order and the Authoritarian State*. Philadelphia: Open University Press.

Gartner, R., and S. Thompson. 2004a. "Trends in Homicide in Toronto." Paper presented at the University of Toronto Centre of Criminology Research Colloquium on Community Safety: From Enforcement and Prevention to Civic Engagement.

_____. 2004b. "Trends in Homicide in Toronto." In B. Kidd and J. Phillips (eds.), *From Enforcement and Prevention to Civic Engagement: Research on Community Safety*. Toronto: Centre of Criminology, University of Toronto.

Gazso, A., and H. Krahn. 2008. "Out of Step or Leading the Parade? Public

Opinion about Income Support Policy in Alberta, 1995 and 2004." *Journal of Canadian Studies* 42, 1.

Gerda, W., and C. Whitzman. 1995. *Safe Cities: Guidelines for Planning, Design, and Management*. New York: Van Nostrand Reinhold.

Gibson, Timothy A. 2004. *Securing the Spectacular City: The Politics of Revitilization and Homelessness in Downtown Seattle*. Lantham: Lexington Books.

Gimson, M. 1980. "Everybody's Doing It." In N. Wates and C. Wolmar (eds.), *Squatting: The Real Story*. London: Bay Leaf Books.

Gingrich, Luann Good. 2002. "Constructing Identity and Drawing Lines: The Textual Work of Ontario's Safe Streets Act." *Journal of Canadian Studies* 37, 3 (Winter).

Giroux, H. 2004. "Neoliberalism and the Demise of Democracy: Resurrecting Hope in Dark Times." *Dissident Voice*.

Gittens, M., and D. Cole. 1995. *Report of the Ontario Commission on Systemic Racism in the Criminal Justice System*. Toronto: Queens Printer.

_____. 1994. *Racism Behind Bars: The Treatment of Black and Racial Minority Prisoners in Ontario Prisons*. Toronto: Queens Printer.

Glasbeek, H. 2002. *Wealth by Stealth: Corporate Crime, Corporate Law, and the Perversion of Democracy*. Toronto: Between the Lines.

Godoy, A. 1999. "Our Right Is the Right to be Killed: Making Rights Real on the Streets of Guatemala City." *Childhood* 6, 4.

Gordon, L. 1994. *Pitied but Not Entitled: Single Mothers and the History of Welfare, 1890–1935*. New York: Free Press.

Gordon, P. 1987. "Community Policing: Towards the Local Police State?" In P. Scraton (ed.), *Law, Order and the Authoritarian State*. Philadelphia: Open University Press.

Gordon, T. 2007. *Cops, Crime and Capitalism: The Law-and-Order Agenda in Canada*. Halifax: Fernwood Publishing.

_____. 2004. "The Return of Vagrancy Laws and the Politics of Poverty in Canada." *Canadian Journal of Social Policy* 54.

Gorlick, C., and G. Brethour. 1998. *Welfare-to-Work Programs: A National Inventory*. Ottawa: Canadian Council on Social Development.

Gray. 2004. "It Was the Wrong Squat." *Toronto Star*, November 14.

Greaves, G. 1986. "The Police and Their Public." In J. Benyon and C. Bourn (eds.), *The Police: Powers, Procedures and Properties*. Oxford: Pergamon Press.

Green, D. 1998. *Hidden Lives: Voices of Children in Latin America and the Caribbean*. Toronto: Between the Lines.

Greene, J. 1999. "Zero Tolerance: A Case Study of Police Policies and Practices in New York City." *Crime and Delinquency* 45, 2.

Gregg, A. 2007. "Another View." *Public Policy Forum Address*. Available at <allangregg. com/?p=50>.

Grossberg, L. 2001. "Why Does Neo-liberalism Hate Kids? The War on Youth and the Culture of Politics." *Review of Education/Pedagogy/Cultural Studies* 23, 2.

Guest, D. 1991. *The Emergence of Social Security in Canada*. Second edition. Vancouver: UBC Press.

Hall, S., et al. 1978. *Policing the Crisis: Mugging, the State, and Law and Order*. London: Macmillan.

Harcout, B. 2001. *Illusion of Order: The False Promise of Broken Windows Policing.* Cambridge, MA: Harvard University Press.

Harding, J. 1966. "Minister Explains Changes in Welfare Act." *The Mail-Star,* July 23.

Harrison, T., W. Johnston, and H. Krahn. 2005. "Language and Power: 'Special Interests' in Alberta." In T. Harrison (ed.), *The Return of the Trojan Horse: Alberta and the New World (Dis)Order.* Montreal: Black Rose.

Harvey, D. 2007. *A Brief History of Neoliberalism.* New York: Oxford University Press.

Harvey, E.B., B. Siu, and K. Reil. 1999. "Ethnocultural Groups, Periods of Immigration and Social Economic Situation." *Canadian Ethnic Studies* 30, 3.

Heller, C. 1987. *Structured Social Inequality.* New York: Macmillan.

Helm, Richard. 1993. "Welfare Abused to Tune of $2M, Minister Says." *Edmonton Journal* February 10: A7

Henry, F., and C. Tator. 2002. *Discourses of Domination: Racial Bias in the Canadian English Language Press.* Toronto: University of Toronto Press.

Hermer, J., and J. Mosher. 2002. *Disorderly People: Law and the Politics of Exclusion in Ontario.* Halifax: Fernwood Publishing.

Hillyard-Little, M. 1999. "The Limits of Canadian Democracy: The Citizenship Rights of Poor Women." *Canadian Review of Social Policy* 49.

hooks, bell. 2004. *Where We Stand: Class Matters.* New York: Routledge.

Hou, F., and T. Balakrishnan. 1996. "The Integration of Visible Minorities in Contemporary Canadian Society." *Canadian Journal of Sociology* 21, 3.

Hou, F., and G. Picot. 2004. "Visible Minority Neighbourhoods in Toronto, Montreal and Vancouver." *Canadian Social Trends.* Statistics Canada. Catalogue 11-008.

_____. 2003. *Visible Minority Neighbourhood Enclaves and Labour Market Outcomes of Immigrants.* Ottawa: Statistics Canada.

Hughes, K. 1999. *Gender and Self Employment: Assessing Trends and Policy Implications.* Canadian Policy Research Network.

Hum, D., and W. Simpson. 1998. *Wage Opportunities for Visible Minorities in Canada.* Ottawa: Statistics Canada.

Human Rights Watch. 1997. *Guatemala's Forgotten Children: Police Violence and Abuses in Detention.* New York: Human Rights Watch

Hunter, A. 2002. "Instead of Criminalising the Poor, Seek Solutions." *Chronicle-Herald,* October 2.

Jackson, A. 2005. *Work and Labour in Canada: Critical Issues.* Toronto: Canadian Scholars Press.

James, C. 1999. *Seeing Ourselves: Exploring Race, Ethnicity and Culture.* Toronto: Thompson Educational Publishing.

_____. 1997. "Distorted Images of African Canadians: Impacts, Implications and Responses." In C. Green (ed.), *Globalization and Survival in the Black Diaspora.* Albany: State University of New York Press.

Johnson, G. 2004. "In Their Own Words." *Georgia Straight,* April 22 <http://www.straight.com/article/in-their-own-words>.

Justice for Girls. 2003. "Justice for Girls says excessive policing of the Downtown Eastside violates numerous domestic and international human rights laws." *Justice for Girls,* Vancouver, April 11.

Katznelson, I. 2006. *When Affirmative Action Was White: An Untold History of Racial Inequality in Twentieth-Century America.* New York: W.W. Norton.

Karabanow, J. 2004a. *Being Young and Homeless: Understanding How Youth Enter and Exit Street Life.* New York: Peter Lang.

_____. 2004b. *Exploring Salient Issues of Youth Homelessness in Halifax, Nova Scotia.* Halifax: Human Resources Development Canada, Supporting Communities Partnerships Initiative.

_____. 2003. "Creating a Culture of Hope: Lessons from Street Children Agencies in Canada and Guatemala." *International Social Work* 46, 3.

_____. 2000. "A Place for All Seasons: Examining Youth Shelters and the Youth-In-Trouble Network in Toronto." PhD dissertation, Wilfred Laurier University

Karabanow, J. et al. In press. "Can You Be Healthy on the Street?" *The Canadian Journal of Urban Research.*

_____. 2005. *Getting Off the Street: Exploring Strategies Used by Canadian Youth to Exit Street Life.* Halifax: National Secretariat on Homelessness, National Research Program on Homelessness

Katsiaficas, G. 1997. *The Subversion of Politics: European Autonomous Social Movements and the Decolonization of Everyday Life.* New Jersey: Humanities Press.

Kazemipur, A., and S. Halli. 2000. *The New Poverty in Canada: Ethnic Groups and Ghetto Neighbourhoods.* Toronto: Thompson Educational Publishing.

_____. 1997. "The Invisible Barrier: Neighbourhood Poverty and Integration of Immigrants in Canada." *Journal of International Migration and Integration* 1, 1.

Keil, R. 2002. "'Common-Sense' Neoliberalism: Progressive Conservative Urbanism in Toronto, Canada." *Antipode* 34, 3: 578–601.

Kelley, R. 1997. *Yo' Mama's Disfunktional! Fighting the Culture Wars in Urban America.* Boston: Beacon Press.

Kelling, G., and C. Coles. 1996. *Fixing Broken Windows: Restoring Order and Reducing Crime in Our Communities.* New York: Martin Kessler Books.

Kelly, P. 2001. "Youth at Risk: Processes of Individualization and Responsibilisation in the Risk Society." *Discourse: Studies in the Cultural Politics of Education* 22, 1.

Kern, Leslie. 2005. "In Place and at Home in the City: Connecting Privilege, Safety and Belonging for Women in Toronto." *Gender, Place and Culture* 12, 3 (September).

Kerstetter, S. 2002. *MSP Premiums: A Really Dumb Tax.* Canadian Centre for Policy Alternatives.

Keynes, J. 1936. *The General Theory of Employment, Interest and Money.* Cambridge: Macmillan Cambridge University Press.

Kipfer, S., and R. Keil. 2002. "Toronto Inc? Planning the Competitive City in the New Toronto." *Antipode* 34, 2: 227–64.

Kitchen, Brigette. 1997. "'Common Sense' Assault on Families." In Diana Ralph, Andre Régimbald, and Neree St. Armand (eds.), *Open for Business, Closed to People: Mike Harris's Ontario.* Halifax: Fernwood Publishing.

Klassen, T., and D. Buchanan. 1997. "Getting It Backward? Economy and Welfare in Ontario 1985–1995." *Canadian Public Policy* 23, 3.

Koskela, Hilli. 1997. "'Bold Walk and Breakings': Women's Spatial Confidence Versus Fear of Violence." *Gender, Place and Culture* 4, 3 (November).

Kufeldt, K., and M. Nimmo. 1987. "Youth on the Street: Abuse and Neglect in the

Eighties." *Child Abuse and Neglect: The International Journal* 11, 4.

Lafrance, J. 2005. "Does Our Path Have a Heart? Children's Services in Alberta." In T. Harrsion (ed.), *The Return of the Trojan Horse: Alberta and the New World (Dis)Order.* Montreal: Black Rose.

Lamble, S., and L. Freeman. 2004. "No Room for Squatters Except in the Big House." *Briarpatch Magazine* October: 19–21.

Larner, W. 2000. "Neo-liberalism: Policy, Ideology, Governmentality." *Studies in Political Economy* 63.

Lave, T. 1995. "Breaking the Cycle of Despair: Street Children in Guatemala City." *Columbia Human.*

Law Commission of Canada. 2004. *What Is a Crime? Defining Criminal Conduct in Contemporary Society.* Vancouver: University of British Columbia Press.

Laxer, G., and T. Harrison (eds.). 1995. *The Trojan Horse: Alberta and the Future of Canada.* Montreal: Black Rose Books.

Lee, K. 2000. *Urban Poverty in Canada: A Statistical Profile.* Ottawa: Canadian Council on Social Development.

Lee, Murray. 2001. "The Genesis of 'Fear of Crime'." *Theoretical Criminology* 5, 4: 467–85.

Lemke, T. 2002. "Foucault, Governmentality, and Critique." *Rethinking Marxism* 14, 3.

_____. 2001. "The Birth of Bio-politics: Michael Foucault's Lectures at the College de France on Neo-liberal Governmentality." *Economy and Society* 30, 2.

Leonard, L., G. Rosario, C. Scott, and J. Bressan. 2005. "Building Safer Communities: Lessons Learned from Canada's National Strategy." *Canadian Journal of Criminology and Criminal Justice* 47, 2.

Levine, S. 2002. "Squatters Issue Trio of Demands." *Ottawa Sun,* July 2.

Lewis, Stephen. 1992. *Report to the Premier on Racism in Ontario.* Toronto.

Linday, C. n.d. *Profiles of Ethnic Communities in Canada.* Statistics Canada, Catalogue 89-621-XIE.

Lindsey, E., et al. 2000. "How Runaway and Homeless Youth Navigate Troubled Waters: Personal Strengths and Resources." *Child & Adolescent Social Work Journal* 17, 2.

Little, Margaret. 2003. "The Leaner, Meaner, Welfare Machine: The Ontario Conservative Government's Ideological and Material Attack on Single Mothers." In Deborah Brock (ed.), *Making Normal: Social Regulation in Canada.* Toronto: Thompson Nelson.

Lowman, J. 1986. "Street Prostitution in Vancouver: Notes on the Genesis of a Social Problem." *Canadian Journal of Criminology* 28, 1.

Luann G.G. 2002. "Constructing Identity and Drawing Lines: The Textual Work of Ontario's *Safe Streets Act,*" *Journal of Canadian Studies* 37, 4: 151–70.

Luxton, Meg. 1997. "Feminism and Families: The Challenge of Neo-Conservatism." In *Feminism and Families: Critical Policies and Changing Practices.* Halifax: Fernwood Publishing.

Lusk, M. 1989. "Street Children Programs in Latin America." *Journal of Sociology and Social Welfare* 16, 1.

MacAfee, M. 2001. "Seven People Arrested as Montreal Police Evict about 30 Squatters." *Canadian Press Newswire,* October 3.

McCarthy, M. 1998. "Begging the Question: While Governments, Business and Anti-Poverty Activities Discuss What to Do, Down-and-Outers Pan City Streets for Silver." *Vancouver Courier*, June 14.

McCarthy, W. 1990. "Life on the Streets." PhD dissertation, University of Toronto.

McClung, Nellie. 1972. *In Times Like These*. Toronto: University of Toronto Press.

Messerschmidt, J. 1993. *Masculinities and Crime*. Lanham, MD: Rowman and Littlefield.

Milan, A., and K. Tan. 2004. *Blacks in Canada: A Long History*. Canadian Social Trends. Statistics Canada Catalogue 11008.

Mink, Gwendolyn. 1990. "The Lady and the Tramp: Gender, Race and the Origins of the American Welfare State." In Linda Gordon (ed.), *Women, the State and Welfare*. Madison: The University of Wisconson Press.

Mitchell, D. 2003. *The Right to the City: Social Justice and the Fight for Public Space*. New York: Guildford Press.

_____. 2001. "The Annilation of Space by Law: The Roots and Implications of Anti-Homelessness Laws in the United States." In N. Blomley, D. Delaney, and R. Ford (eds.), *The Legal Geographies Reader*. Oxford: Blackwell.

Moar, K. 2002. "Cops Ticket Intersection Panhandler." *Halifax Daily News*, October 27.

Moody, K. 1997. *Workers in a Lean World*. London: Verso.

Moon, R. 2002. "Keeping the Streets Safe from Free Expression." In J. Hermer and J. Mosher (eds.), *Disorderly People: Law and the Politics of Exclusion in Ontario*. Halifax: Fernwood Publishing.

Morissette, R. 2006. "Revisiting Wealth Inequality." *Perspectives on Labour and Income* 7, 12. Statistics Canada.

Morrissette, P., and S. McIntyre. 1989. "Homeless Youth in Residential Care." *Social Casework* 70, 10.

Moscovitch, A. 1997. "Social Assistance in the New Ontario." In D. Ralph, A. Régimbald, N. St-Armand (eds.), *Open for Business, Closed to People: Mike Harris's Ontario*. Halifax: Fernwood Publishing.

Mosher, J. 2008. "Welfare Fraudsters and Tax Evaders: The State's Selective Invocation of Criminality." In C. Brooks and B. Schissel (eds.), *Marginality and Condemnation*. Second edition. Halifax: Fernwood Publishing.

Mosher, J., and J. Brockman (eds.). Forthcoming. *Interrogating the Concept of "Crime" and Its Deployment*. Vancouver: University of British Columbia Press.

Mosher, J., and J. Hermer. 2005. *Welfare Fraud: The Constitution of Social Assistance as Crime*. Ottawa: Law Commission of Canada.

Mosher, J., et al. 2004. *Walking on Eggshells: Abused Women's Experiences of Ontario's Welfare System*. Toronto: Woman and Abuse Welfare Research Project.

Munck, R. 2002. *Globalization and Labor*. London: Zed Books.

Murphy, J. 1997. "Alberta and the Workfare Myth." In E. Shragge (ed.), *Workfare: Ideology for a New Under-Class*. Toronto: Garamond.

_____. 1995. "Workfare Will Make You Free: Ideology and Social Policy in Alberta." In G. Laxer and T. Harrison (eds.), *The Trojan Horse: Alberta and the Future of Canada*. Montreal: Black Rose.

Myers, T., and B. Myers. 2000. "It's One Thing for Us to Take Shots at Our City, but Tourists?" *Vancouver Province*, September 13.

National Anti-Poverty Organization. 1999. *Short-Changed on Human Rights: A NAPO Position Paper on Anti-panhandling By-laws.* Ottawa: National Anti-Poverty Organization.

National Council of Welfare. 2005. *Welfare Incomes 2005.* Ottawa: National Council of Welfare.

_____. 2000. *Welfare Incomes 1997 and 1998.* Ottawa: Minister of Public Works and Government Services.

_____. 1998. *Profiles of Welfare: Myths and Realities.* Ottawa: Minister of Public Works and Government Services.

Nelson, J. 2008. *Razing Africville: A Geography of Racism.* Toronto: University of Toronto Press.

Neocleous, M. 2000. *The Fabrication of Social Order: A Critical Theory of Police Power.* London: Pluto.

Nova Scotia Department of Justice. 2007. *Safer Streets and Communities, Report to the Minister of Justice.* Nova Scotia Department of Justice.

Nova Scotia Department of Public Welfare. 1958. *Welfare Services in Nova Scotia.* Halifax, Nova Scotia.

Nova Scotia Minister of Public Works and Mines. 1943. *Thirteenth Annual Report of the Director Administering the Mothers' Allowance Act.* Halifax: King's Printer.

_____. 1937. *Seventh Annual Report of the Director Administering the Mothers' Allowance Act for the Year Ending November 30, 1936.* Halifax: King's Printer.

_____. 1932. *Third Annual Report of the Director Administering the Mothers' Allowance Act for the Year Ending September 30, 1932.* Halifax: King's Printer.

_____. 1931. *First Annual Report of the Director Administering the Mothers' Allowance Act.* Halifax: King's Printer.

Nova Scotia Department of Social Services. 1973–77. *Nova Scotia Annual Reports.* Halifax, Nova Scotia.

Nunn Commission of Inquiry. 2006. *Spiraling Out of Control: Lessons Learned From a Boy in Trouble.* Available at <nunncommission.ca/home/index.cfm?id=22>.

O'Grady, B., and R. Bright. 2002. "Squeezed to the Point of Exclusion: The Case of Toronto Squeegee Cleaners." In J. Hermer and J. Mosher (eds.), *Disorderly People: Law and the Politics of Exclusion in Ontario.* Halifax: Fernwood Publishing.

O'Grady, B., R. Bright, and E. Cohen. 1998. "Sub-employment and Street Youths: An Analysis of the Impact of Squeegee Cleaning on Homeless Youths." *Security Journal* 11.

O'Grady, B., and S. Gaetz. 2004. "Homelessness, Gender and Subsistence: The Case of Toronto Street Youth." *Journal of Youth Studies* 7, 4.

O'Grady, B., and C. Greene. 2003. "A Social and Economic Impact Study of the Ontario Safe Streets Act on Toronto Squeegee Workers." *Online Journal of Justice Issues* 1, 1.

O'Malley, P. 1998. *Crime and the Risk Society.* Brookfield: Ashgate.

O'Reilly, P., and T. Fleming. 2001. "Squeegee Wars: The State versus Street Youth." In T. Flemming, P. O'Reilly and B. Clark (eds.), *Youth Injustice: Canadian Perspectives.* Toronto: Canadian Scholars Press.

Office of the Mayor. 2006. *Project Civil City.* Vancouver: City of Vancouver.

Olsen, G. 2002. *The Politics of the Welfare State: Canada, Sweden, and the United States.*

Toronto: Oxford University Press.

Olsen, J. 2007. "European Anarchists Join Rioters in Danish Capital." *Globe and Mail*, March 3 <www.ainfos.ca/07/mar/ainfos00044.html>.

Ontario Association of Interval and Transition Houses. 1998. "Locked In, Left Out: Impacts of the Budget Cuts on Abused Women and Their Children." In L. Ricciutelli, J. Larkin, and E. O'Neill (eds.), *Confronting the Cuts: A Sourcebook for Women in Ontario*. Toronto: Inanna Publications.

Ontario Coalition Against Poverty. 2004. "Mayor Miller's Summer Social Cleansing Begins: Bathurst St. Bridge Residents Evicted, Spadina and Gardiner Residents Next." Available at <update.ocap.ca/node/349> .

Ontario Ministry of Community and Social Services. 2000. "Ontario's Zero Tolerance on Welfare Cheats Effective Today." Press release, April 1.

_____. 1997. "Ontario's Social Assistance Caseload Declines by Almost 210,000." Press release, August 5.

Ornstein, M. 2000. *Ethno-Racial Inequality in the City of Toronto: An Analysis of the 1996 Census*. Toronto: City of Toronto.

Ortiz-de-Carrizosa, S., and J. Poertner. 1992. "Latin American Street Children: Problems, Programmes, and Critique." *International Social Work* 35, 4.

Ottawa Citizen. 2002. "Police tactics bring quiet end to house occupation: More takeovers likely, politicians warn." July 4: B1.

Pain, R. 2001. "Gender, Race, Age and Fear in the City," *Urban Studies* 38, 5–6: 899–913

_____. 1991. "Space, Sexual Violence, and Social Control: Integrating Geographical and Feminist Analyses of Women's Fear of Crime," *Progress in Human Geography* 15, 4: 415–31.

Palmer, B. 1992. *The Working-Class Experience: Rethinking the History of Canadian Labour, 1800–1991*. Toronto: McClelland and Stewart.

Panter-Brick, C., and M. Smith. 2000. *Abandoned Children*. Cambridge: Cambridge University Press.

Parenti, C. 2000. *Lockdown America: Police and Prisons in the Age of Crisis*. London: Verso.

Parkes, D. 2005. "Prisoner Voting Rights in Canada: Rejecting the Notion of Temporary Outcasts." In C. Mele and T. Miller (eds.), *Civil Penalties, Social Consequences*. New York: Routledge.

Parnaby, Patrick. 2003. "Disaster through Dirty Windshields: Law, Order, and Toronto's Squeegee Kids," *Canadian Journal of Sociology* 28, 2 (Summer): 281–307.

Patriquin, M. 2001. "Squatters 1, Montreal 0 in Battle Over Housing." *Toronto Star*, August 18.

Philp, M. 2000. "Poor? Coloured? Then it's no vacancy." *Globe and Mail*, July 18.

Picot, G., and F. Hou. 2003. *The Rise in Low Income Rates Among Immigrants in Canada*. Statistics Canada. Analytical Studies Branch Research Paper Series, Catalogue 11F0019MIE, 198.

Picot, G., F. Hou, and S. Coulombe. 2007. *Chronic Low Income and Low Income Dynamics Among Recent Immigrants*. Statistics Canada. Analytical Studies Branch Research Paper Series, Catalogue 11F0019MIE, 294.

Pivot Legal Society. 2002. *To Serve and Protect: A Report on Policing in Vancouver's Downtown*

Eastside. Vancouver: Pivot Legal Society.

Platt, A. 1996. *The Child Savers: The Invention of Delinquency*. Chicago: University of Chicago Press.

Pollard, C. 1998. "Zero Tolerance: Short Term Fix, Long Term Liability?" In N. Dennis et al. (eds.), *Zero Tolerance: Policing a Free Society*,. London: IEA Health and Welfare Unit.

Porter, M., and M. Campbell, M. 2001. "Three Neighbourhoods grapple with shootings: Black-on-Black violence baffles police, residents." *Toronto Star*, July 28.

Powell, B. 2008. "Police went too far, judge rules." *Toronto Star*, March 20.

Power, B. 2002. "Halifax Mayor Vows Crackdown on Slumlords; Group Protests Homelessness, Calls for Affordable Housing in City." *Chronicle-Herald*, November 23.

Pratt, A., and M. Valverde. 2002. "From Deserving Victims to 'Masters of Confusion': Redefining Refugees in the 1990s." *Canadian Journal of Sociology* 27, 2 (Spring).

Pratt, M. 1991. "Arts of the Contact Zone." *Profession* 91: 33–40.

Ranasinghe, P., and M. Valverde. 2006. "Governing Homelessness Through Land-use: A Sociolegal Study of the Toronto Shelter Zoning By-law." *Canadian Journal of Sociology* 31, 3 (Summer).

Rankin, J., et al. 2002. "Singled Out: An Investigation into Race and Crime." *Toronto Star*, October 19.

Raphael, D. 2007. *Poverty in Canada*. Toronto: Canadian Scholars' Press.

Razack, S. 2002. *Race, Space and the Law: Unmapping a White Settler Society*. Toronto: Between the Lines.

Reichwein, B.P. 2003. *Benchmarks in Alberta's Public Welfare Services: History Rooted in Benevolence, Harshness, Punitiveness and Stinginess*. Edmonton: Alberta College of Social Workers.

Reid, B. 1998. "The Political Economy of Densification: Looking for Signs of the Postmodern City: A Case Study of Urban Transformation in Greater Vancouver." Ph.D. diss., University of Manitoba.

Roberts, Julian. 2001. *Fear of Crime and Attitudes to Criminal Justice in Canada: A Review of Recent Trends*. Ministry of the Solicitor General of Canada, Public Works and Governmment Series Canada, Catalogue no. JS42-99/2001.

Rose, N. 1999. *Powers of Freedom: Reframing Political Thought*. Cambridge, UK: Cambridge University Press.

_____. 1996. "Governing 'Advanced' Liberal Democracies." In A. Barry, T. Osborne, and N. Rose (eds.), *Foucault and Political Reason: Liberalism, Neo-liberalism and Rationalities of Government*. Chicago: University of Chicago Press.

Roy, F. 2004. "Social Assistance by Province, 1993–2003." *Canadian Economic Observer* 17, 11 (November).

Ruddick, S. 2002. "Metamorphosis Revisited: Restricting Discourses of Citizenship." In J. Hermer and J. Mosher (eds.), *Disorderly People, Disorderly People: Law and the Politics of Exclusion in Ontario*. Halifax: Fernwood Publishing.

Ruppert, E. 2006. *The Moral Economy of Cities: Shaping Good Citizens*. Toronto: University of Toronto Press.

Safer City Task Force. 1993. "Final Report." City of Vancouver.

Sanger, Carol. 2001. "Girls and the Getaway: Cars, Culture, and the Predicament of Gendered Space." In Nicholas Blomley, David Delaney, and Richard T. Ford (eds.), *The Legal Geographies Reader: Law, Power, and Space*. Ottawa: Blackwell.

Schneiderman, D. 2002. "The Consitutional Disorder of the Safe Streets Act: A Federalism Analysis." In J. Hermer and J. Mosher (eds.), *Disorderly People: Law and the Politics of Exclusion in Ontario*. Halifax: Fernwood Publishing.

Sears, Alan. 2003. *Retooling the Mind Factory: Education in a Lean State*. Aurora: Garamond.

_____. 1999. "The 'Lean' State and Capitalist Restructuring." *Studies in Political Economy* 59 (Summer).

Sennett, R. 1970. *The Uses of Disorder: Personal Identity and Social Life*. New York: Knopf.

Shaw, M., and C. Andrew. 2005. "Engendering Crime Prevention: International Developments and the Canadian Experience." *Canadian Journal of Criminology and Criminal Justice* 47, 2: 1293–316.

Sheldrick, B. 2004. *Perils and Possibilities: Social Activism and the Law*. Halifax: Fernwood Publishing.

Shillington, R. 1998. *Social Assistance and Paid Employment in Alberta, 1993–1996*. Edmonton: Population Research Laboratory of the University of Alberta.

Simon, J. 2007. *Governing through Crime: How the War on Crime Transformed American Democracy and Created a Culture of Fear*. New York: Oxford University Press.

Skogan, W. 1990. *Disorder and Decline: Crime and the Spiral of Decay in American Neighborhoods*. Toronto: Collier MacMillan Canada.

Sommers, J. 2001. "The Place of the Poor: Poverty, Space, and the Politics of Representation in Downtown Vancouver, 1950–1996." Ph.D. diss., Simon Fraser University.

Sommers, J., and N. Blomley. 2003. "The 'Worst Block in Vancouver'?" In R. Shier and S. Douglas (eds.), *Every Building on 100 West Hastings*. Vancouver: Arsenal/ Pulp Press.

Sommers, J., C. LaPrairie, M. Berti, and T. Laviolette. 2005. "Policing Homelessness: The Report on the Research Project on the Regulation of Public Space and the Criminalization of Homelessness in Vancouver." National Homelessness Initiative: National Research Program. (CSGC# 0666305).

Staff Report of the City of Toronto. 2005. "From the Street into Homes: A Strategy to Assist Homeless Persons Find Permanent Housing."

Stanford, J., and L. Vosko. 2004. *Challenging the Market: The Struggle to Regulate Work and Income*. Montreal/Kingston: McGill-Queen's University Press.

Stanko, E. 2001. "Victims R Us: The Life History of 'Fear of Crime' and the Politicization of Violence." In T. Hope and R. Sparks (eds.), *Crime, Risk and Insecurity: Law and Order in Everyday Life and Political Discourse*. New York: Routledge.

_____. 1998. "Warnings to Women: Police Advice and Women's Safety in Britain." In Susan Miller (ed.), *Crime Control and Women: Feminist Implications of Criminal Justice*. Thousand Oaks, CA: Sage.

_____. 1997. "Safety Talk: Conceptualizing Women's Risk Assessment as a 'Technology of the South'." *Theoretical Criminology* 1, 4: 479–99.

Stein, J. et al. 2007. *Uneasy Partners: Multiculturalism and Rights in Canada*. Waterloo: Wilfred Laurier University

Stiglitz, J. 2002. *Globalization and Its Discontents*. New York: W.W. Norton.

Strathcona Research Group. 2005. "Policing Homelessness: The Report on the Regulation of Public Space and the Criminalization of Homelessness in Vancouver." Vancouver: Strathcona Research Group/PHS Community Services Society. Available at <city.vancouver.bc.ca/commsvcs/cnrp/pdf/policinghome-lessness05feb.pdf>.

Strong-Boag, V. 1979. "'Wages for Housework': Mothers' Allowances and the Beginnings of Social Security in Canada." *Journal of Canadian Studies* 14, 1.

Suljit, C. 2001. "Protecting Equality in the Face of Terror: Ethnic and Racial Profiling and the s.15 of the Charter." In R. Daniels and K. Roach (eds.), *The Security of Freedom: Essays on Canada's Anti-Terrorist Bill.* Toronto: University of Toronto Press.

Swanson, J. 2001. *Poor Bashing: The Politics of Exclusion.* Toronto: Between the Lines.

Taft, K. 1997. *Shredding the Public Interest: Ralph Klein and 25 Years of One-Party.* Edmonton: University of Alberta Press/Parkland Institute.

Teeple, G. 1995. *Globalization and the Decline of Social Reform.* Toronto: Garamond Press.

Thompson, B. 1991. *Single Mother's Survival Guide.* Halifax: Public Interest Research Group, Dalhousie University.

Toronto Mayor's Homelessness Action Task Force Report. 1999. *Taking Responsibility for Homelessness: An Action Plan for Toronto.* City of Toronto.

UNICEF. 2005. *Child Poverty in Rich Countries.* Florence: Innocenti Research Centre.

United Way of Greater Toronto and the Canadian Council on Social Development. 2004. *Poverty by Postal Code: The Geographical Neighbourhood Poverty, 1981–2001.* Toronto: UWGT/CCSD.

Urquhart, S. 1966. "Only small amount spent on drinking, betting." *The Mail Star,* June 28.

Vancouver Board of Trade, Tourism Vancouver, Downtown Vancouver Business Improvement Association, Vancouver Hotel Association, Vancouver Taxi Association, Retail B.C., Downtown Vancouver Association, Vancouver Hotel General Managers' Association, Building Owners and Managers Association of B.C., Council of Tourism Associations of B.C., B.C. Restaurant and Food Services Association of B.C., and B.C. and Yukon Hotel Association. 2006. "Letter to Prime Minister Stephen Harper, Premier Gordon Campbell, and Mayor Sam Sullivan." Available at <boardoftrade.com/policy/StreetDisorder-letter3oct06.pdf >.

Vonn, M. 2004. "Safe Streets: Laws for Us, Laws for Them." B.C. Civil Liberties Association. Available at <bccla.org/othercontent/04safestreetsvonn.htm>.

Vosko, L. 2006. *Precarious Employment: Understanding Labour Market Insecurity in Canada.* Montreal/Kingston: McGill-Queen's University Press.

_____. 2000. *Temporary Work: The Gendered Rise of a Precarious Employment Relationship.* Toronto: University of Toronto Press.

Wacquant, L. 2001. "The Penalization of Poverty and the Rise of Neoliberalism." *European Journal on Criminal Policy and Research* 9.

_____. 2001. "Deadly Symbiosis: When Ghetto and Prison Meet and Mesh." *Punishment & Society* 3, 1.

Wardaugh, J., and J. Jones. 1999. "Begging in Time and Space: 'Shadow Work' and the Rural Context." In H. Dean (ed.), *Begging Questions: Street-Level Economic Activity and Social Policy Failure.* Bristol: Policy Press.

Webber, M. 1991. *Street Kids: The Tragedy of Canada's Runaways.* Toronto: University of Toronto Press.

Weber, T. 2005. "Police Stop Blacks, Natives more than Whites: Report." *Globe and Mail,* May 26.

Wekerle, Gerda, and Carolyn Whitzman. 1995. *Safe Cities: Guidelines for Planning, Design, and Management.* New York: Van Nostrand Reinhold.

Welsh, B., and D. Farrington. 2005. "Evidence-based Crime Prevention: Conclusions and Directions for a Safer Society." *Canadian Journal of Criminology and Criminal Justice* 47, 2.

Wente, M. 2007. "So, what did you learn in school today?" *Globe and Mail,* June 12.

Wiegand, E. 2004. "Trespass at Will: Squatting as Direct Action, Human Right, and Justified Theft." *LIP Magazine* <http://www.lipmagazine.org/articles/featwiegand_squat.shtml>.

Wilson, J., and G. Kelling. 1982. "Broken Windows: The Police and Neighbourhood Safety." *Atlantic Monthly* 34.

Winnipeg Police Service. 1998. *Annual Report.* Winnipeg: Winnipeg Police Service.

Wortley, S. 2005. *Bias Free Policing: The Kingston Data Collection Project.* Toronto: Centre of Excellence for research on Immigration and Settlement.

_____. 1997. "The Usual Suspects: Race, Police Stops and Perceptions of Criminal Injustice." Paper presented at the 48th annual conference of the American Society of Criminology, Chicago.

Wortley, S., and J. Tanner. 2004. "Social Groups or Criminal Organizations? The Extent and Nature of Youth Gang Activity in Toronto." In B. Kidd and J. Phillips (eds.), *From Enforcement and Prevention to Civic Engagement: Research on Community Safety.* Toronto: Centre of Criminology, University of Toronto.

_____. 2003. "Data, Denials, and Confusion: The Racial Profiling Debate in Toronto." *Canadian Journal of Criminology and Criminal Justice* 45, 3.

Yalnizyan, A. 2007. *The Rich and the Rest of Us: The Changing Face of Canada's Growing Gap.* Ottawa: Canadian Centre for Policy Alternatives.

Young, Iris Marion. 2003. "The Logic of Masculinist Protection: Reflections on the Current Security State." *Signs: Journal of Women in Culture and Society* 1 (Autumn).

Zeytinoglu, I., and J. Muteshi. 2000. "Gender, Race and Class Dimensions of Non-Standard Work." *Industrial Relations* 55, 1.

Ziff, B. 2000. *Principles of Property Law.* Third edition. Toronto: Thompson Canada.